The Myth
of the Powerless
State

A volume in the series
Cornell Studies in Political Economy
EDITED BY PETER J. KATZENSTEIN

The Myth
of the Powerless
State

LINDA WEISS

Cornell University Press
Ithaca, New York

For John,
fellow enthusiast for life, love and learning

First published in the United States of America in 1998 by
Cornell University Press.

First published in Great Britain in 1998 by Polity Press
in association with Blackwell Publishers Ltd.

Reprinted 1999

ISBN 0–8014–3547–1
ISBN 0–8014–8543–6 (pbk)

Library of Congress Cataloging-in-Publication Data
Weiss, Linda, 1952–
    The myth of the powerless state/Linda Weiss.
        p.   cm.—(Cornell studies in political economy)
    Includes bibliographical references (p.   ) and index.
    ISBN 0–8014–3547–1 (cloth:alk. paper)—ISBN 0–8014–8543–6
(pbk. : alk. paper)
        1. Economic policy.   2. Industrial policy.   3. East Asia—Economic
policy.   4. Sweden—Economic policy.   5. Japan—Economic
policy—1989–   6. Germany—Economic policy—1990–   I. Title.
II. Series.
HD87.W45   1998
338.9—dc21   97–48666

Typeset in 10 on 12pt Times
by Wearset, Boldon, Tyne and Wear.
Printed in Great Britain by MPG Books Ltd, Bodmin, Cornwall.

This book is printed on acid-free paper.

CONTENTS

Chapter 3: TRANSFORMATIVE CAPACITY IN EVOLUTION: EAST ASIAN DEVELOPMENTAL STATES

Chapter 4: LIMITS OF THE DISTRIBUTIVE STATE: SWEDISH MODEL OR GLOBAL ECONOMY?

Chapter 5: DUALISTIC STATES: GERMANY IN THE JAPANESE MIRROR

Chapter 6: THE LIMITS OF GLOBALIZATION

Chapter 7: THE MYTH OF THE POWERLESS STATE

PREFACE

Whether as enthusiasts or critics, analysts or observers, many contemporary thinkers subscribe to the influential view that globalization is the master concept of our time. Those who adhere to the global idea firmly believe that as the integration of the world economy advances, national governments are becoming less relevant, losing their powers not only to influence macroeconomic outcomes and to implement social programmes, but also to determine strategies for managing the industrial economy. From their globalist perspective, the string of currency crises in the East Asian region in the second half of 1997 are simply one more piece of incontrovertible evidence that, when push comes to shove, the nation-state is but a pawn in the invisible hand of the global market.

As its title suggests, this book questions such claims of *state powerlessness*. It starts with the idea that the impact of external economic pressures on national economies and public policies depends to a large degree on the strength or weakness of domestic institutions. Specifically, the present study is concerned with that constellation of institutions and orientations that strengthens or weakens the state's transformative capacity.

The important questions that this concern raises are why state capacity is robust in some cases and weak in others; why state responses to international pressures are managed effectively or poorly; and why state involvement gets such mixed results, producing relatively robust effects in some settings but poor or perverse outcomes in others. Answers to these questions can only be arrived at by looking in each case at the particular combination of a state's fundamental priorities, its architecture, and its linkages with key economic actors. Thus the argument fashioned in this study turns on the synergy of goal-oriented state agencies closely interacting with key economic actors.

Where these arrangements are configured in such a way as to bolster the state's transformative capacity, I call this constellation 'governed interdependence'. In those cases where governed interdependence has taken a definite form and adapted to the changing tasks of economic management (e.g. Japan, Germany and Taiwan) states have retained or are in the process of reconstituting a fairly robust capacity for guiding and coordinating economic change. In such cases, adjustment to economic crisis is likely to mobilize and reinvigorate core state capacities. In other cases where interdependence has become partially, though increasingly, 'ungoverned' (e.g. South Korea in the 1990s), state capacity has been relatively weakened, the potential for business failure has increased, and the response to economic crisis is likely to be more protracted and uncertain.

Quite clearly, then, the argument has naught to do with that fictional domain of state omnipotence. What it does seek to highlight, in contrast to globalization orthodoxy, is that states are rendered far from powerless and passive as they confront global market forces. In principle at least, if not always in practice, there is much that states can do to foster wealth creation and social wellbeing. The tasks of national economic management are not fixed and finite, but ever-changing; and since the tasks are always evolving, it stands to reason that the policy tools must also vary over time. Contrary then to much current thinking about the state's place in economic management, such changes imply state *adaptivity*, not state retreat, and tighter rather than looser connections with economic actors. There are, in short, numerous areas where state involvement in the industrial economy remains important and vital to national prosperity, even as economies develop and mature.

Studies such as this one, which aim to shed light on real world processes must be prepared to deal with changing reality. As this book goes to press, some very significant changes are underway in the East Asian region. I refer in particular to the series of financial crises that have engulfed South East Asia (mainly Thailand, Malaysia and Indonesia), and most recently South Korea. In many quarters, the occurrence of severe financial dislocation in the region is being taken as evidence of the final unravelling of the East Asian 'miracle', as a sign of the profound pitfalls of state-guided development, and as final triumphant proof of the overwhelming force of global markets disempowering national governments. Since some (though not all) of the countries examined in this book are located in this troubled part of the world, and since these events have occurred since the text of this book was completed, I shall use this Preface to spell out how the perspective developed herein can make sense of the recent economic disruptions in the region.

Financial dislocation of the kind we are witnessing in the late 1990s definitely gives some muscle to the otherwise flabby notion of a globalizing economy that has loomed so large in contemporary debates. Indeed, as this study acknowledges, money markets are perhaps the only true face of global capitalism in the late twentieth century. As such, the emergence of a generalized crisis involving nation-states and global financial markets *could hardly offer a tougher test of the argument of this volume.*

So what does this whole episode of apparent financial meltdown in North and South East Asia imply for the present study? For many commentators, what began as a currency crisis and developed successively into a stockmarket and banking crisis seems to be a clear case of strong states being brought to heel by global markets, or of markets exacting revenge on excessive state involvement. Dramatic currency devaluations of up to 30 per cent, effectively reducing the hard-won benefits of rapid growth, seem to leave no doubt that global markets rule. Or do they?

On the face of it, East Asia's financial woes offer an open-and-shut case, reminiscent of the classical detective tale where the butler is found, knife in hand, bent over the corpse. The verdict seems irresistible: the butler was there, so the butler must have been the perpetrator. It is tempting to read the East Asian story in similar fashion: the state is heavily involved in the economy, so the strong state must be the source of the problem. The neoliberal message could not be clearer: state involvement earns the revenge of the market. What this viewpoint overlooks, however, is that state *involvement* is not equivalent to state *transformative capacity.*

This important point can be restated in a slightly different way. Transformative capacity is not widely diffused throughout the region. The point deserves emphasis because many commentators, including the World Bank (1993a), have helped to perpetrate the view of an undifferentiated East Asia. In this view, it seems as if each of the region's component parts was moving in roughly the same direction, following basically similar goals with institutionally similar means. The differences, however, most notably those between South East and North East Asia, remain stark.

Thus, for example, in the second-generation NICs of South East Asia, the constellation of political priorities, state structures and government-business relations that prevailed during their high-growth phase has differed remarkably from that more typically found in North East Asia. At the most basic level, there are major differences to be observed in public priorities, as well as in the number, quality and organizational commitment of career bureaucrats who might be mobilized to coordinate transformative projects. One important consequence

– evident as much in Thailand and Indonesia as in Malaysia – has been the absence of investment coordination to ensure that resources are directed to more productive ends. A substantial proportion of domestic and foreign finance has been allocated to speculative projects (especially to property development and showcase projects) rather than to industrial production. In Thailand in the 1990s, for example, the availability of easy finance coupled with the virtual absence of investment guidelines contrasts dramatically with the highly coordinated investment strategies put in place earlier by the Taiwanese, Koreans and Japanese at a similar stage of development. Whereas the state-guided strategies of the Northern states generated high levels of investment in high-growth industries, the Thais' uncoordinated approach, coupled with the availability of easy money, encouraged intense speculative activity, leading to a frenzy of over-investment in the property sector and ultimately contributing to the currency crises of 1997.

Slightly different versions of this basic tale can be told for Malaysia and Indonesia. What all of them point to is the *weakness* of domestic institutions: the relatively weak transformative capacities of these states have assisted in the massive inflation of asset values that rapid growth and easy money allowed. The South East Asian economies have thus become ever more vulnerable to the disruptive potential of global money markets. Viewed from this perspective, the South East Asian crisis provides little support for the thesis of 'strong states at the mercy of global markets'. If the state turns out to be part of the problem in this setting, it is more precisely a problem of *too little state capacity*, rather than too much state involvement. This is what has left these countries vulnerable to global (and domestic) speculators.

The Korean crisis of November 1997, leading to an IMF rescue package and an adjustment programme that by the end of the month had yet to be agreed, is undoubtedly more challenging to the argument of this book. With good reason as it now turns out, the Korean case of transformative capacity has emerged as the least stable of those examined in this book. Though superficially similar to those of South East Asia, Korea's difficulties have quite different roots. According to *The Economist* (1997 [November]: 23–4), a long tradition of state-guided development is the fundamental cause of the problem. But this verdict seems rather wide of the mark, for it is aimed at a moving target. It completely overlooks a number of important changes that, in combination, have substantially altered the structure of 'state-guidance'.

Where the South East Asians have typically maintained little control over the pattern of domestic investment, the South Koreans have increasingly *relinquished* state control over the past decade. With partial liberalization of the financial system, the state progressively loosened its grip over the type and level of industrial investment sustained by the Korean *chaebol*; the *chaebol* in turn achieved greater independence of the state-run financial institutions. Instead of depending on state-directed credit to feed their huge investment requirements, they turned increasingly to foreign capital markets, taking advantage of competitive interest rates. But these conglomerates hedged their bets, on the one hand seeking financial independence in international markets, while on the other hand looking to the state for support in times of trouble.

In this half-way house of economic management, the Korean system of governed interdependence became ever more 'ungoverned' in critical areas. Increasingly, the *chaebol* were doing their own thing, spreading their tentacles into other *chaebols*' areas of production even when – in spite of all the economic bureaucracy's warnings and protestations – overlapping investments threatened to result in overcapacity (as occurred in petrochemicals, steel and, most recently, automobiles).

In short, the Korean system since the late 1980s has witnessed a gradual unravelling of the three fundamentals of transformative capacity. First, as returning US-trained economists have colonized the economic ministries, preaching state retreat from economic affairs, there has been mounting disagreement over the definition of public priorities, hence over the nature of the national system of economic management. Second, with regard to the state's architecture, there has been a dismantling of the Economic Planning Board, the key pilot agency of industrial transformation since the 1960s. Finally, concerning state-industry linkages, the *chaebol* have achieved greater financial independence, thus loosening the government–business ties that underpinned the strong transformative capacity of the high-growth era. In this context of diminished coordination of investment behaviour, Korean companies have rushed to invest in each other's areas, and failed to develop the self-governing collaborative structures through which to regulate excess production. The results are now all too clear: a weakening of state capacity, the slowing of industrial and technological upgrading, and substantial overinvestment in mature industries. On this reading, the Korean crisis shapes up as a crisis, not of a strongly intrusive state, but of weakened institutional capacity for governing the economy.

The South Korean experience raises two important questions. One is whether the transformative capability of developmental states – i.e. synergistic government-industry coordination – has had its day. The experiences of Taiwan and Japan, analysed in this book, would seem to argue against such a view. The other question is whether, once unravelled, core capacities can be recomposed or knitted together once again. Germany's postwar experience, especially of the past two decades, examined in chapter 5, would indicate that recomposition to meet new tasks is indeed possible, even after a lengthy period of state submergence.

In the Korean case, the current crisis would seem to provide an extraordinary opportunity for state recomposition. Above all, it offers strong potential for the very restructuring of the conglomerates and their financing that the government has long sought to institute. But while the depth of the crisis provides an opportunity for organizational reform of the *chaebol* and for recomposition of state capacity, the outcome will be decided in the realm of domestic politics, not global markets.

ACKNOWLEDGEMENTS

This book was completed in the glorious setting of the European University Institute in Fiesole, which nestles in the Tuscan hills overlooking Florence. I count myself fortunate to have had during those three months as visiting fellow the intellectual companionship, support and hospitality of Colin Crouch and Gianfranco Poggi.

Since 1994 when I first began thinking through the ideas for this book, I have accumulated many debts of gratitude to friends, colleagues and institutions. I would like especially to thank Dal-Joong Chang and Kyung-Sup Chang at Seoul National University, Yun-Peng Chu and Wan-wen Chu at the Academia Sinica, Chao-cheng Mai at the Chung-Hua Institution of Economic Research, my bases in Seoul and Taipei during five months of fieldwork in 1994 and 1997. Sigurt Vitols and Steven Casper at the Wissenschaftszentrum in Berlin introduced me to the relevant debates on *Modell Deutschland*.

I would like to thank the following people for helping me in one way or another to improve or clarify points of the argument: Robin Blackburn, William Coleman, Colin Crouch, James Fulcher, David Held, Richard Higgott, John Hobson, John Hutchinson, Chalmers Johnson, Rikki Kersten, David Levi-Faur, Jane Marceau, Michael Mann, John Mathews, Helen Nelson, Gianfranco Poggi, John Ravenhill, Martin Rhodes, Richard Robison, and Robert Wade. Special thanks are due to Michael Mann for reading the entire manuscript, to Colin Crouch for written comments on several chapters, to John Ravenhill for enjoining me to think more deeply about globalization, and to Chalmers Johnson for encouraging me to pursue the Germany–Japan comparison. Whether the results of their efforts will meet their expectations remains to be seen. For their good humour and support I also thank my colleagues in the Department of Government. John Hobson's friendship and passion for scholarship and debate are especially appreciated. For the opportunity to speak on different aspects of the argument in many parts of the world, including Brazil, Israel and Taipei and, closer to home, Brisbane and Canberra, I wish to thank Rene Dreifus, David Levi-Faur, Wan-wen Chu, Geoff Dow, John Ravenhill and James Richardson.

My former student, Tianbiao Zhu, now a PhD candidate at Cornell, provided exacting help with the savings and investment data. My research assistant, Elizabeth Thurbon, now pursuing her own dissertation on Japan, has contributed to the project in countless ways. For her many intelligent suggestions and not least her unfailing sense of humour, I am most grateful.

The Australia Research Council awarded me a large grant for 1996–1998, some of which has helped to advance this project. Their support is gratefully acknowledged.

Julia Harsant and Pamela Thomas at Polity Press deserve special mention for their fine efforts in seeing the book through the demanding production phase.

I thank David Held for his enduring enthusiasm and support for the project, and for his wise and generous ways as editor of Polity. I am grateful to Peter Katzenstein for his interest at a crucial moment, and to Roger Haydon at Cornell University Press for his support for the project in its final stages.

Finally, my largest debt is to John Mathews who has learnt more about state capacity than he ever wished to know and contributed more to the outcome than he could ever realize. This book is dedicated to him.

1

THE STATE IS DEAD: LONG LIVE THE STATE

> [Nation states] have become unnatural – even dysfunctional –
> as actors in a global economy ... [They] are no longer mean-
> ingful units in which to think about economic activity.
>
> *Kenichi Ohmae 1995*

Introduction

In 1985, the state had just been resurrected to a prominent place in social science analysis. *Bringing the State Back In* (Evans et al. 1985) confidently announced a programmatic agenda for exploring the multifarious ways in which states could be seen as important society-shaping institutions. Thirteen years on one can only be struck by the confidence with which, in many quarters, the state is being pronounced a moribund institution.

It is deeply ironic that an institution which has so insistently structured vast areas of social life should come to depend so heavily on the vagaries of academic fashion to determine its analytical fate. For most of the time, and with few notable exceptions, the state was an analytical object which social scientists in the English-speaking world were trained either to ignore or to conceptualize in reductionist terms.[1] Quite exceptional in this regard was the decade or so spanning the late 1970s and 1980s when the state enjoyed a brief revival as an object of 'serious' study. Whatever the broader structural changes involved in that revival, macro-sociologists made an important contribution, particularly through comparative historical analysis that sensitized the research community to the role of inter-state conflict and competition in structuring society.[2] As one would expect, political scientists clearly played their part as well in 'bringing the state back in' to the centre of enquiry. The task of restoring the state to political science of course was by no means unanimously admired or accepted.[3]

But the state is no longer in vogue. 'Who reads *Bringing the State Back In* these days?', queried one of the panellists at the 1996 meeting of American political scientists, as if challenging those present to declare their outmodish tastes. If admirers of that substantial text were to be found among the audience, they had long ago taken shelter in the proverbial closet.[4] From the vantage point of the 1990s, the 'bringing the state back in' (BSBI) movement appears to have been killed off in its youth. Indeed, the state itself is in its death throes, we are constantly told. For this is the era of 'civil society' and 'postmodernity', of 'global society' and the transnational market.

The Phenomenon of 'State Denial'

Wherever we look across the social sciences, the state is being weakened, hollowed out, carved up, toppled or buried. We have entered a new era of 'state denial'. This one may well be more intense and encompassing than ever before, for the state is being killed off not so much by the appearance of new perspectives, but by the emergence of allegedly new tendencies in the world at large – from social movements and democratization to the new regionalism of the European Union (EU) and the globalization of markets.

Unlike the BSBI movement, which sought to counter the long history of state trivialization, this book addresses the more recent phenomenon of 'state denial'. What defines the new spirit of the age – in comparison with the pre-BSBI era – is less a conceptual de-emphasis or blindness towards the state than an assertion of its impending demise as an active centre.

There are many forms of state denial currently in evidence. Most converge on the same set of claims and presuppositions: viz. the loss of national autonomy, the powerlessness of governments in the face of transnational capital, the obsolescence of the nation-state as an organizing principle. Underlying all these 'endist' and convergence arguments is the conception of a globalizing economy integrated only by transnational capital and the market. As the twentieth century draws to a close, the notion of a 'global' economy, dominated by stateless corporations and borderless finance, has captured the imagination of countless commentators. 'Globalization', with its empowerment of market players, it seems, is rapidly eroding the power of the nation-state as capital, finance and technology flow effortlessly across its borders. In this view, not only the sovereignty of nation-states but the very idea of a 'national' economy and the capacity of central governments to manage it are being undermined. Thus the regnant view projects an era of global convergence, where transnational corporations (TNCs) stride across the world at random, and where national governments – from Tokyo to Timbuktu – are increasingly irrelevant and powerless to influence the economic welfare of their citizens.

State denial thus refers to the proliferation of theses which portend the diminution or displacement of states as power actors in the domestic and international arenas. These range from the 'collapse of the welfare state' and the 'death of industrial policy' to the 'end of national diversity' and the 'demise of the nation-state'. As such the image they portray is quite different from the images of corruption, capture or ineptitude generally reserved for developing country states. Nevertheless, they are of a piece in one key respect: they remain quite blind to the *variety* of state responses to international pressures, and to the *sources* and *consequences* of that variety for national prosperity.[5] These are key analytical concerns of the present study to which I return below.

The phenomenon of state denial has, of course, long roots in the tendency in social science to ignore or conceptually de-emphasize the state's importance in structuring social relations.[6] Although at times influential in culturally diverse settings, state denial has none the less remained a fundamentally Anglo-American institution. Indeed, to a large extent, it would seem that this phenomenon is culture bound. But the strength of state denial has tended to wax and wane along with episodic events and changes in the world historical context: becoming somewhat softer in the immediate aftermath of World War II, then hardening during the height of the Cold War, and now regaining intensity after the collapse of the Soviet Union. Intellectual traditions no doubt play some part in shaping the strong underbelly of the state-denial orientation. But traditions rarely tell the whole story. For it is probably not coincidental that the more vociferous proponents of state-denial (read 'globalization') are located in the very countries where the industrial economy has been seen to suffer more than most, and where the capacity for governing industrial adjustment is at its weakest among the advanced countries.

In sum, if American and British analyses generally project passive or ineffectual states as victims of external forces, this is because their authors daily confront such a reality: that is to say, political institutions with weak capacities for *domestic* adjustment strategies. Whatever the precise mix of reasons – historical, ideological, experiential – state denial has once again been reinstated as the dominant tendency of the social sciences in the English-speaking world.

Scope of the Argument
State capacity defined

State capacity has usually been discussed with reference to *general* capabilities – whether in the domestic or international arena, and whether in the industrial, foreign or social policy sectors. But analysis at this level of generality has yielded few insights. At most, it has served as a reminder of the simple but important point that states are not uniformly capable across all policy areas. Thus, for example, the prowess of the United States in pursuing foreign economic policy has long been offset by weakness in governing domestic industrial adjustment.

Indeed, for reasons to be discussed more fully in chapter 2, the idea of a generalized state capacity is meaningless. The capacity 'to get one's way in spite of opposition', for instance, shares little with the capacity 'to mobilize consent' or 'to institutionalize cooperation'. Similarly, the provision of social welfare entails a very different array of capabilities from those required for raising the nation's investible surplus. One might well consider the latter far more exacting, given the proliferation of 'welfare' states and the relative rarity of 'developmental' states (i.e. those prioritizing production and growth), or indeed states combining dual capabilities.

In short, there can be no such thing as state capacity in general, merely capacities in particular arenas. Indeed it may well be that it is the *unevenness* of state capacity that is most significant for understanding state behaviour in certain spheres (Skocpol 1985). America's strong focus on foreign policy and international capacity may well be a consequence of its weakness in the domestic arena.

I therefore focus on the second, more specific sense in which state capacity has been discussed. This is with reference to capabilities in the industrial economy. Some nation-states are notably more successful than others in anticipating and responding to economic change. Whether the aim is to catch up with the more industrialized countries, or to keep abreast of one's competitors, or to achieve technological leadership, comparative analysis reveals considerable variation between states in their capacity for mobilizing a collective investment effort, for raising the level of manufactured exports, and for coordinating technological upgrading. Transformative capacity in this sense refers to the ability of a state to adapt to external shocks and pressures by generating ever-new means of governing the process of industrial change.

Understanding the sources of such capacity – that is to say, why some states are more effective than others in managing the industrial economy and the benefits that flow from that difference in a highly internationalized system – are key issues for analysis. It is thus the capacity to devise and implement policies that *augment* a society's investible surplus, as opposed to merely *redistributing* existing resources, that is the major focus of this book (although, as I show in later chapters, these are complementary rather than competing objectives).

Advantages of state capacity in a global economy

The proposition that state capacities for domestic transformative strategies provide a competitive advantage lies at the heart of this study. Governments and the scholarly community alike increasingly evoke the 'global economy' as the force responsible for domestic troubles, or else to justify or explain the adoption of unpopular policies. But just how uniform are national responses to the external environment? Why do industry sectors in some countries seem more able than in others to upgrade technology rapidly and conquer new export markets? Why is it that highly coordinated market economies such as Japan and Germany (and one might add the newly industrialized countries [NICs] of Korea and Taiwan), recent adjustment pressures notwithstanding, have sustained a greater capacity for growth with equity than the least coordinated market economies, Britain and America? And why is it that a once vibrant industrial nation, like Sweden, now finds it necessary to trim its social policy sails and de-emphasize full employment, thus redefining national priorities? What do such differential responses mean in an increasingly integrated world economy? Can current difficulties in the industrialized North be explained solely as a result of changes in levels of economic integration?

To shed light on these sorts of issue, this book develops a counter-argument to the new global orthodoxy. Far from becoming an anachronism, state capability has today become an important advantage in international competition. State capacity in this context refers to the ability of policy-making authorities to pursue domestic adjustment strategies that, in cooperation with organized economic groups, upgrade or transform the industrial economy.[7] Such strategies encompass both structural shifts: from declining to expanding sectors, as well as technological diffusion and innovation; and the creation of new industries, products and processes.

This is not to suggest that the state is the only institution capable of coordinating change in leading sectors or technologies.[8] The main point is that when possessed of domestic adjustment capability, the state can provide a potentially more powerful locus for coordinating change. This is because the state's institutions can offer the most encompassing organizational complex for overcoming a number of widely recognized obstacles to change, including problems of collective action, bounded rationality and short-term horizons, as well as unprecedented time compression in technological transformation. Most important of all, perhaps, only the state can readily absorb and socialize risk to the extent required by modern production technologies.[9]

In economics, the benefits of state coordination have been noted for a range of areas, including: coordinating complementary investment decisions, organizing the specialization of smaller firms (as producers of non-traded intermediate goods), promoting the sharing of information as well as technological acquisition, learning, and diffusion. Economists have tended to discuss these benefits – that is, to justify state coordination – in terms of 'market failures'.[10] But the new institutional economics, along with many business and organizational analysts, now suggests that market 'failure' is beside the point. State coordination, in principle, is vital to induce firms to engage in activities where the risk level would be so great as to deter firms acting alone. Such cases arise whenever investments are not only large scale but interdependent and, therefore, need to be made concurrently. Examples include the linkages between petrochemicals and successful mid- or down-stream producers in plastics or synthetic fibres, between semiconductor fabrication and a computer industry, and between robotics engineering and a robot-using industry. The cases can be multiplied. But the point remains the same: in order to effect change (and thus to ensure the industries necessary to each other's existence), some central coordinating device seems essential. The state has few if any equals for that particular job description. The new institutional economics comes to similar conclusions, but uses different language: the state can resolve many important problems of coordination better than the market by virtue of reducing 'transaction costs' in the wider economy.[11]

While there has been much discussion of these issues in the context of newly developing countries, it must be said that these are problems common to developing and mature industrial countries alike. Just as capitalism spreads geographically, so its geographical expression changes the nature of competition. Nowadays, successful adaptation to economic change within the developed world is no more automatic and hardly less difficult than successful development within the late industrializing ('latecomer') world. The sheer time compression in technological change, for example, has blurred the once developmentally distinctive boundaries between industrializing and industrialized. In some ways, though, industrialized-country firms face even greater competitive challenges, since their lot is not to copy or borrow technology from those ahead in order to advance, but to innovate constantly in order to maintain position.

The problem is that while *some* firms may have the capabilities to read the rapidly changing technological terrain, most do not, let alone the means to act on such capabilities *with sufficient speed* to meet the competition. Does this mean that the state will read the situation any better than individual firms? Not necessarily, and transformative states do not attempt to do this in ivory-tower isolation from the industry practitioners. But by providing the infrastructure, socializing the risks and encouraging cooperation, the state is in a position to orchestrate more nationally effective responses to technological competition.

The sources of state capability

So much for the advantages, but what of the *sources* of state capacity for governing industrial transformation? To reiterate, I am concerned not with capacity *per se*: the ability of the state to pursue its goals whatever they may be. Instead, my primary focus is on what can be called 'transformative' capacity: the ability to coordinate industrial change to meet the changing context of international competition. As the following chapter makes clear, transformative capacity is not to be elided with any particular set of policies. The agents of transformative states seek to shape and coordinate resources across a broader spectrum than that of 'industry' policy proper. However, it is in the state's actions aimed at the industrial economy that one can most readily trace the presence or absence of transformative capacity.

Clearly state capacity in this sense does not lend itself to precise measurement, in the way that is possible, say, for extractive (revenue-raising) capacity.[12] Moreover, there is no clear correlation between extractive and transformative capacity. States with very high extractive capacities, for instance Sweden, exhibit little of the transformative capacity of a low-taxing state like Japan, as argued in chapter 4.

Among the main understandings of this whole issue is the assumption that state capacity is a function of economic openness; that the more open or internationalized an economy, the weaker the state's capacity to govern industrial change. To follow this line of reasoning, in a highly integrated nation-state like Sweden one would predict relatively weak state capacity. To put this hypothesis to the test, I examine transformative capabilities in other highly integrated economies, such as Singapore and Germany. Such comparisons, however, reveal that differential capabilities have less to do with levels of economic integration than with the nature of domestic linkages and national strategies.

A much more influential hypothesis turns on the nature of 'policy instruments'. According to this reasoning, state capacity depends upon a predetermined set of policy instruments; hence, as the industrial economy matures and specific policy tools are no longer necessary or useful, capacity inevitably diminishes. Policy-instrument theorists, when looking at Japan for instance, are thus led to conclude that 'industrial policy is dead'. This view, however, assumes a static economy. It implies unvarying tools for unvarying tasks. But if the tasks change (e.g. from export promotion and industry creation to coordination of innovation and technology diffusion, as well as management of trade disputes, currency realignments and economic integration) – as indeed they must in a dynamic economy – then so too must the means for their accomplishment. My analysis of the Japanese case (in chapter 3, and again in chapter 7) suggests a state that is constantly creating new tools for new tasks, where industrial policy is very much alive, though its scope and targets are ever being redefined to meet changing domestic and international circumstances.

A third approach assumes that weakness in the business sector is somehow vital to state capacity, and that the latter is about the state having its way against or in spite of resistance from dominant economic groups. A corollary of this view is that such a situation is rarely, if at all, possible in democracies, and that therefore in developed countries – which are mostly democracies – transformative capacity is most unlikely.

In contrast with these approaches, I draw upon a more recent literature to argue (in chapters 2 and 3) that state capacity is a product of institutions governing domestic linkages, rather than of policy 'tools' or level of international integration, or private-sector weakness. This implies an approach that goes well beyond 'statism' so called. For we shall see that, with rare historical exceptions, *the state as such is not the sole source of its transformative capacity*. In recently and maturely industrialized settings, the latter depends very largely on the nature of the state's domestic linkages. Indeed, it would appear that the more industrialized the country and the more sophisticated the technology becomes, the more critical the policy linkages between economic bureaucracy and industrial sector for transformative success.

The powers of government to promote domestic adjustment, however, have long been highly differentiated across countries. Changes in the world economy would appear to have done little to even out these differences, though in the long run they may well work to deepen them.

Moreover, where states appear weak in responding to international change, we should view this as a sign less of the power of 'global' forces than of pre-existing frailty in the institutions governing domestic linkages. Indeed, as I seek to show with regard to the Swedish case, certain types of domestic linkage appear more robust than others in enabling transformative adjustment strategies.

State adaptation versus state decline

To conduct an interesting experiment, count the number of papers and books on the theme of state decline. Then do the same for those presenting the counter-view on the theme of state adaptation. It is a fair bet that one will be hard pressed to find more than a trickle of contributions on the latter subject. Yet consider that, over the long run, most states have (with some notable revolutionary exceptions) proved highly adaptive to changing circumstances. Failure to recognize or acknowledge adaptation has led too readily to the conclusion that the nation-state is in decline.

. If we exclude the current period, it is possible to identify at least three main episodes of 'adaptation' (occurring unevenly as nation-states emerge and develop at different rates). Modern states have defined themselves initially as tax-seekers for the conduct of military affairs (having primacy up to the eighteenth century); secondarily as protectors of the national economy and agents of industrialization (from the nineteenth century onwards); thirdly as builders of 'the nation' through the expansion of social citizenship (largely a twentieth-century phenomenon). The shift in tasks has meant not abandoning the old, but adding and overlaying new functions and institutions. For some countries, most notably Japan and Germany, militarism and industrialism were historically conjoined, and this had devastating consequences. But it also left in those settings a legacy of state capacity for guiding economic change, a capacity which I shall argue has evolved rather than diminished over time.

Military competition, industrialization and nation-building have thus formed three core challenges to which modern states have responded and in relation to which they have 'crystallized' different, and at times unrelated, functions. In responding to these challenges, states have gradually enhanced their 'infrastructural' capacities and generally shed arbitrary 'despotic' powers. But differences in infrastructural capacities – to penetrate society, to extract resources, and above all to mobilize and coordinate social energy – remain striking, especially in the developed world.[13]

Moreover, the pace and weight of military, economic and social challenges *vis-à-vis* individual nation-states have been historically uneven. This unevenness in turn has not been without consequences. Arguably, it has had a strong influence in shaping contemporary *differences* in the architecture and adaptive capacities of states. Thus some states have greater capacity for military mobilization, or for managing epidemics and natural disasters, than for economic transformation. Translated into the language of public policy, this means that, as Stephen Krasner (1978b: 58) noted many years ago,

> There is no reason to assume a priori that the pattern of strengths and weaknesses will be the same for all policies. One state may be unable to alter the structure of its medical system but be able to construct an efficient transportation network, while another can deal relatively easily with getting its citizens around but cannot get their illnesses cured.

Given the different rate, timing and situational circumstances of individual state development, this unevenness of capacities should come as no surprise. It is perhaps the key source of the state's widely noted 'incoherence' as an institutional complex.[14] This lack of coherence is in part a source of the state's partial autonomy. If we accept that states are not unitary or monolithic structures, then we must also recognize that their actions cannot be explained simply by noting the alignment of forces (domestic and international) in their environment. In other words, states do not behave uniformly just because they might face similar environmental conditions.

Globalization *versus* social caging?

It is now widely believed that nation-states are currently undergoing a fourth challenge or period of adaptation, the so-called challenge of 'globalization'. Many consider this to be a novel process, in the sense of being both more intensive and extensive in scope than in any preceding period.

What is different about globalization in the late twentieth century is that the process departs from (and depends upon) an environment structured quite differently from the global movements of a pre-industrial era. The fundamental difference is succinctly captured in Mann's conceptualization of state power as social 'caging'. As Mann has argued in a larger time frame contrasting pre-industrial and modern states,

> The 'power' of the modern state principally concerns not 'state elites' exercising power over society but a tightening state–society relation, caging

social relations over the national rather than the local-regional or transnational terrain, thus politicizing and geopoliticizing far more of social life than had earlier states. (1993a: 61)

The key idea conveyed by the 'caging' metaphor is not territorial confinement, but the notion that, with the nationalization of social life, much of the activity and social relations that were previously constituted at local or supra-national levels came to be regulated through the nation-state, hence depending increasingly on the latter for its existence. Thus, for example, while 'globalization' or transnationalism was the original context for early capitalism and state formation, the caging process, whereby states nationalized social life, came to provide a necessary structure for the development of the modern capitalist economy.

The central question is whether society is 'uncaging' (the usual meaning of globalization). Is genuine economic globalization occurring; and if so, does it mean that national networks of social interaction are being undermined? The answer to such questions depends on whether, in general, the new 'transnationalism', in contrast to earlier forms, goes through (i.e. exists by virtue of) the nation-state, or bypasses it altogether.

Globalization, which I argue is more appropriately termed 'internationalization', is often misunderstood as something imposed by microprocesses, such as the revolution in information technology. A number of sophisticated studies, however, have begun to attribute global economic change to the actions of state authorities as they have set about responding to domestic economic crisis precipitated, in turn, by a series of external shocks, by US financial deregulation to support extraordinary levels of deficit financing, and ultimately by prolonged world recession. Once set in train, however, the process of internationalization has acquired a certain momentum of its own – especially in finance. It is in this fourth era of adaptation that we see not only the expansion of capitalism on a world scale, but also the contest of different models or varieties of capitalism, as internationalization proceeds and as the domestically more robust states seek to 'externalize' aspects of their own model (see chapter 7).

Thus, the argument of this book implies that as we move into the next century, the ability of nation-states to adapt to internationalization (so-called 'globalization') will continue to heighten rather than diminish national differences in state capacity, as well as the advantages of national economic coordination.

The Book in Outline

The argument gets off the ground in chapter 2. This chapter builds on conceptual and empirical advances which analyse state capacity as an institutional complex, rather than as a product of policy tools, regime characteristics, class structure or level of openness. The argument is then advanced via three studies in 'comparative capitalism', each based on a distinctive institutional complex, and each chapter dealing with a different thesis about state denial.

Taking up the first thesis of state denial, we turn our attention in chapter 3 to the evolution of transformative capabilities (so-called 'developmentalism') in Japan and the NICs. Such a focus enables us to evaluate the endist-school prediction of the imminent demise of developmental or 'state-guided' capitalism and the death of industrial policy in East Asia.

Chapter 4 analyses the so-called crisis of the Swedish model of national economic management. It considers whether the much-admired Scandinavian model of domestic adjustment (so-called 'distributionism') has been steadily overpowered by increasing integration into the international economy or, rather, placed under stress by internal contradictions which may have reduced exposure to the global economy.

In the final case study, in chapter 5, I look to Germany, where its larger international environment – the EU – has supposedly usurped national policy-making capabilities. The chapter focuses on the adjustment strengths and potential weaknesses of *Modell Deutschland* and considers the extent to which the federal state's transformative capacity represents part of the problem or the solution to German adjustment.

From these chapters emerges a picture of different institutional complexes structured around distinctive projects – variously referred to as 'distributive', 'transformative' (or 'developmental') and 'dual' – with correspondingly varying consequences for transformative capacity. The argument of chapter 5 suggests that, while developmentally coordinated market economies generally tend to do better in international competition than either distributively coordinated or non-coordinated market economies, 'dual' polities (like Germany and Japan), which combine both developmental and distributive capabilities – in short, growth with equity – may have more long-run potential.

Having established in earlier chapters the continuing significance of state capacity, I turn in chapters 6 and 7 to a more general assessment of the globalization thesis. Chapter 6 analyses the extent of globalization, drawing on recent findings on trade, foreign direct investment (FDI), finance and multinational behaviour. While lending strong support to the notions of internationalization and regionalization, it finds little evidence of genuine globalization. Moreover, the stronger tendency towards regionalization has important implications for the viability of the nation-state. For regionalism draws attention not only to the importance of physical proximity between producers and suppliers, and hence of institutional embeddedness, but also to the importance of a home base for multinationals.

Finally, chapter 7 seeks generally to demolish the myth of state powerlessness and to take further the core argument that state capacity is an asset in an internationalized economy. This chapter proposes that 'strong states' tend to be midwives (even perpetrators), rather than victims, of 'globalization'. Thus we find strong states like Japan and the NICs adapting to external pressures for change (e.g. currency realignments, trade disputes and economic integration) by pursuing internationalization strategies in collaboration with their business sectors.

This book, then, is about state capacity: its sources, varieties, and consequences for industrial vitality in the late twentieth century. The question at the centre of these concerns is: what makes some nation-states better at domestic transformative strategies (e.g. Germany better than Sweden, Japan better than the United States, Taiwan better than Brazil)? The book's general argument emphasizes state adaptivity and its continued advantages rather than diminution of state capacity in an increasingly 'global' environment. State capacity, far from becoming irrelevant, has acquired new significance in a changing world economy. Such an argument implies that the contest between competing capitalisms (between, say, the producer-oriented East Asian and the consumer-oriented Anglo-American varieties) will be increasingly a contest between strong and weak state capacities in the domestic industrial arena.[15] The book therefore takes issue with the current orthodoxy according to which states are at most hapless or harmless victims of change that traverse their borders and yet are beyond their control. So-called 'globalization' is not likely to displace state power. If anything, it will make it more salient.

2

THE SOURCES OF STATE CAPACITY

Introduction

Interest in the nature and sources of state capacity has a firm foothold in comparative and international political economy. In the seventies and eighties, as the long postwar boom subsided, many studies set about exploring the issue of comparative economic performance within the Organization for Economic Cooperation and Development (OECD). Why had some countries responded more effectively than others to common economic problems? In this literature, the key problems were identified as falling growth rates, rising unemployment, and inflation. In an environment defined by soaring oil prices and US war-induced inflation, controlling costs was thus perceived as key to maintaining competitiveness. Consequently, much of the literature that emerged in this period probed the (corporatist) institutional arrangements that best afforded some measure of wage restraint in the new inflation-driven environment. The state emerged as a central player in these accounts, both in orchestrating cooperation of the main organized partners, and in coordinating resources essential to their bargaining.[1]

But what also emerged from these accounts of the 'merits of corporatism' was the sense of a highly delimited sphere of state capability. For, typically, the states presiding over so-called democratic or social corporatism have shown much more capacity for social and labour-market policies than for industrial-technological change. 'Distributive' rather than 'transformative' capacity is one way of encapsulating this distinction (as argued for Sweden in chapter 4). Such a contrast suggests, on the one hand, a group of states which are more at home distributing the costs of change (in order, for example, to assist the transfer of labour from declining industries) and, on the other hand, a group of transformative states, which are more routinely involved in strategies for upgrading the industrial economy. While the former category includes Sweden and some of the smaller states of northern Europe, the latter more appropriately describes the so-called 'developmentally oriented' states of East Asia (Japan, South Korea and Taiwan), and their European counterparts, Germany, Austria, and postwar France. While, as we shall see, the East Asian states also share corporatist institutional features with their European counterparts, their state–society relations are organized more narrowly and accordingly focused more directly on transformative tasks.

The dramatic emergence of Japan as an industrial leader outpacing America in many sectors, and the astonishing 'catch-up' success of the East Asian NICs, have offered in recent years a new and more sustained source of interest in state capacity. As emphasis within the OECD nations has shifted from inflation to the trade balance and to the need to increase exports, attention has switched from cost-driven to the challenge of innovation-driven, competition and the role of states in national competitiveness.[2] The dramatic industrial transformation of North East Asia, in particular, has posed the question of why some states have been able to play a more effective role than others in co-ordinating industrial change. This issue has given rise to a literature that highlights the importance of policies and institutions quite different from those analysed in the earlier corporatist accounts. For where the latter placed primary emphasis on the *organization of social groups* and the sorts of policy necessary to institutionalize political exchange (e.g. wage control for employment), the former has *also* given much attention to the orientation and *organization of the state* and the sorts of policy necessary to transform the industrial economy.[3]

This is what I have called transformative capacity, whereby emphasis is placed on domestic strategies for industrial change. Arguably, it is the type of state capacity of most importance to the nation-state in a globalizing economic environment. It is of primary interest to the present study.

The Problem of State Capacity

Delimiting state capacity

As the more anodyne term for state power, state capacity is impossible to define in the abstract. The reason for this is straightforward. States are not unitary or monolithic structures. They are organizational complexes whose various 'parts' represent different ages, functions and (at times) orientations. Mann makes the point in a novel way that states lack systemic coherence. The modern state is not unitary but 'polymorphous and factionalized in its structure', with military, capitalist and nationalist elements (1993a: 796). Mann has theorized this lack of coherence, drawing on the notion of diverse 'political crystallizations'. Here is an illustration:

> Today, the American state might crystallize as conservative-patriarchal-Christian one week when restricting abortion rights, as capitalist the next when regulating the savings and loans banking scandal, as a superpower the next when sending troops abroad for other than national economic interests. These varied crystallizations are rarely in harmony or in dialectical opposition to one another; usually they just differ. They mobilize differing, if overlapping and intersecting, power networks, and their solutions have consequences, some unintended for each other. (Mann 1993a: 736)

Taking seriously this notion of the state as a conglomeration of varied crystallizations has two important consequences for state theory. First, it implies an anti-reductionist theory of the state: there is no one particular crystallization that can ultimately determine the overall character of the state. Second, however, crystallization theory does allow for the possibility of 'imbalances' whereby one crystallization may weigh more heavily on state behaviour, with more or less direct consequences for other crystallizations. Thus, it can help to make sense of differential capabilities as between the domestic and international spheres. A state that is strong at home is not necessarily also a state that is strong internationally. The weight of the military crystallization in the United States, for example, lends greater legitimation to foreign policy and externally oriented activity, downplaying capacity to act in the domestic arena and thus the economic crystallization.

As well as large differences between domestic and international capabilities, exemplified by the United States where even basic extractive capacities are among the weakest in the Western world, states often show surprising variability in their domestic capabilities. On closer inspection of course this may not be so surprising, given the earlier point that the state's various organizational parts, its legislative bodies and executive agencies, are not of a piece.

Indeed different tasks often make for competing interests, not to mention variable competencies. Thus the German Foreign Office has often opposed the free-trade stance of the Economics Ministry on the grounds that foreign economic policy is an instrument of foreign policy which should not be sacrificed to economic ideology. In Japan, the competence of the elite bureaucrats of the Ministry of International Trade and Industry (MITI) and the Ministry of Finance (MOF) is now legion, but this feature cannot be generalized to the executive bureaucracy as a whole. The Ministry for Post and Telecommunication, for example, is considered by the elite ministries as little more than a 'third-rate business bureaucracy' dramatically different from MITI-type 'policy ministries'.

This is not to deny the potential for some larger 'coherence', however limited this may be. After all, it is possible to distinguish 'liberal states' from, say, 'fascist' and 'corporatist' states, as so ably shown by Simon Reich (1990). But the overall point bears emphasis. It makes little sense to speak of the powers or capacities of states *in general*.[4]

Speaking of state capacity in the abstract is of little use for understanding substantive issues. Whether or not state capacity exists in a given context can only be determined on the basis of specific issues that interest us. Accordingly, one must always ask: 'capacity for what?' A state's capacity tends to vary across issue areas, some of which will be more far-reaching in their ramifications than others, depending on the larger environment. In the present historical juncture, it is hard to doubt the importance for national prosperity of the capacity for coordinating industrial change, for diffusing innovation, and for generally ensuring permanent upgrading of the industrial structure. This applies to developed and industrializing countries alike. It must be emphasized, however, that transformative capability is not synonymous with 'intervention', since all states intervene to some degree; yet much intervention is ineffective or inappropriate in inducing change. And such capability is not inimical to the enforcement of market processes, for that is simply one of the many and shifting techniques, as we shall see, that states can deploy to control their environment.

The problem of government failure

Whether among industrializing or developed industrial states, the presence of transformative capacity has not been the norm. Not so much exceptional as atypical, it is the restricted rather than generalized presence of state capacity that has underlined the need for a special explanatory effort. That effort has been shaped in large part by a tendency to assume that all states are essentially alike – predatory or self-serving in motivation, incompetent or inefficient in economic affairs. Attempts to unravel the sources of state capacity have thus been shaped by two quintessentially neoclassical premises.

The predatory/rent-generating state   The first such premise posits the primary motivation of state actors as one of predatory or self-serving behaviour.[5] Given this starting point, the central question then becomes: 'What are the structural attributes and environmental conditions that enable a bureaucracy to pursue collective goals rather than disintegrating into a collection of self-serving revenue-maximizers?' A variation on this theme sees bureaucracies dominated by vote-maximizing politicians whose interventions generate rents which private agents seek to capture.[6]

The main difficulty with this *a priori* form of reasoning, however, is the sweeping assumption that all states will act in a particular way, regardless of how they are configured, how their incumbents are recruited, or how they are linked to other social groupings. The premise that all states (hence also state elites) are somehow 'naturally' oriented to self-enrichment rather than to broader institutional and collective goals is simply asserted, not demonstrated. Where welfare economics erred in naively assuming that the state would always serve the public, intervening to correct market failures, the neoclassical political economy literature has often veered too far in the opposite direction, assuming that states are fundamentally self-seeking revenue maximizers (e.g. Colander 1984).

For reasons well known to historical-institutional analysis, pre-industrial states and some third world states, particularly fledgeling states, have appeared more prone to predatory and self-serving behaviour.[7] Such state forms have typically lacked both established bureaucracy and legislature, and more generally the social base for a stable authority structure (Migdal 1987). But the predatory/rent-generating-state approach would appear to be of little value in analysing the majority of contemporary modern polities with their more complex institutional configurations. Indeed, among the most distinctive features of the modern state is the institutional constraint on the exercise of *arbitrary* power (Poggi 1990: 74–6). The obverse of this reduced 'despotic' power is a heightened 'infrastructural' power, giving the modern state a far-reaching ability to penetrate society and mobilize social energies across vast distances (Mann 1984/1988).

The distinction between advanced industrial and developing states is by no means absolute or watertight. But it is sufficiently marked to suggest that the level of *institutionalization* is of major significance. The important point is that institutions matter, for once in place, they condition and constrain the actions of individuals *qua* individuals. Conversely, where state-building is fragile or incomplete, as is the case in many African countries, there will be far greater scope and incentives for individualized interventions, including predatory behaviour.

At a deeper level still, the degree and character of institutionalization is strongly influenced by the historically and geopolitically formed international environment in which state-building takes place. Where nation-states have experienced sustained threats to national security – whether in the form of military challenge, resource scarcity or economic pressure, or some combination of these – this has perhaps done more than anything else to galvanize elites of newly formed (or re-formed) states to widen and deepen institutionalization. The model cases are Meiji Japan and postwar Taiwan and South Korea. While *institutional depth* refers to the degree to which the boundaries of the state and the orientations of state actors define a public sphere distinguishable from larger society, *institutional breadth* refers to the density of the links between state activities and those of other social entities.[8] Together, institutional depth and breadth bring a measure of *insulation* and *embeddedness* to the complex of organizations that constitute all modern states.[9] Thus, I shall argue below, if industrialized states differ in their capacities, this cannot be simply because some have more constraints on self-serving behaviour than others. Rather, *the difference owes much to the **degree** and **type** of institutional depth (insulation) and breadth (embeddedness)*, not to their simple absence or presence.

The incompetent state   Another influential assumption that informs contemporary understanding is that state involvement in the economy is more likely to stifle or obstruct industrial transformation than to induce it. This is based on the (neoclassical) tenet that markets are necessarily more *efficient* than governments in anticipating or adjusting to change, that only markets can provide the sort of information necessary to enable producers to stay abreast of new developments, that government failure is more pervasive and more costly than market failure, and that attempts by public agencies to provide guidance or leadership in the process of change are bound to fail due to information problems and rent-seeking.[10]

Thus, the key question here becomes: 'What are the attributes that enable public policy-makers to pursue industrial adjustment strategies relatively *effectively*, and thus to succeed more often than to fail?'

While the problems of information asymmetry and rent-seeking have been much exaggerated (Chang 1994: 25–30), the so-called government-failure literature has none the less provided a valuable corrective to the view that, given the right sorts of policy, governments can readily achieve what they set out to do. Similarly, as the focus on state capacity as a problem to be explained implies, I too clearly reject such a crudely 'statist' view.

My position nevertheless differs from the government-failure view in assuming neither generalized predation nor generalized incompetence. Rather, I suggest a more fruitful approach is to posit that, for path-dependent reasons, *state orientations* or regime goals and their associated *state–society linkages* have evolved in different ways. In some settings, both orientations and linkages have become more tightly focused on long-term projects for industrial transformation and the continuous organizational learning necessary to that task. In many other contexts, exposed to markedly different industrialization experiences, regime goals and domestic linkages have been given over to the more or less self-conscious avoidance of transformative projects and their associated learning processes. Following this reasoning, one might therefore argue that the relatively weak domestic capacities of some industrialized states to respond to economic change (or to achieve such stated goals) would appear to be due less to endemic or insurmountable problems of rent-seeking and information gaps than to an historically formed regime predisposition hostile to government coordination and public–private cooperation.

This is notably the case for liberal states. Liberal states are primarily those of the English-speaking world: Britain and the settler societies of the United States, Australia, Canada and New Zealand. They can be usefully distinguished by their regulatory goals and by their state–society relations, in particular the government–business relationship and the state's role in the economy. With a state tradition built on the primacy of individual over collective rights, the suspicion of state power and the celebration of free markets as key to prosperity, liberal states have long approached their economic role, and the interventions that must perforce be carried out from time to time, as something to be tolerated, however momentarily, rather than improved and perfected. At the opposite end of the spectrum lie so-called 'developmental' states like Japan and Germany, which have, on the whole, assumed a more project-oriented and transformative approach to economic management. As subsequent chapters argue, these states have overseen a more production-centred regime of industrial policy involving varying forms of bureaucratic coordination and government–business cooperation. In between these two major types lie variously constituted corporatist states, like Sweden or Norway, which tend to lean more towards distributive intervention (or what Katzenstein [1985] has called 'domestic compensation') than direct industrial transformation to foster growth.

Weak capability and the liberal state: situational imperatives and domestic orientations

One implication of the discussion to this point, which anticipates later arguments, is that in the advanced states at least, 'incapacity' is rarely cement-like, requiring some kind of revolutionary blasting to reconfig-ure social and organizational structures. Weak capability appears much more fundamentally a matter of changing state *orientations* (by no means a simple matter). Thus, for example, a state may change its poli-cies quite dramatically, or develop islands of expertise for managing this or that issue area, but without a sea change in underlying orientations, the general mode of intervention and policy instruments in particular are likely to remain unaltered.

Consider the recent adjustment experience of a liberal democratic state, Australia, and its free-trade policy. Australia shares elements with the Anglo-American experience more generally: like America and Britain, it is a liberal state strongly opposed to an industrial policy, faced since the 1980s with massive restructuring of its traditional indus-tries. This has involved *inter alia* removing protection from the textile, clothing and footwear (TCF) industries and providing massive subsidies for their upgrading. While the whole episode serves to underline weak state capacity, somewhat unexpectedly, it also does much to explode the myth that liberal states are simply captives of organized interests. In this case, it was against intense community and industry protest that the Labor-led government decided in 1987 to slash protection (by gradually removing quotas by 1995). Adding insult to injury, the government intensified business and union opposition by announcing to an aston-ished industry in 1991 that market opening would be accelerated (removing all quotas by 1993, bounties by 1995, and tariffs by 2000).[11]

But autonomy – however great or small – is a poor predictor of capacity. Herein lies the problem. The government, attracted by the elegant simplicity of liberal economics as a recipe for prosperity, proved quite capable of moving ahead on the 'free-trade' front (i.e. removing protection regardless of industry and union demands or interests). But in implementing the programme to upgrade the industry and equip it for the coming competition, the liberal state – through the newly consti-tuted TCF Development Authority (TCFDA) – demonstrated precisely those problems predicted by its economic ideology: an absence of industry expertise within the bureaucracy (a largely contrived outcome to ensure that the staff of the fledgeling TCFDA had no allegiance to protection-seeking industry or unions); distrust of formalized *industry input* in upgrading programmes (whose cooperation had not been sought in devising the new policy and which could therefore hardly be relied upon to go along with it); and heavy dependence on outside 'consultants' (who at times had little knowledge of the industry and who absorbed a disproportionate share of the funds). As a consequence, coordination was non-existent: while a few textile manufacturers used subsidies to upgrade facilities in (mistaken) anticipation of new orders from local clothing producers and retailers, many of the latter deployed their subsidies to upgrade warehousing facilities to receive greater quantities of *imports*. The result was: $1 billion expended in subsidies, the loss of 40,000 jobs, and an industry in shreds.[12]

The point to underline in this example is that liberal states may not lack the *ability to impose* new policies on industry (which is what often passes for state capacity); indeed imposing market solutions, as in the removal of TCF protection, may well be their *forte* (see e.g. Ikenberry 1986). However, while sometimes indicative of a state's crude 'strength', such imposition may be of little or no relevance at all to its transformative 'capacity'. This has indeed been the Australian experience in TCF. Similar examples of *strength without capacity* could no doubt be found for quintessentially liberal Britain and America.

Move somewhat 'upstream' in the economic bureaucracy and one finds an island of expertise in the form of Austrade, a trade promotion agency within the Department of Foreign Affairs and Trade whose success in achieving its goals stands in stark contrast to most other areas of the administration. Recently reconstituted under a Labor government to encourage Australian exports, Austrade stands apart from most of the executive bureaucracy for its commitment and ability to provide effective export guidance to Australian industry. Perhaps 'oasis in the desert' is a more fitting metaphor than 'jewel in the crown', for Austrade appears as something of an exception in the sphere of economic guidance.

Success stories like Austrade can be found even in the more classically liberal states of Britain and America. It is, for instance, widely recognized that American agriculture and high-tech have benefited massively from public–private coordination. But the point is that this type of federal involvement in industry has not been routine. It has been forthcoming only to the extent that it could be justified as a national security issue.[13]

These sorts of episode remain the exceptions which prove the rule that liberal states have relatively weak transformative capacity and that they are reluctant to generalize their organizational 'successes'. This reluctance within the industrialized world at least is, I have suggested, a by-product of historically formed regime goals. For these provide the foundation for the development or underdevelopment, as the case may be, of the relevant institutional apparatus and policy instruments that support a regime of industrial policy. In a comparison of postwar British and German policy towards the automobile industry, Simon Reich (1990: 34–5) summarizes the problem of ideological constraints well, observing that 'The principles of liberal ideology lead to the development of few interventionist instruments, and the absence of examples of effective intervention sustains a belief in the efficacy of limited intervention.'

In the deepest sense, then, regime goals are the foundation stone on which the pillars of state capacity are erected. They throw some light at least on why it is that liberal states generally do not modify their structures or modes of intervention, even when only slight modifications might mean greatly enhanced effectiveness. Historically formed regime goals also help to explain why some states – like Japan, France and Germany – have adopted a more coordinated, production-centred approach to the industrial economy, while others – like America and Britain – have long favoured a consumer-centred, market-led approach to economic issues.

Thus in a search for the environmental-situational determinants of state orientations, one would certainly have to include developmental timing – that is, a nation-state's point of entry into the world system – as well as geopolitics – that is, the resource and locational pressures, security imperatives and other external challenges that latecomers face in the race to catch up. Different environmental conditions have thus played a large part in shaping subsequent developmental patterns. Faced with fewer competitors and less demanding technologies, early industrializing liberal states like Britain and America have thus traditionally pursued market-led, consumption-centred development. But for late industrializers like nineteenth-century Japan and Germany – as well as the more recently industrialized Asian NICs – the forced pace and overlapping pressures of security and technology gaps have typically meant a more state-coordinated, production-oriented pattern of development in the catch-up effort.

I have stressed here the primacy of regime goals for the simple reason that they are all too often taken for granted in discussions of state capacity, and in order that I may set them to one side in the following analysis. To investigate the origins of different state orientations would take us too far into the developmental-geopolitical histories of different states and too far from the core task, which is to understand the more proximate, institutional sources of state capacity.[14]

Probing institutional arrangements rather than origins of orientations also makes sense for those countries which would seek to learn from their more dynamic neighbours. For while one cannot recreate the historical conditions in which particular state orientations were formed, we do know from the history of the geographical spread of capitalism, for example, that the difficulty of building supporting institutions in apparently 'culturally' hostile or inappropriate environments should not be exaggerated, and that orientations can be modified if not entirely reshaped by such institution-building.

Let us begin then with the principal approaches to state capacity.

Approaches to State Capacity

From the literature on comparative economic performance, it is possible to extract four principal hypotheses to explain cross-national differences in state capacity (and thus economic performance).

Capacity as social bargaining: corporatism

The first hypothesis places most emphasis on social organization, especially on the organization of social interests. In particular, concentrated, centralized interest groups are seen as the key to a system of social partnership based on stable, long-term political bargaining. Otherwise known as 'corporatism', this system emphasizes the relationship of organized interests to the state. It implies encompassing representation of organized interests (labour and capital), which, in turn, enables them to exercise strong negotiating powers in policy formation with government, and strong implementation powers in delivering member compliance. Thus, corporatism – especially in its tripartite version involving power-sharing arrangements among business, labour and the state – has often figured in comparative analysis as the key to state capacity and superior economic performance in modern democracies (see e.g. Katzenstein 1984; Schott 1984; Goldthorpe 1984).

In this literature, the relationship between corporatism and state capacity arises in at least two ways. First, the state facilitates corporatist bargaining via legal recognition of organized interests and provision of policy resources as a *quid pro quo* in labour–industry negotiations over wages. Second, corporatist bargaining, in turn, underpins the state's macro-economic efforts to control inflation and oversee modest industrial adjustment.

From the perspective of explaining state capacity, however, the corporatist literature has a number of limitations. First, given its focus largely on comparative responses to the oil shocks of the 1970s, corpo- ratist analysis has necessarily pursued a somewhat restricted explana- tory target. From our vantage point of the 1990s, it appears to have concentrated on economic outcomes which are either too narrow (i.e. low inflation) or too fleeting (i.e. low unemployment) to allow sustained analysis of transformative capacity and comparative industrial perfor- mance.

Second, as a result of the emphasis on wage bargaining and social policy provision, the corporatist approach has tended to overplay the significance of tripartite arrangements, and thus overlook the impor- tance of government–industry relations, in economic management. However, as Colin Crouch (1993a) has cogently argued, the essence of corporatism is revealed less by the structure of political bargaining (tri- partism) than by the mode of interaction with the state (power-sharing or the 'sharing of public space'). If we follow this line of reasoning, tri- partite arrangements – while important in specific spheres of economic management – may have a more restricted role in industrial transforma- tion than is conventionally understood in the corporatist literature. Conversely, various forms of power-sharing may contribute to state capacity in ways unanticipated in corporatist analysis. Indeed, we shall see in the following chapters that power-sharing arrangements involv- ing government and industry (though not necessarily labour) are a fea- ture common to all transformative states.[15]

Finally, while corporatism contributes something to our understand- ing of state capacity, it does so largely from the point of view of *social organization*. Whereas the latter is given centre stage in corporatist analysis, the *organization of the state* itself receives little treatment. These emphases are reversed in the next approach.

Capacity as coercion: the 'strong-state' thesis

The end of the long boom gave rise in the 1970s to a body of literature concerned with the capacity of states to intervene in their economies to restructure industry. Widespread concern with comparative economic performance throughout the industrialized world led many studies to focus on different responses to industrial adaptation and the sources of that variety. Some writers, concerned especially with the sources of fail- ure, such as Stephen Blank (1978) and Andrew Gamble (1981) writing on Britain's decline, drew attention to state weakness and inability to coordinate 'industrial modernization'. Others sought to explain why advanced industrial states appeared to differ so significantly in their capacity to respond to economic problems (e.g. Zysman 1977, 1983; Katzenstein 1978b, 1985; Krasner 1978a; Gourevitch 1978; Ikenberry 1988).

Part of this literature relies on a 'strong-state' versus 'weak-state' formulation to account for the observed differences in industrial adaptation. Advanced industrial states are grouped into particular categories of 'weak' and 'strong' capacity, according to the historically formed balance of power between state and society. Accordingly, Britain and the United States are paired as 'weak' states marked by incoherent or fragmented administrative structures. At the other extreme of this typology are France and Japan, both classified as 'strong' states for their highly centralized, insulated bureaucracies staffed by a technocratic elite, able to resist and transform private preferences.[16]

The test of a strong state – generally understood as the national political executive and the bureaucracy which serves that executive office – includes three core capacities: the ability to formulate policy goals and evolve strategies for implementing them independent of societal pressures; the ability to alter the behaviour of important domestic groups in order to further its policies; and the ability to restructure the domestic environment (e.g. property rights and industrial structure) in pursuit of its goals. Clearly such ability will vary across issue areas, warns the author of this strong-state formulation. But should it show generally positive on all three areas, 'then one is dealing with a relatively strong state' (Krasner 1978a: 60). This ability in turn is seen to reside in aspects of the state's organizational structure which enhance the autonomy of the state elite.

For the most part, this is a rich and innovative literature. It has a common feature, however, which marks the limits of its explanatory power. That is to say that much analysis in the strong-state genre has drawn its language and assumptions from the dualism of Cold War politics, which counterposes state (plan) against market. This influence seems evident above all in the assumption central to the concept of state strength: namely, that strong states (read 'autonomous' or 'capable' states) are such because they have *power over* society.

The orthodox notion of strength as an autonomous state wielding power over a relatively weak or subordinate society can be most appropriately called the 'statist' conception of state power. It is what most people have in mind when characterizing this or that approach as statist or state-centred theory. As one writer puts it in an effort to assemble a state-centred theory of development,

Support for a 'statist' view [state-centred theory] of development should ... come from evidence that agencies and actors within the national government routinely implemented adjustment policies *different from those advocated by the best-organized societal interests*. (Tillotson 1989: 341, *emphasis added*)

This statement encapsulates the conventional thinking on the question of state capacity: the state is seen to be good at industrial adaptation if it is strong; it is strong in so far as it is able to achieve those tasks and goals that it sets for itself, *over and against opposition* from dominant groups in society. Numerous influential texts emphasize this *coercive* sense of capacity. As Gourevitch (1978: 902) has noted, a strong state is typically defined as one 'whose unitary structure allows it to impose [its objectives] *over the objection of particularistic interests*' (emphasis added).[17] A similar understanding is reiterated in Skocpol's (1985: 9) introductory essay, 'Bringing the State Back In', where she defines state capacity as the ability of states 'to implement official goals, *especially over the actual or potential opposition of powerful social groups* or in the face of recalcitrant socioeconomic circumstances' (*emphasis added*).

Even the capacity of the state to provide economic guidance or *leadership* tends to be defined in coercive or abrasive terms. This idea has perhaps been most extensively debated for the Japanese economic bureaucracy, where the distinction between 'leading' and 'following' has been posited as 'a make-or-break matter for the strong state thesis' (McKean 1993: 82). The problem, however, is that by insisting on a coercive view of leadership as the 'ability to make others do what they would rather not' (McKean 1993: 89), one is led to the confident but arguably bizarre conclusion that the Japanese state has little capacity or strength.

Somewhat ironically, then, statism has become both the most influential understanding of state power theoretically, and at the same time the most contested empirically. Indeed, it is a point surely worth emphasizing that **state power has been conceptualized in a way that makes it virtually impossible to apply to modern states**. Not surprisingly, this provides plenty of scope for mounting critiques of statism, and such critiques have been readily forthcoming, assuming an almost ritualized character. The general point is worth restating in a slightly different way: since few if any industrial states in the capitalist world conform to the essentially coercive notion of power implied by the definition of a strong state, so-called 'statism' has become an all-too-easy target.

However, the critique of statism may well be misplaced precisely because, as I shall presently argue, state power has been fundamentally misconceived. In this regard, it is worth emphasizing that even the most vociferous critics of the 'strong-state' approach have not disputed the *conceptualization* of state power so much as the *reality* to which it is meant to apply. Hence, for example, they would today reject the notion of the Korean state as a capable state on the grounds that democratization has compromised its *ability to impose unilaterally* certain measures on the business sector (a point we return to in chapter 3). Critics of statism, in other words, generally accept the conventional, coercive view of state capacity. But they question its *existence* in given settings.

The critique of statism

Strong-state arguments have generated a rather large critical commentary, from which four main objections can be extracted.

The monolithic state   The first objection is the somewhat banal point that 'strength' is not generalizable across issue areas.

The state is not a unified organization; some parts are stronger, others weaker. Indeed, according to Skocpol 'one of the most important facts about the power of a state may be its unevenness across policy areas' (1985: 17). Thus Japan's effectiveness in industry policy has not been matched in the area of earthquake relief, while Sweden's capacity for social policy finds no equivalent in the sphere of industry. Others have pointed to sectoral evidence of exceptions to state strength and state weakness, so that weak states like Britain and the United States sometimes appear unexpectedly strong, while strong states like France and Japan appear sometimes subservient to private actors (Samuels 1987: 6; Wilks and Wright 1987: 284ff). At the same time, it is worth noting that such 'exceptions' themselves are often the outcome of quite particular interpretations, hence rarely constituting unambiguous evidence against the thesis in question.

Thus while the undifferentiated notion of strength and of state structure as 'unitary' has been widely criticized (see e.g. Zysman 1983: 297–8; Wilks and Wright 1987: 284–7), this characterization is not automatically posited by strong-state theorists. Some in fact have been careful to emphasize that strength is not an aggregate property of states (Krasner 1978a). It is probably therefore fair to say that even though the labels 'weak' and 'strong' are offered for comparative purposes, they are often intended more as convenient markers of state attributes in areas of particular importance than as general ideal types.

Strength versus policy orientation   Another criticism is that strength or autonomy is a poor predictor of policy orientation. Autonomy may be a good predictor of a state's ability to achieve its objectives, but a very poor predictor of the content of those objectives. Thus a state may be 'strong' in the sense of achieving its (highly circumscribed) goals – i.e. to leave the work of industrial transformation to the play of market forces – precisely because it has little transformative capacity in its own right. The Australian case of TCF adjustment mentioned earlier is an obvious example.

It is important to distinguish the question of transformative capacity and developmental effectiveness from that of 'strong' versus 'weak' states', which refers to the capacity of a state 'to carry out effectively those functions which it claims to be able to perform' (Crouch 1993a: 298). A strong state is not necessarily a highly interventionist one, while a weak state may well be interventionist. As Crouch explains,

> Although a state that occupies only a fragment of potential political space is likely to be a weak one, a restricted state which nevertheless carries out all the functions needed to secure basic order may well rate as very strong precisely because it concentrates its power and does not try to achieve 'too much'. Indeed, a need to restrict the state precisely in order to make its strength effective was part of the new right's critique of the arguably over-extended states of the 1970s. (1993a: 298–9)

Notions of strength and weakness, then, can only be useful if one is assessing the capacity of a state to achieve its goals. They are of little use in distinguishing between the capacity of a 'restricted' state that is strong precisely because it does not try to achieve too much, and the capacity of a 'catalytic' state that has a transformative project. (On the notion of a catalytic state, see the final chapter.)

Autonomy versus effectiveness Weak–strong portrayals have also tended to conflate autonomy with effective capacity. The fact that a state may choose its goals and successfully implement them is not a reliable predictor of effectiveness from a developmental point of view. History is strewn with examples of autonomous states which have proven highly ineffective from a transformative perspective (Weiss and Hobson 1995). At issue then is the capacity not simply to pursue projects broader in scope than the interests of any particular group, but also to coordinate economic change in a way that is growth enhancing rather than growth retarding.

As an example of the distinction between strength (autonomy) and effectiveness (capacity), consider an episode in the South Korean experience in semiconductors. In nurturing the establishment of the industry, the state insisted that the semiconductor industry export 100 per cent of its production. This had the (calculated) effect of breaking

up the Japanese–Korean alliance between Sony and Samsung, ultimately leading to the creation of Samsung's independent venture into
micro-electronics. The state's requirement succeeded in stifling Sony's
plan, in allying with Samsung, to capture the domestic market. It is a
clear example of the state getting its policy goals implemented, even
when in conflict with private-sector preferences (Yoon 1989). But the
action itself is silent on the issue of state *effectiveness vis-à-vis* national
economic enhancement. It may be that the end result – namely, forcing
Samsung into an independent venture in micro-electronics – eventually
worked in favour of national improvement. But this is a separate issue
to be determined empirically. The point is that strength (or autonomy)
vis-à-vis capital, and capacity *vis-à-vis* performance outcomes cannot be
assumed to coincide.

Statism: 'power over' versus 'power to'   Finally, a more fundamental
criticism turns on a larger conceptual weakness which strong-state
theorists and their critics share. Without exception, the strong-
state–weak-state literature (and its critique) have employed a concept
of state power as coercive–arbitrary, and portrayed state–society power
relations as adversarial and zero sum. This is what is usually meant by
statism: 'the state's tendency to act *against* the (short- or long-term)
economic interests of particular dominant classes' (McLennan 1989:
230).

So pervasive is this way of conceiving state power that even the more
insightful critiques of the strong–weak dichotomy remain caught within
its logic. Thus, for example, Ikenberry, who rejects simple notions of
strong and weak as crude and misleading, still sees domination as key to
the state's strength (1986: 106). Indeed, Ikenberry is primarily concerned not to overturn but to *broaden* this notion of strength, arguing
that the capacity 'to impose market solutions' is also a strength. While
this may be so, it simply restates the logic of domination and subordination at the heart of the strong-state approach that it criticizes.

The point worth stressing, however, is that neither state autonomy
nor business subservience can be taken as evidence of the presence of
transformative capacity. To advance beyond these unsubtle notions of
strength and weakness we need a way of conceptualizing state power
that takes seriously both the strength of the state and the strength of
organized groups in society. To this task we return in due course.

Capacity as 'policy instruments': the role of national financial systems

In earlier research within the statist perspective, autonomy from society was assumed to endow the state with the capacity to ensure its goals were implemented (Skocpol 1979; Trimberger 1978; Levi 1981). More recent research has distinguished the state's ability to *formulate* its goals from the capacity to devise and *implement* strategies to achieve them (Evans et al. 1985). But the issue of whether those strategies are effective from a developmental-transformative point of view, and what makes them so, has only begun to receive the sustained attention it deserves (see Evans 1995).

One of the first efforts in this direction was Zysman's (1983) highly innovative analysis of the different financial systems of comparative capitalism. In a wide-ranging comparison, Zysman outlines two characteristics of a state with transformative capacity (1983: 296ff). The first is independence from continuous specific pressures exerted by particular political groups and the legislature. Rather than reflecting the wishes of those who may have captured it, the state has sufficient autonomy (i.e. insulation) to develop and implement policies of its own. The question of 'autonomy from whom' is important. For, as Haggard and Moon have argued,

> If the state were 'autonomous' only from the working class, peasants, and marginal groups, there would be no way of differentiating an institutionalist perspective from societal theories of public policy; policy could be parsimoniously explained by the preferences of the dominant coalition. (1990: 214)

A critical test, then, is 'whether state structures can insulate political elites from the demands of powerful interest groups' (Haggard and Moon 1990: 214).

State insulation from such specific pressures is seen to derive from three features that define state structure. These chiefly concern the mode of recruitment of the national civil service (i.e. whether top bureaucratic positions are recruited from the civil service or filled by political appointment); the degree to which power is centralized; and the extent to which the political executive has autonomy from detailed legislative scrutiny. Together these three features suggest the ability of senior executives to formulate and impose their views of the economy on government policy (Zysman 1983: 298, 300). But in order to understand capacity for effective implementation, Zysman adds a further consideration.

The second feature of state capacity emphasized by Zysman is the ability to act on relevant groups in economy and society. This presupposes two quite important organizational arrangements. The first is, in Zysman's terms, the ability to structure access points for particular groups and to deny access to others. The other concerns the executive's ability to act effectively and thus selectively in the economy. This ability, argues Zysman in developing his central thesis, is enhanced or diminished according to the structure of financial institutions (so-called 'policy instruments') (Zysman 1983: 298).

Thus, in a major departure from strong-state (state-autonomy) approaches, Zysman offers instead a highly original argument, outlining what I have called a 'policy instrument' explanation of state capacity and variations in industrial adjustment. This attempts to establish a causal connection between the character of a country's financial system and the capacity of the state to intervene effectively in the economy. It argues that state capacity for industrial adjustment is powerfully shaped by the structure of a country's system of capital allocation. This identifies three types of financial system and three models of industrial change. 'State-led' systems are those typical of France and Japan, (and one might add Korea and Taiwan), where credit-based, price-administered finance allows bureaucrats to coordinate the flow of investment. 'Company-led' models of change occur where there are extensive capital markets and therefore minimal means of state-coordinated change, as in Britain and the United States. Finally, Zysman describes a pattern of 'negotiated' (or tripartite-bargained) adjustment, ostensibly typical of the former West Germany, where the financial system was led by banking institutions.

This is a powerful argument about differential capacities for strategic versus short-term approaches to industrial adaptation, and subsequent elaborations of this kind of approach have yielded important results (e.g. Ikenberry 1988; Y. Woo 1991). Nevertheless, it is not entirely clear whether the policy instruments approach *explains* or simply *restates* the problem of differential state capacities.

As many studies have shown, the use and efficacy of particular instruments will vary over time, depending on the phase of development and its associated tasks; but it does not follow that state capacity must thereby ebb and flow.[18] In Japan, for example, one can trace the shift in policy instruments from control of tariffs and exchange and import licence controls to administrative guidance and liberalization of the credit system; but in spite of the changing importance of various tools of policy, the capacity of MITI to coordinate industrial change appears to be relatively stable, as the arguments of chapters 3 and 7 suggest. As

Okimoto, along with many others, has observed for Japan, the 'harder' instruments have gradually lost ground to the 'softer' means of governing industrial change:

> MITI's influence today rests less on control of credit allocation or the possession of formal authority than on its powers of persuasion and coordination vis-a-vis the private sector, its capacity to gather and process information, set directions and priorities, promote private-sector and collective interests, and serve as an intermediary between domestic and international economies. (Okimoto 1989: 144)

Similarly, in the heartlands of so-called 'state-led' systems of finance – Japan, Korea and Taiwan – there is nowadays much less emphasis on increasing and coordinating investment for the purpose of export promotion and industry creation, and much more on developing and disseminating new products and technologies. Thus in the 1990s, Korea, Japan and Taiwan give much more prominence to the R&D side of industry policy (promotion and diffusion of technologies) than to that of investment banking (export and sectoral promotion). In the German case (analysed at length in chapter 5), we find even more dramatic changes, *vis-à-vis* the policy instrument. Indeed, in the 1990s, the major task of economic restructuring and integration of the east has highlighted the important role of state-led investment and a diminished role for the industrial banks – contrary to what one would predict from Zysman's model. None the less, one should not overplay the importance of the financial instrument. Tax systems too can be used in a highly creative manner to shape the upgrading and innovation process, as Taiwan and Japan have shown.[19]

The more general point to emphasize is that as the relevant tasks of economic transformation have evolved so have the instruments for achieving them. Indeed, evidence of the state's shifting techniques of economic management would suggest, as Ikenberry (1986: 136) notes, that it is this very ability to transform the instruments of policy that go to the heart of state capacity.

More generally, in the policy instrument formulation, analytic emphasis still falls for the most part on state autonomy and *state structure*. More recent research, especially on East Asian development, has developed a different institutional explanation, which brings the state and its organizational *linkages with industry* more centrally into the picture.

Capacity as embedded autonomy: organization of state and society

In thinking about state capacity, many writers have gone beyond state structure, noting that capacity also depends on the organization of groups in society (e.g. Katzenstein 1978b; Krasner 1978a; Evans et al. 1985). Most frequently, however, the assumption has been that organizational weakness, or fragmentation, of dominant groups in society is the key condition of the state's capacity to formulate and implement policy.

In the most important theoretical and empirical advances on the makings of a capable state, this thinking is reversed: encompassing organization of industrial interests makes effective policy-making more likely. Arguments of this kind have been fashioned by scholars working on comparative policy innovation in Europe and the comparative performance of newly industrializing countries. In his seminal work on the differential capacity of British and French governments for policy innovation, Peter Hall (1986) specifies three arenas which structure state capacity:

1 *the state's internal structure* (including the relationship between political and career executives, and internal decision-making attributes);
2 *the relationship between state and society* (i.e. the kind of leverage government has over society via, for example, the control of finance);
3 *the structure of society*, which can facilitate or constrain effective intervention (e.g. the kinds of industry organization which enhance policy implementation).

Chalmers Johnson has perhaps done most to alert us to the importance of the first of these arenas in his classic study of MITI (1982), which outlined the makings of an elite bureaucracy endowed with talent, commitment and a sense of mission.[20] With regard to the second feature, John Zysman's work – as we saw earlier – has been most influential in drawing attention to the role of the financial instrument in providing the state with policy leverage. But recent thinking on this issue has drawn attention to the different phases of industrial transformation and the different kinds of coordination task demanding changing policy tools. Thus instead of state leverage via specific *policy instruments*, the new emphasis is on leverage via coordination of *domestic linkages*, and the search for the kind, extent and function of such linkages. With some notable exceptions, there has been relatively little empirical work on this issue (see Johnson 1984a; Okimoto 1989; Evans 1995; Kuo 1995).

Peter Evans has recently taken these ideas further in his comparative political economy of third-world states (1989, 1995). This fourth approach involves the notion that state capacity in the industrial arena is founded upon a set of institutions which simultaneously *insulate* the economic bureaucracy from special interests, and establish cooperative *links* between bureaucrats and organized business. Evans argues that states which are more effective in achieving their transformative goals tend to be not merely sufficiently *autonomous* to formulate their own goals, but also sufficiently *embedded* in particular industrial networks to implement them.[21] In the notion of 'embedded autonomy', Evans gives us an important intellectual tool, not merely for differentiating third-world state capacities, but also for making sense of differential capabilities within the advanced industrial world.

The concept of *embedded autonomy* has been coined to solve the puzzle of why some highly 'interventionist' states, such as Korea, have been able to translate their developmental goals into practice, while others like Brazil and India have been far less effective in economic management. The answer, as Peter Evans has explained, is that certain attributes internal to state structure must heighten insulation or autonomy from pluralistic interests. But autonomy is not sufficient if goals are to be implemented successfully. For that to occur, autonomy must be embedded in specific social ties: 'It is an autonomy embedded in a concrete set of social ties which bind the state to society and provide institutionalized channels for the continual negotiation and renegotiation of goals and policies' (1992: 162). Thus he explains the apparent paradox of states which are at once sufficiently 'insulated' to avoid capture by special interest groups, yet sufficiently 'connected' to key social groupings who can ensure smooth implementation.

With the concept of embedded autonomy, Evans shifts the analytic focus from state structure and autonomy *per se* to the effectiveness with which the state carries out its transformative tasks, and so to state–economy linkages. Embedded autonomy thus draws attention to the capacity of the state to combine two seemingly contradictory aspects: 'Weberian bureaucratic insulation' with 'intense immersion in the surrounding social structure' (1989: 561). In one of the earliest formulations of this idea, Evans explains with regard to the 'developmental states' of East Asia that

the efficacy of the developmental state depends on a meritocratic bureaucracy with a strong sense of corporate identity and a dense set of institutionalized links to private elites ... Embedded autonomy depends on the existence of a project shared by a highly developed bureaucratic apparatus with interventive capacity built on historical experience and a relatively organized set of private actors who can provide useful intelligence and a possibility of decentralized implementation. (1989: 561, 575)

But is embedded autonomy simply a property of successful late industrializers, as Evans's analysis suggests? It could be argued that embedded autonomy applies, to some degree, to all or most contemporary industrial states, *qua* modern states. Few are without some degree of organizational insulation from special interests; and no modern state lacks multiple linkages and connectedness with its civil society (hence the common refrain that state boundaries are 'blurred' or hard to define). In the modern era, a modicum of *generalized* insulation and embeddedness defines the norm. Historical comparison helps to illustrate this point. For the contemporary norm diverges dramatically from that of pre-industrial states which, as Mann (1983/1988) has shown, were strong on autonomy by virtue of being almost entirely *disconnected* from 'their' surrounding society.

So how can the concept of embedded autonomy (which pertains in part to *all* modern states) illuminate the transformative capacity of *some* states? The answer, I would contend, lies in the more *specialized* nature of embedded autonomy in such states. *While all (or most) industrialized states have developed a generalized insulation and embeddedness, only some states have developed these features also in a form and degree of particular benefit to the* **industrial economy.** In these settings, state–economy linkages are tight but often highly selective, with structured access points for particular groups and exclusion of others from access: hence a *selective embeddedness.*

But for all its fruitfulness in Evans's own work, the notion of embedded autonomy suffers from a certain ambivalence. On the one hand, there is a clear sense in which it is being contrasted with statism (i.e. top-down, insulated, non-connected decision-making). On the other hand, 'embeddedness' appears to be 'negotiation'-neutral. For the thrust of Evans's account suggests that when a state has embedded autonomy it can use business networks with relative ease to implement its own policies.

The question, then, is how does a situation of 'embedded autonomy' differ from a situation of 'state corporatism' (*qua* top-down decision-making of the statist variety, but using organized groups as instruments of public policy)? Consider for a moment the typology in box 2.1. From this it would appear that embedded autonomy sits more comfortably with the 'state corporatist' policy network than with either the 'statist' or 'social corporatist' variety.

The problem, however, is that none of these categories conceives of a

Box 2.1 Industrial policy networks and the strong state

1 *Statism* applies where the state is 'strong' (goal-oriented, insulated from pluralist pressures) and the social group is fragmented or weakly organized, making domestic linkages difficult or unstable; resulting in top-down decision-making, relatively frequent information failures and implementation blockages.

2 *State corporatism* applies where the state is 'strong' and the social group is highly organized, yet is more an instrument of public policy than a negotiating partner – a situation conforming most closely to the notion of 'embedded autonomy'; effective within highly circumscribed political and technological boundaries (e.g. interwar Japan, 1960s South Korea).

3 *Concertation (social corporatism)* applies where the state is moderately insulated and the social group is highly organized in a robust negotiating relationship, but where domestic linkages are broadly constituted – a situation in which self-governance tends to prevail over other modes of state guidance (e.g. Sweden).

4 *Governed interdependence* applies where both state and social group are 'strong', i.e. the state is insulated and industry is highly organized in a robust negotiating relationship, but where domestic linkages for industrial transformation are relatively narrowly yet tightly constituted – a situation in which government provides leadership, and self-governance is only one aspect of a broader system of state guidance (e.g. postwar Japan).

situation in which a strong state *and* a strong society coexist. The categories continue to reflect the standard despotic theory of state power as negative-sum power of A over B. What they each fail to allow is the possibility of a strong state in combination with a strong capital sector.

In Peter Evans's formulation, the state can have transformative capacity only while capital remains in a relatively dependent–subordinate relationship to the state. Ironically, perhaps, this may be why Evans leans towards the view that the transformative states of East Asia are destined to have a short shelf life. Embeddedness is both their strength and their eventual undoing: by making capital strong they bring about their own gravediggers.[22]

What is needed, therefore, is **a concept able to incorporate both the strength of the state and that of the private sector.** Moreover, such a concept should be able to make sense of *a range of different situations* which involve *different forms of government–business cooperation*, thus reflecting the *changing tasks of economic management*. The concept of 'governed interdependence', discussed below, seems useful for this task.

Capacity as a special form of infrastructural power: 'governed interdependence'

'Governed interdependence' (GI) refers to a negotiated relationship, in which public and private participants maintain their autonomy, yet which is nevertheless governed by broader goals set and monitored by the state. In this relationship, leadership is either exercised directly by the state or delegated to the private sector where a robust organizational infrastructure has been nurtured by state policies.

GI is intended to convey a reality in which both state and dominant economic groups are 'strong': i.e. the state is well insulated and industry is highly organized and linked into the policy-making framework via a robust negotiating relationship. MITI's relationship with Japanese industry associations (*gyokai*) is a classic instance. A key distinction between the two concepts in question can be summarized as follows: While 'embedded autonomy' solves conceptually the problem of how, when the state is strong, to control the state's autonomy without compromising its effectiveness, GI solves the problem of how conceptually to preserve state effectiveness, when capital is strong, without compromising autonomy.

Interdependence is of course a generalized aspect of government–business relations. Firms rely on their governments to establish and nurture conditions essential for capturing world markets and for access to stable markets. Governments, on the other hand, depend on firms to increase wealth by generating jobs and growth. The key difference between this ordinary 'interdependence' and systems of GI is that in the latter, mutual dependence is given far greater formal recognition through opportunities for institutionalized cooperation, and therefore 'governed'. Rather than leaving mutual dependence to chance, the state takes a proactive role, drawing business into a negotiating relationship in order to further its developmental projects.

States can embed their autonomy in 'strong' or 'weak' social organization (thus resulting in various forms of state and social corporatism). Increases over time in the strength of social organization should not be read as corresponding diminutions of state capacity. Rather, they may provide a new basis for a reinvigorated state capacity, in line with the changing nature of transformative tasks in industrial society. As the following chapter argues, this has taken place most clearly in Japan. It appears to be increasingly the case in Taiwan, while recent Korean experience is somewhat ambiguous.

Thus, in contrast to existing approaches, GI theory rejects the notion that the state's ability to 'impose' its decisions is central to its transformative capacity. Unilateralism is more likely to be a developmental minus than a plus. It implies the capacity to act, but not necessarily to act effectively. Of central importance is the state's ability to use its autonomy to consult and to elicit consensus and cooperation from the private sector. I call this a special kind of infrastructural power because, through its linkages with key economic groupings, the state can extract and exchange vital information with producers, stimulate private-sector participation in key policy areas, and mobilize a greater level of industry collaboration in advancing national strategy.[23]

GI encompasses both the coordinated and the cooperative quality of that power. It describes a system of central coordination based on the cooperation of government and industry. Policies for this or that industry, sector or technology are not simply *imposed* by bureaucrats or politicians, but are the result of regular and extensive consultation and coordination with the private sector. Because of insulated policy-making, the government's transformative project does not lose out to clientelistic or sectional interests; because of institutional connectedness, business does not lose out to remote and bumbling bureaucrats.

As chapter 3 will seek to show in a discussion of its various forms and dynamics, GI refers to a relationship that evolves over time, whereby the state exploits and converts its autonomy into increasing coordinating capacity by entering into cooperative relationships with the private sector, in order thereby to enhance the effectiveness of its economic and industrial policies. If the state begins from a position of institutional insulation, this makes it more likely that cooperation over public policy will not degenerate into clientelism or be reduced to private sectional interest; rather, it will be subject to rules laid down by state agencies. The issue is not whether instances of clientelism or interest-group politics are absolutely ruled out, but instead whether such instances are isolated rather than the rule, especially in the sector of value-added tradables, where national competitiveness is most at stake.

Conclusion

Can there be a definitive conception of the makings of transformative capacity? The thrust of my analysis in this chapter (argued more fully in the following) has been to argue that this is not possible. It is not possible for the banal but important reason that the conditions for industrial success – and therefore the nature of the transformative tasks that need to be undertaken – change over time. As elaborated in chapter 3, 'statist' states may be effective under very restricted historical circumstances, such as forced-march industrialization; and 'state corporatism' has been most fruitful in catch-up phases of industrialization when the road ahead was relatively straight and fledgeling industrial groups depended heavily on state resources. By contrast, GI tends to yield more advantages for participants in a highly internationalized environment where competition is driven by continuous innovation.

By keeping these changing tasks of economic management firmly in view, we are therefore able to consider the possibility, usually ignored by existing approaches, that domestic and global changes are not undermining state capacity in general (hence leading to convergence on the 'weak' liberal state), but rather producing shifts in the *basis* of state capacity as transformative tasks alter. To follow this line of reasoning is to argue that differences in state capabilities are being not flattened but preserved, and that while being preserved they are also taking on more complex forms. Indeed, I shall endeavour to show in chapter 3 that GI itself can take a *variety of forms*, sometimes appearing more 'top-down' in character, yet at other times (especially in recent years) involving more private-sector initiative. The task of the following chapter will be to analyse the institutional underpinnings of such a system, focusing on the East Asian experience.

3

TRANSFORMATIVE CAPACITY IN EVOLUTION: EAST ASIAN DEVELOPMENTAL STATES

> the forces of production are the tree on which wealth grows, and ... the tree which bears the fruit is of greater value than the fruit itself. ... The prosperity of a nation is not ... greater in the proportion in which it has amassed more wealth ... but in the proportion in which it has more developed its powers of production.
>
> *Friedrich List 1966: 144*

Introduction

List's quotation captures the spirit of 'producer economics',[1] a system of political economy which emphasizes the value of production rather than consumption as the primary measure of national well-being.[2] In the primacy given to developing and deepening their industrial and technological powers, the so-called developmental states of East Asia – Japan, South Korea and Taiwan in particular – appear to have been exemplary students of List.[3]

The rise of high-performance market economies in East Asia – specifically those just mentioned – has generated a very large and commanding literature on the subject of East Asian development, including its strengths and weaknesses, its facilitating conditions and causes. Three major issues have emerged from this research. The first concerns the role of government, specifically the contribution of industrial policy; the second relates to why intervention has worked relatively well; and the third touches on the changing relationship between government and business.

Debate on the first issue has more or less run its course and this chapter takes as its premise the outcome of that debate: that active governments pursuing strategic trade and industrial policies have constituted an important component of East Asia's high-performance economies. This proposition is not defended here. But the reader is referred to the considerable body of supporting evidence marshalled elsewhere.[4]

That literature includes the work of both economists and political scientists. A growing number of economists have begun to document not the 'absence' or 'failure' of intervention in East Asian economies, but its 'effectiveness'. Accordingly, they have begun to highlight the importance of 'institutions', 'insulated technocracies' and 'bureaucratic capacities'.[5] Thus, even World Bank authorities now concede that it is no longer possible to ignore the importance of state activism in East Asian dynamism. Indeed, the most recent wave of World Bank reports represents a substantially toned-down version of free-market orthodoxy. A number of titles in the 'Lessons of East Asia' series are explicit about the leading role of government; whereas the more widely cited *East Asian Miracle* (1993a) goes so far as to include an entire chapter on the developmental role of governmental institutions, in which a series of market failures is shown to raise 'the problem of coordination'. More striking still is the emphasis given to state effectiveness in the World Bank's latest *World Development Report* (1997). The report's core acknowledgement that an effective state is essential for a prosperous society is by no means novel outside the neoclassical community. But it would seem to mark a dramatic shift in the bank's (and, therefore, in neoclassical) thinking about how economies develop. Rather than an exercise in 'paradigm maintenance' (see Wade 1996b), this latest effort inclines one to ask whether some sort of paradigm shift is under way. The more immediate point, however, is that by retaining the idea of prudential macro-economic management, yet rejecting the notion of 'neutral' or 'intervention-free' trade regimes, and embracing the idea of state effectiveness, neoclassical thinking can be seen to share common ground with the institutional analysis of the so-called 'new political economy'.

This latter refers to a body of work in comparative and international politics, loosely rather than rigorously unified by an explicit emphasis on strategic policies, and a more or less implicit one on government capacities and institutions as a major component of East Asia's strong economic performance.[6] Much of the region's analytic appeal stems from this unanticipated combination of impressive administrative ability with strong market performance. Such economies tend to defy Western expectations and deserve perhaps a distinctive label. We might call them 'coordinated market economies'.[7] Whether to establish new industries and create new products, or to upgrade quality, technologies and skills, the East Asian experience has emphasized the advantages of a publicly coordinated approach to industrial innovation.

The important questions for our purposes therefore relate to the second and third issues. What shared features of the East Asian states have made them relatively effective as agents of industrial change? How has their transformative capacity changed over time, and in what ways has the government–business relationship evolved as a result? Finally, I ask to what extent the tasks of industrial transformation have changed with domestic maturity and global change, and how this has altered the national system of economic management. In short, is industrial policy (and thus transformative capacity) obsolete?

Sources, manifestations and outcomes of state capacity

This chapter therefore takes as demonstrated the important role of the state in coordinating industrial transformation in East Asia. It does not seek to demonstrate the *effects* or outcomes of the state's industrial policies, a topic already extensively analysed in the literature. Nor shall I focus primarily on the *nature* of industrial policies themselves, although many of their features are integral to the analysis that follows. Indeed, as figure 3.1 indicates, it is in the design and implementation of particular policies that one has perhaps the clearest indicator of the presence or absence of a state's capacity for a transformative project: that is, in the extent to which its policy measures (in both design and implementation) on behalf of the industrial economy are *coordinated, selective* and *disciplinary*.[8] All three aspects of policy-making and implementation will be evident in the course of the discussion that follows.

Rather than retell a tale so amply told in other pages, my general objective here is to develop the institutional analysis of state capacity in East Asia, specifying the common institutional arrangements that enable a coordinated and cooperative approach to change. Empirically, I seek to show how the government–business relationship provides a core element of the state's transformative capacity, and to elaborate the main forms of that relationship and their changing importance over time. On a theoretical level, I seek to show how government–business cooperation – in which the strength of the state is matched by the strength of the private sector – can be accommodated in a theory of state capacity.

My general argument is that government–business cooperation is integral to a theory of state capacity; that – in the more industrially vibrant systems – the forms of cooperation have **adapted** over time to the changing tasks of transformation; and that the most robust form of

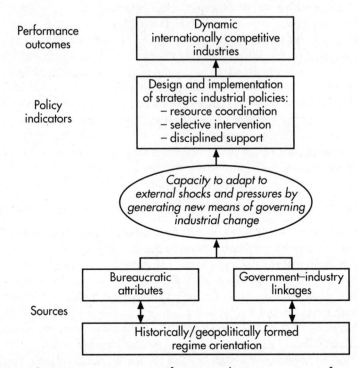

Performance outcomes

Dynamic internationally competitive industries

Policy indicators

Design and implementation of strategic industrial policies:
– resource coordination
– selective intervention
– disciplined support

Capacity to adapt to external shocks and pressures by generating new means of governing industrial change

Bureaucratic attributes

Government–industry linkages

Sources

Historically/geopolitically formed regime orientation

Figure 3.1 A state capacity framework: sources, manifestation in policies, and outcomes of their application

state capacity (and consequently industrial vitality) issues from the linkage between strong (cohesively organized) capital and strong (insulated) state agencies. Different forms of cooperation can coexist in the same system (some of which appear more state led, others more corporate driven); however, some forms will tend to predominate over others in particular phases of industrial change. Thus, for instance, in the industrialized settings of Taiwan and Korea, there is nowadays both far less scope for, and far less value in, top-down decision-making with whose outcomes industry simply passively concurs. In the most advanced countries, the more encompassing and cohesive the organization of industry, the more cohesive and insulated the executive bureaucracy, and the tighter the links between the two, the greater the capacity for innovation (i.e. for rapid and coordinated responses to economic change). Conversely, where industry has lacked organizational cohesion (as in the case of textiles in Taiwan), the state may be less disposed and less able either to stimulate industry input or to provide vital guidance.

The argument advanced in this chapter therefore diverges sharply from the standard view of state capacity. Most influential in this regard is the claim that organizational weakness (or fragmentation) of dominant groups in society is a condition of the state's capacity to formulate and implement policy (Skocpol 1985; Krasner 1978a). My argument takes an altogether different tack. As I will seek to show, in a fully developed system of GI where transformative capacity is high, one finds an established corporate sector that is both expected and required to take initiatives, and thus to assist governing agencies to target their activities and resources to greater effect.

This chapter will therefore seek to advance two propositions. The first has a distinguished pedigree but has not been adequately elaborated for the East Asian experience. This is the proposition that the East Asian capacity for coordination has an institutional basis. A number of writers have propounded this idea, notably Chalmers Johnson (1982), who first presented the evidence for Japan in his famous study of MITI; Robert Wade (1990a), who extended this idea to the NICs in his pioneering account of Taiwanese industrialization; and Peter Evans (1995), who followed up these accounts with an innovative attempt to highlight third-world differences in state capacity.

The second proposition advanced in this chapter is novel. It is proposed that the institutional arrangements in question result in a distinctive kind of government–business relationship, referred to here as GI. In this relationship, coordination and cooperation go hand in hand. Economic projects are advanced by public–private cooperation, but their adoption and implementation are disciplined and monitored by the state. The claim is not that existing accounts ignore the existence of 'cooperation' in East Asian government–business relations.[9] Rather, the problem is that they are unable to integrate the reality and idea of public–private cooperation into a theory of state capacity.

In their haste to dispute the 'developmental state' idea – to knock down the notion that the East Asian state is in some sense 'strong' or distinctive – many recent studies fail to pay sufficient attention to the possible importance of cooperation to a theory of state capacity. Cooperation is usually seen as a sign of the *diminution* or dilution of state power; its absence as a sign of the state calling the shots. Consequently, much analysis has lined up under either state-led or society-led approaches, where each admonishes the other to take either the state or capital seriously. The weakness of the most recent wave of 'business-led' accounts, however, is that in seeking to bring capital back in, the state is being marginalized or diminished, in a negative-sum manner (e.g. Calder 1993; Callon 1995).

So what would a theory look like in which both state and capital are taken seriously, and where strong states and strong industry go hand in hand? I contend that it would approximate a theory of GI. In a system of GI, the state acts as a catalyst in coalitions of government officials and industrial actors. The following analysis seeks to provide the substantive building blocks of such a theory in two ways. First, I analyse institutional arrangements in the Asian Three, complementing and extending upon the work of Johnson, Wade and Evans. Second, by examining particular policy measures, I distinguish different types of state–industry interaction – some apparently 'state led', others apparently 'business led' – all of which can be accommodated in a theory of GI. More generally, the analysis suggests how the basis of transformative capacity changes over time, becoming more rather than less robust with the strengthening of industry participation.

Institutions and Economic Performance

Most analyses of the East Asian experience are heavily indebted to the pioneering studies of Chalmers Johnson and Robert Wade for advancing empirical and theoretical understanding of East Asian development. The present study is no exception, notwithstanding important differences, as we shall see.

Wade's work, like that of Johnson's before him, is important not merely for demolishing market-led accounts of East Asian success, but for building a new view of that experience in which active governments and strategic industrial policy play a central part. But Wade, like Johnson, goes further than this to draw attention to the importance of institutional arrangements that make such a strategic approach possible. The result is what Wade has called 'governed market theory' (GMT).

GMT advances three main propositions (see figure 3.2). First, the superior performance of Japan and the NICs is the result of heavy investment in internationally competitive, high-growth industries. Moreover, the patterning and level of investment are different from what would have been the case if market mechanisms alone had operated. Second, the exceptional levels of investment in increasingly high-tech sectors is the deliberate outcome of a set of 'strategic industrial policies'. Third, at a deeper level of causality, these policies were pursued with more consistency, and were more effective than in other

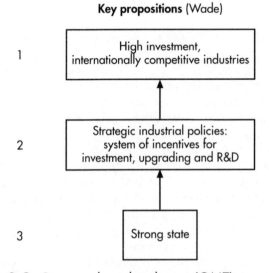

Key propositions (Wade)

1

High investment,
internationally competitive industries

2

Strategic industrial policies:
system of incentives for
investment, upgrading and R&D

3

Strong state

Figure 3.2 Governed market theory (GMT)

developing countries, because of a particular set of institutional arrangements, in this case a strong 'autonomous' state.

The point of Wade's argument is not that industrial policies are the whole story, but rather that in the absence of some form of *coordination*, there is no guarantee that savings and investment will be channelled towards productive rather than speculative activities, or that technological upgrading rather than cost-cutting strategies will prevail. Though it uses different language, GMT highlights this aspect of the state's coordinating role in the region.[10] Industrial strategies seek to ensure the industries essential to the nation's long-run welfare, rather than merely reward short-term consumption. Such policies entail flexibility and therefore generally involve three arms: an investment banking arm for promoting exports and/or particular sectors; a restructuring arm for streamlining or upgrading sectors in decline; and an R&D arm for developing and disseminating new products and technologies. All three are interconnected, but the importance of each will vary according to different phases in the development process. Thus, for example, in the 1990s, Korea, Japan and Taiwan give much more prominence to the R&D arm (promotion and diffusion of technologies) than to that of investment banking (export and sectoral promotion).

GI theory

My approach differs from GMT in two key respects. The first difference to note concerns the larger 'system' nurtured by public policies, which institutionalizes a dynamic response from industry. The proposition is that the ability of East Asian firms and industry more generally to adapt quickly to economic change is based on a system that socializes risk and thereby coordinates change across a broad array of organizations – both public and private.

In this system, firms are relieved from bearing the entire burden of four major 'risks': (1) raising capital; (2) developing new products and technologies; (3) finding new markets; and (4) training skilled engineers and workers. A significant proportion of the costs of upgrading technology, new product development, industrial training, market expansion and so forth is shared by, or embedded in, a thick network of state-informed (i.e. public–private) institutions.

This system is perhaps the most tangible by-product of the state's strategic industrial policies (the latter being the focus of Wade's analysis). But beneath that system, what makes the policies so effective is a particular kind of state structure and a particular kind of relationship between the state and industry. I call this institutional arrangement GI. As discussed in chapter 2 (and in more detail below), it describes a system of central coordination based on the cooperation of government and industry. Policies for this or that industry, sector or technology are not simply *imposed* by bureaucrats or politicians, but are the result of regular and extensive consultation, negotiation and coordination with the private sector.

It is this institutional level of analysis (discussed at length in the following section) that remains the least developed aspect of Wade's GMT. In its present form it does not offer a convincing explanation of the capacity for coordinating industrial change, or what Wade and others refer to as 'strategic industrial policy'. Why have the Taiwanese, Koreans and Japanese been able to pursue 'their' developmental projects so effectively? Wade, like many other analysts, appears to rely on the idea of a relatively 'hard' state, able and willing to *impose* its own objectives and decisions, regardless of private opposition. He is therefore led to emphasize the authoritarian, corporatist character of the East Asian state, especially with regard to the NICs.

But as indicated in the previous chapter, the state's ability to 'impose' its decisions is a poor predictor of developmental effectiveness. Such a 'hard' state may be relatively effective in the early phase of industrialization when the transformation tasks are relatively simple, as suggested below. Over the long run, however, what really matters is whether the state is able to use its autonomy to consult and to elicit cooperative responses from the private sector. This is not the kind of power 'over' society that one associates with authoritarian government; it is power 'through' society, which is much more potent in developmental terms.[11]

Institutional Capacities for Industrial Transformation

So how did Japan and the NICs do what they did so well? What helped to make active industrial policies relatively effective in the region, especially in the light of neoclassical predictions about rent-seeking and information gaps?

The general argument highlights key features of the organization and interaction of government and business, which make effective coordination of the market a more likely outcome in the East Asian Three. As we shall see, there is no monolithic 'East Asian model', but different ways of achieving a coordinated outcome.

Bureaucratic structures of coordination

Peter Evans has paved the way for a nuanced understanding of the whole issue, concentrating on the notion of 'embedded autonomy', as outlined in chapter 2 above. On the features contributing to state autonomy, however, Evans's account seems too narrow. He stresses bureaucratic coherence (through meritocracy and personal networks) as the key to the state's insulation (1992: 163). But such a state would constantly run the danger of being under-insulated and over-embedded. If we are to grasp the makings of state capacity and government–business relations in the region, we need to add to Evans's 'coherence'.

A number of conditions are essential if a state's policies are to be consistent with a transformative or developmental project and growth-oriented goals. One is that the bureaucracy be competent and committed to organizational objectives. The other is that the state's key policy-making agencies be sufficiently insulated against special interest groups and clientelistic pressures generally. Though Evans tends to treat these together, the conditions for each are not identical.

Three main features of the East Asian state's internal organization are relevant in this regard: the quality and prestige of the economic bureaucrats (the main focus of Evans's analysis of state autonomy); a strong in-house capacity for information gathering; and the appointment of a key agency charged with the task of coordinating industrial change. These conditions are significant in so far as they contribute to the *insulation* or autonomy of the bureaucracy, preserving policy-making from domination by private interests, and thereby enhancing the likelihood that state agencies will pursue projects broader than the interests of any one particular group. But even a creatively structured civil service may count for very little if the broader political system is at odds with a growth agenda. Thus, one must also take account of the relations between the civil service and the broader political environment in which it functions, a point to which I return shortly.

High-quality bureaucrats   As many writers have noted, in East Asia, government service has traditionally conferred high status. Merit-based recruitment and promotion of officials, rather than political appointment, have tended to minimize political manipulation of the bureaucracy. Consequently, governments have been able to attract highly qualified individuals. But one should not overstate the 'rational' Weberian characteristics of these bureaucracies. For the cohesiveness that provides a measure of insulation can come from a variety of sources. The formation of the postwar Taiwanese and Korean civil service was not solely merit-based. In addition to talent, ethnic homogeneity (the mainland factor in Taiwan) and in some cases shared military background (in Korea) were important attributes in the recruitment process. These 'non-bureaucratic' forms of recruitment bound such groups more tightly to the state and thus served to foster the kind of bureaucratic culture in which individuals take as their own objectives the goals of their organization. In this sense, they contributed a further important mechanism of insulation.[12]

   Also at odds with the Weberian ideal are the high levels of internal competition, especially marked in Japan's civil service, which provide another means of fostering high-quality performance. More generally, however, the combination of talent and prestige has made for a highly motivated, competent and cohesive civil service which has internalized national objectives.[13]

Intelligence-gathering infrastructure   The second, related feature of the core economic ministries is their powerful capacity for marshalling and analysing economic information in-house. In Japan, MITI's dedicated research institute yields much of the data, analysis and conceptual equipment that make possible the Ministry's powerful 'think-tank' role

(Johnson 1984a). More generally, MITI's acknowledged strengths in analysis of technology and market conditions for manufactured products and raw materials derives from its central, nodal position in a vast information network. Having command of a robust intelligence-gathering infrastructure has thus enabled MITI to identify new technology areas with important commercial potential and to alert companies to, and encourage them to act on, the opportunities for change.[14] It is perhaps the most important resource at MITI's disposal as the ministry's role in industrial policy continues to evolve (Johnson 1984a: 62).

Striking parallels with Japanese capability can be found in Korea and Taiwan. Prior to its recent restructuring, the capacities of Korea's Economic Planning Boards (EPB) were outstanding in this regard. More generally, Korea's key economic ministries each maintains an efficient information network of its own. This includes the numerous research institutes attached to particular ministries, one of the largest being the Korean Institute for Science and Technology (KIST), which serves the Ministry for Trade, Industry and Energy, as well as state agencies like the Korean Trade Promotion Corporation (KOTRA), whose role has been crucial to the export drive of Korean firms. Indeed, in its knowledge of product demand, quality standards and foreign market trends generally, KOTRA has often been better informed than the private sector (Jones and Sakong 1980).[15]

A key aspect of the information-gathering network in Korea has been the establishment of a mandatory reporting system. This allowed the bureaucracy to keep close track of priority industries throughout the high-growth period. In return for significant state support, these industries were required regularly to report on their export performance and on other areas of business activity. Failure to do so would incur sanctions ranging from fines and withdrawal of support to bankruptcy or even prison sentences. The important point is that through this monitoring system, the state gained access to up-to-date knowledge of production conditions in priority sectors (cf. Chang 1994: 142).

Similarly, in Taiwan, the web of public research agencies that surround the state sector provides both firms and individual ministries with a range of vital information that feeds into both private production and public policy. The public research institutes like the Industrial Technology Research Institute (ITRI), for instance, are the vitally important implementation arms of the Industrial Development Bureau (IDB) within the Ministry of Economic Affairs. ITRI, which houses the innovative and industry-dedicated laboratories such as the Electronics Research and Service Organization (ERSO) and the Computing and Communications Laboratory (CCL), mediates between industry and bureaucracy, monitors the new technologies, products and production processes of international competitors, organizes technology transfers, and coordinates new projects in alliance with local firms. Hence, in addition to 'implementation' – carrying out R&D and diffusing the practical results to the private sector – these agencies form part of the policy-making process itself. The highly successful 'technology alliances' – joint public–private projects coordinated by ERSO and CCL, discussed in more detail below – are among the most recent policy outcomes of this information-saturated public sector.[16]

The contrasting case is where the public sector 'contracts out' most or a large part of its research and information requirements, as occurs more typically in Anglo-American settings. (In Australia, for instance, it appears that even the definition of national 'visions' is something better entrusted to a commercial consultancy firm like McKinseys!) The significance of these differences can be seen in the differential impact on state capacity.

Two important consequences follow from the development of an in-house information-oriented capacity. One is that it equips state agencies with a formidable *competence* in areas normally left to the private sector. The other is that it nurtures bureaucratic *independence vis-à-vis* sectoral interests within the business community. As is well known, none of the Anglo-American economies can boast similar attributes.

Insulated pilot agencies and policy coordination   The third important condition for effective policy-making in the region is the existence of what Chalmers Johnson has referred to as 'pilot agencies' charged with the task of coordinating economic change. MITI's horizontally organized policy bureaus, Korea's EPB, and the Council for Economic Planning and Development (CEPD) in Taiwan have all figured in this capacity for much of the postwar period. While structurally quite different, they can be viewed as functional equivalents of the idea of a super-ministry in the industrial policy-making apparatus. The key feature in common is that each agency engages in the task of policy coordination, and each is removed from *direct* contact with special economic constituencies.

Korea's superministry, the EPB, restructured in 1994, was perhaps the most famous of the three for its broad mandate, combining planning, budgetary and economic management functions. One reason for the EPB's ability to provide such a strong coordinating role is the way it was organized. Standing outside and astride the individual ministries, the EPB during its thirty-three years of existence had no *direct* relationship with the private sector. Before seeking to initiate major policy proposals, individual economic ministers were required to consult with the head of the EPB, the deputy prime minister. For its part, the EPB sought to protect its institutional 'insulation', and thus its broad political mandate, by resisting close identification with any particular sector or group. It was therefore more likely to uphold more encompassing initiatives against parochial or group interests (cf. Choi 1991: 7–8).[17] The rise of a new generation of US-trained neoclassical economists within the bureaucracy, however, began to generate conflict and confusion over the structure and role of Korea's system of national economic management, leading to the dismantling of Korea's key pilot agency, the EPB, in late 1994, thus compromising the state's transformative capacity (cf. Johnson 1994; Amsden 1994).

Taiwan's institutional 'equivalent' to the EPB is the CEPD. Like its predecessor, the Economic Stabilization Board of the 1950s, CEPD operates independently of the ministerial bureaucracy, having its own planning and budgetary functions. At the same time, however, CEPD integrates the leadership of the individual ministries, which are thereby inclined to act as a unit rather than to represent client interests. In this respect, CEPD has assumed an 'encompassing' character similar to that of Korea's EPB, hence relatively insulated from special interests and accordingly well placed to fulfil a coordinating role. One should be careful, however, not to overstate the power of these two pilot agencies, for in spite of their importance as centres of economic decision-making, their power relative to that of particular ministries has varied over time and across issue areas.[18]

Though much more has been written on the Japanese bureaucracy, it is perhaps not often appreciated that MITI's so-called 'horizontal' bureaus are functionally, if not organizationally, quite similar to the Korean and Taiwanese pilot agencies. MITI's horizontal agencies (such as the Industrial Policy Bureau, responsible for overall industrial policy) develop and coordinate policy across industries. The vertical divisions (which represent specific industries, such as machinery and information) represent the needs of their own sectors, solve problems and develop programmes at individual-industry level.[19] As in the case of the Korean EPB, this structure provides a degree of insulation – or 'built-in safeguard' – against the tendency (very noticeable in Anglo-American economies) to respond politically to particular business demands, which may clash with a more long-term approach to industrial vitality.

From what has been said thus far, we can therefore conclude that the Asian countries in question have an institutional advantage at governmental level: the existence of a talented, technically able and prestigious public service, which is charged with a broad institutional mission and relatively insulated from special interests, and which has developed an impressive in-house capacity for acquiring and managing production-relevant information. This situation contrasts not only with the more porous bureaucracies of developing countries, such as the Latin American NICs, but also with the low status and narrow competence of public administration in the more mature industrial economies, such as the USA.

The political environment

While these are the three main internal organizational features that help to foster a cohesive civil service relatively insulated from politics, their overall effect depends critically on the wider political environment. In particular, bureaucratic capabilities can be retarded or advanced, depending on the relations between the civil service and the political leadership. As Pempel and Muramatsu (1995: 30) note, even the most perfectly structured civil service can have little economic impact if political leaders – whether elected or otherwise – do not share a growth agenda.

In this regard, it is notable that in all three countries, consistent regime goals (informed by an ideology of growth and, in Japan's case, of technological independence) have supported civil-service commitment to production-centred policies. In Taiwan, it was the Kuomintang (KMT) leadership that became the catalyst for a transformative project, first establishing a civilian government distinct from military influence, which was run by a professional civil service, then ensuring the recruitment of competent persons to manage economic transformation. Even in Japan, where electoral politics has had a lengthier existence than in Korea and Taiwan, the Liberal Democratic Party (LDP) leadership has long embraced the project of industrial transformation. Indeed, the LDP's relationship with the elite economic bureaucrats has been primarily one of collaboration rather than confrontation (Pempel and Muramatsu 1995: 34–40). One may conjecture that this elite cohesion over core national goals has to do with factors that go well beyond the LDP's lengthy rule. Arguably, it is bound up with a shared national experience which gave rise to the drive for technological independence.[20]

Ultimately, then, while structural features of the state are important to state capabilities, one should not overlook the character of the political system or the factors which make for elite cohesion, in so far as these may impede or support bureaucratic capability. To the extent that the political leadership may use administrative structures to weaken or strengthen a transformative project, a country's political system will have an important influence on the operation of its civil service. In the East Asian Three, it is clear that even where the bureaucracy has been ultimately answerable to a higher political authority, a shared and pervasive ideology of growth forged out of a common national experience has served to complement and fortify the transformative capacities of the executive bureaucracy.

State–industry linkages: insulation but not insularity

Bureaucratic 'autonomy' or insulation from pressure groups is hardly a sufficient explanation for the state's coordinating capacity in the Asian Three. History is strewn with examples of autonomous states which have proved either inept or diffident (or both) in matters of industrial management. Tsarist Russia and twentieth-century Britain offer two such examples at different points on the developmental spectrum. One important feature lacking in such cases of 'autonomy without capacity' can be described as industrial 'connectedness' or what Evans has referred to as 'embeddedness'. In practical terms, embedded autonomy implies the existence of what I have called 'domestic linkages'. These include the array of institutional ties, policy networks, deliberative councils and the like, which link government and industry in the information-exchange and policy-making process.

In all three of the East Asian countries, various state agencies have established an elaborate set of links with the private sector, which are maintained through both formal and informal mechanisms. These domestic linkages provide the relevant agencies with a vital mechanism for acquiring adequate information and for coordinating agreement with the private sector over the content and implementation of policy. Somewhat surprisingly, the East Asian Three provide many more venues and networks for joint decision-making than one would expect in relatively 'youthful' democracies (and rather more than the older democracies).

Japan boasts the most extensive set of institutional arrangements for reaching agreement between government and industry. The bureaucracy can count on more than 200 deliberating councils – forums for public–private consultation on key policy issues. Of these, MITI sponsors around twenty, which gives the ministry a power of consultation and coordination with the private sector that is relatively smooth and rich in vital industry-related information (Johnson 1984a: 192–3; Okimoto 1989). Arguably, there are more critical aspects of this joint decision-making arrangement. One is the highly systematized mode of continuous consultation between MITI officials and the Japanese scientific-technological community (Freeman 1987). Another is the prior informal process whereby government officials consult closely and extensively with industry experts about their products, technologies and business environment.[21] But regardless of where the key decisions are initiated, and where they are hammered out (whether in informal consultations or in the deliberation councils), it seems that postwar industrial policies, at least in the past two to three decades, have become as a matter of routine much more of a joint, negotiated effort. More than at any time previously, as Johnson emphasized in the MITI study, the postwar regime of industrial policy was the product of a genuine collaboration between MITI and the related industries (Johnson 1982: 196, 240, 256, 310; see also Dore 1987: 199–200; Mabuchi 1995). The point is not that conflict is eliminated through such negotiated relationships, but that it is *institutionalized* (cf. Samuels 1987, 1994).

In contrast with Japan, business input in Taiwan's postwar policy-making process is widely believed to have been minimal. Economic policy-makers in the IDB none the less fostered the creation of business associations and generally encouraged industrialists to set up organizations to communicate with government. According to the authoritative accounts, however, the Taiwanese approach was a decidedly top-down affair. While Japan's industry bodies interacted with the state on behalf of their members, Taiwanese business organizations ostensibly served more as a conduit for transmitting government policies to the private sector, and hence a form of 'state corporatism' (cf. Gold 1986: 127, 171; Wade 1990a).

However, more recent research into Taiwan's two leading export sectors of the postwar period – textiles and electronics – overturns this interpretation. Top-down, state-corporatist-style decision-making was only ever partially true; that is, when the industry sector was divided, inconsistent, or indecisive on issues critical to its future. The relationship between government and business has depended critically on the capacity of the relevant sector to organize its members and to act decisively as a unitary body in its dealings with ministry officials. Where producer cooperation has occurred – increasingly problematically in textiles after the first oil crisis, but quite effectively in electronics – participatory policy-making has flourished. Thus, for instance, officials in the Council for Economic Cooperation and Development (CIECD, later CEPD) institutionalized producer participation early on in the decision-making process. In 1967, two months after the first meeting with the industry association TEAMA to discuss the development of the local electronics industry, the Committee on Electronics Industry was established. The first long-term development plan for the industry, moreover, was formulated in 1975 at industry's request and in response to the oil crisis. TEAMA not only helped formulate the new proposal, but closely monitored its monthly progress.[22] Indeed, Kuo's evidence and conclusions provide ample support for the argument advanced here. Regarding the electronics industry, he argues that '[o]nly after intimate cooperation between the state and TEAMA had begun did a significant class of indigenous industrialists emerge and expand' (1995: 182).

More pointedly, among the various development plans, 'the only plan that was effectively implemented was the one producers had consulted on beforehand'. When manufactured in the CEPD's 'ivory tower', as was the 1980 Ten-Year Plan for the industry's development, proposals 'died in anonymity'. In comparing the fate of textiles and electronics, Kuo concludes that 'the rapid and stable growth of Taiwan's electronics industry was due to the existence of a strong industrial association and a cooperative state' (1995: 184, 191).

Policy networks have also been strengthened over the past decade through the institution of joint 'industry task forces' which meet at two-monthly intervals. These have flourished especially since the Economic Innovation Commission (composed of government, business and academic leaders) was set up in 1985 as a provisional advisory organ to help draft industrial and economic policies to deal with Taiwan's international economic difficulties. In short, the evidence points to a conclusion at odds with the conventional wisdom. It indicates that *the capacity for industrial transformation in Taiwan has been enhanced not by a hard state acting over or against capital, but by a project-oriented state working in coalition with a well-organized private sector.*

In the Korean case, links between government and industry were also forged through the state sponsorship of business organizations and deliberation councils. The latter functioned most effectively in the famous monthly export promotion meetings held at the presidential Blue House from the mid-1960s to propel the export drive.[23] Under the presidential leadership of Park Chung Hee (1961–79), the Korean government gained great leverage over industry by securing foreign capital and by controlling its allocation to private firms. To gain industry's cooperation and assist the implementation of its export policies (and later its heavy industrialization drive), the government instituted routinized meetings in which the details of policy implementation and thus the rules of eligibility for state support were made clear to all participants (Root 1996: 25–6). Thus, in the 1960s at least, rather than being fully fledged policy-making forums, Korean deliberation councils functioned more as a vehicle for generating trust and motivating the business sector by making the underlying rules transparent to all. In the current era, however, when export success has made such meetings irrelevant, the Korean bureaucracy is seeking to revive the so-called 'private councils for industrial development' as a means of encouraging more intra-industry coordination and private initiative.

To foster new industries and in order to involve the private sector in their development, the Korean bureaucracy also established special intermediate organizations such as trade associations and industry promotion societies. To promote the important electronics sector, for example, the government in 1967 established the Korea Electronics Industry Promotion Society (KEIPS), with membership drawn from the leading electronics producers. Authorized by the then Ministry of Trade and Industry (MTI, now the Ministry of Trade, Industry and Energy) as the exclusive body representing the interests of the industry, KEIPS became the major link between bureaucracy and firms. Through its specially constituted deliberation council, KEIPS interacted with the EPB, MTI and other government agencies to fashion and implement development strategies for the sector (KEIPS 1967).

In the Korean context, deliberative councils have taken different forms, sometimes devoted to information gathering and exchange between industry representatives and MTI bureaucrats; at other times, involving a more collaborative form of decision-making (Campos and Root 1996: 90–1). Although it is hard to establish with any precision, it would appear that collaborative decision-making has tended to gain more prominence over time, not only as an industrial class has matured (cf. E. Kim 1987), but as the tasks of technology transformation have become more complex.

Why are such institutional linkages important? In a nutshell, because they are about the state doing things not in isolation from the private sector, but in concertation with industry. In so far as public and private decision-makers get together to exchange information and to coordinate actions, information gaps are minimized and each generally ends up making better decisions than if trapped in isolation. Rather than engaging in purely top-down decision-making, abstracted from the real conditions of production, the economic bureaucracy therefore has a vital mechanism for acquiring production-related information and for coordinating agreement with the private sector in order to design and implement policies better.

Moreover, institutional linkages, the forums of negotiation between government and business, make industrial policy decisions more open to public scrutiny – 'transparent' in Dore's terms (1987: 200) – thus reducing the risks of corruption or political favouritism. Being 'in daily contact' with industry experts, having formal meetings on a regular basis with industry representatives, establishing performance-monitoring systems that provide constant feedback to enable policy adjustments – these are among the more tangible features of institutionalized public–private cooperation, which increase the effectiveness of the policy-making apparatus. It is important to note that the organization of industry itself is by no means incidental to this outcome, as we shall see shortly.

Okimoto, another astute observer of the Japanese system, has put the case concisely in his account of industrial policy instruments for high-tech. He observes that through its extensive network of contacts with the private sector, MITI can regularly tap in to a vast system of up-to-date information. Rigorous discussions with 'people in the know' – industry leaders, researchers, financial analysts, engineers – put MITI in a strong position to determine 'where technology is headed, and where the most promising commercial opportunities lie'. Accordingly,

> The information it collects and processes is about as thorough as could be obtained. National research projects thus emerge from an ongoing process of national consensus building based on extensive give and take between government and the private sector. (Okimoto 1989: 73)

This section has made two points that are important to the argument. First, on a general note, in addition to being *insulated* in certain areas, other parts of the bureaucracy need to be closely *connected* with organized industry. Both insulation and connectedness are important conditions of the state's capacity to coordinate change. Second, public–private *cooperation* is much more *institutionalized* in the East Asian Three than in most other countries. One major consequence of these institutional capacities is the enhancement of policy effectiveness.

Organization of industry

The final condition of transformative capacity is essentially a means of facilitating the linkages between state and industry. This third feature turns on the organization of industry itself, a topic we have touched on in the previous section. Business structures in East Asia differ widely. They range from the giant diversified groups of Korea (*chaebol*) and the more specialized industrial corporations of Japan to the thriving small and medium-sized firms of Taiwan. But beyond this diversity at the enterprise level, the organization of industry exhibits a number of common features which facilitate its relationships with government.

One organizational feature that merits particular attention is the *encompassing* rather than fragmented nature of business representation in the region, which is a legacy of statism. Industry or trade associations tend to be highly centralized and increasingly active in the design and implementation of policy. This participation of organized industry has long been true across industry as a whole for Japan, where the *gyokai*, or industry-specific manufacturing trade associations, provide the basic level for execution of policy (Sone 1993: 300–3). It has also been the case in the major export sectors for Taiwan, notably in textiles and electronics. As noted earlier, however, the greater strength of the electronics sector has enabled it to benefit from more consistent developmental programmes and thus more vibrant prospects than has been the case for textiles. Traditionally weaker in Korea owing to the rise of the *chaebol*, trade associations have only recently begun to acquire greater significance in the policy community. But here, as we shall see, they encounter a significant obstacle. We turn to an elaboration of these points in the Korean and Taiwanese settings.

Korea   As a means of coordinating Korea's developmental drive in the 1960s, the central authorities set up a Japanese-style system of industrial organizations. These included national organizations like the Federation of Korean Industries, the Korean Chamber of Commerce and Industry, the Central Association of Small Business Cooperative Associations, and numerous sector-level organizations representing producer interests.

As in Japan, these organizations represented their industries and coordinated interests within their sectors. But as subsidies nurtured the growth of large groups in the 1960s, the bureaucracy came to rely more and more on big business groups for policy implementation. Industry associations in some sectors took on an increasingly passive role, especially from the mid-1970s. Since the *chaebol* organized so much economic activity in the Korean setting, (the top thirty *chaebol* now accounting for 95 per cent of GNP), they often operated as functional alternatives to the encompassing trade associations.

Over the past decade or so, the Korean government has introduced a series of measures designed to streamline the unwieldy activities of industrial groups and to stimulate more organized industry initiative in development planning. The aim is to maintain a coordinated approach to industrial affairs, for which the *chaebol*, having left behind their adolescent dependence on government nurturing and having become so diversified, are proving increasingly difficult 'partners'.

In overall terms, the evolution of Korean government–business relations is much harder to draw than for Japan or Taiwan. In the early stages of industrialization, 'top-down' directives were more prevalent than participatory decision-making. This was due to the underdevelopment of the Korean business class and the absence of a whole range of industries. But even in Korea, the trust and cooperation of private industry was more often than not vital to effective policy implementation. Indeed, Korean officials and industrialists consider the high-growth period to be the high point in government–business cooperation.

In some significant respects, however, government–business cooperation has diminished in Korea in recent years. This has occurred as various governments – first under Chun Doo-Hwan, more recently under Kim Young Sam – have sought, partly for economic and partly for political reasons, to control the unwieldy activities of industrial groups and thus limit their concentration of economic power. Governments have with little success sought to encourage the *chaebol* to concentrate on their core activities and to limit their cross-equity investments. From the mid-1980s, the economic bureaucracies also began phasing out the use of policy loans and loosening (but not abandoning) their grip on the financial system. Meanwhile, the leading industrial *chaebol* – Samsung, Goldstar, Hyundai – have increasingly internationalized their operations. The result is reduced business dependence on state finance for new investment and thus diminished cooperation over its level and patterning. What has emerged, therefore, is a perverse half-way house, wherein the *chaebol* have over-invested in areas of their own choosing, while turning to the state for financial support in times of distress. At the same time, there has been a shift from 'hard' to 'softer' policy instruments in which the role of business input is heightened. Especially since the late 1980s, government has sought to encourage much more private self-governance and intra-firm cooperation, though with little success, particularly in the basic and mature industries more vulnerable to surplus capacity.

One difficulty hampering Japanese-style cooperation is not so much the lack of 'policy instruments', as is sometimes claimed; rather, it concerns the peculiar features of Korea's industrial organization. Public–private cooperation has taken place largely through the *chaebol*, which worked well for a time. It is not simply that Korean groups are now financially independent enough to thumb their noses at the state which made them strong. Though there is some truth to this, considerable financial dependence remains. Nevertheless, a key test for sustaining Korean competitiveness is whether the conglomerates can be sufficiently 'streamlined' and the trade associations sufficiently reinvigorated to enable the recomposition of core capacities and to prevent the collapse of public policy into private interest politics. The Korean case may therefore be seen as pushing at the limits within which GI remains possible in an economy which is not only highly concentrated, but whose business structures are highly diversified.

Taiwan In Taiwan, government mandated the establishment of a number of trade associations at an early stage of industrial development, and by 1985 counted more than 150 such bodies. It was pointed out earlier that these are widely believed to have occupied a less prominent position in the policy-making community than in Japan or Korea (cf. Wade 1990a; Evans 1995). None the less, the significant exceptions to this statement reaffirm rather than deny the importance of co-operative coordination in the Taiwanese political economy.

Indeed, the postwar history of Taiwan's two major export industries – electronics and textiles – suggests that the organizational cohesion of the industry has been central to the kinds of policy and of development outcome that have characterized these two important sectors. The larger organizations, such as the Taiwan Textile Federation (TTF, the recently reconstituted textile association) and TEAMA (which encompasses electronics) have played major roles in interfacing with government, collecting and publishing data, and implementing policy. The electronics industry began organizing after the arrival of FDIs in the mid-1960s. In TEAMA's formative years, the Taiwanese government took steps in several areas to strengthen the association's influence over its members. It supported TEAMA's bid to enrol FDIs and underground factories and ordered the latter to be closed if they refused to join. It delegated the authority to TEAMA to issue export licences, and it prioritized local products in government procurement programmes, making (member) firms dependent on TEAMA for access to the list of such programmes. From its formative years, the industry thus developed as a strong interlocutor with government.[24]

By contrast, the organization of the textile industry, which has been restructured and renamed several times since 1946, has never matched the cohesion or authority of electronics. This has clearly had something to do with ethnic divisions: the mainlanders became dominant in the association in 1955 when it was reorganized into the current Taiwan Cotton Spinners Association (TCSA). None the less, the need to avoid price wars and to increase exports encouraged producers to cooperate and to gain credibility in policy negotiations with government throughout the high-growth period. By the 1970s, however, serious rifts within the industry began to surface, as small producers disputed their export quota allocations. But once the industry lost its credibility with the IDB, as occurred when producers refused to implement a merger proposal and a labour-saving initiative suggested by the producer association itself, the government withdrew its support (Kuo 1995: 102). Today, the coordination of the textile industry as a whole falls to TTF. Indeed, due to Taiwan's peculiar geopolitical and diplomatic situation, the role of TTF has for the past two decades been that of a quasi-government agency. Taiwan's vigorous textile trade made it the subject of American and European quotas in the 1970s. This has meant the deputizing of the textile association to engage in direct trade negotiations with foreign governments, and its authorization to administer export quotas for the industry at home. TTF's growing competence in representing the industry, together with its confidence in undertaking tasks in the 'national' interest, have endowed the federation with the authority and cohesion to take an active role in devising strategies for the industry. In particular, by shifting emphasis to design, TTF has convinced the government of the advantages of upgrading rather than bypassing a traditional industry beset by low-cost competitors.

A key condition for this routinized negotiation is of course a relatively strong industry association able to act as an interlocutor with government. It was precisely with that aim in mind that the Economic Innovation Commission in 1985 proposed that Taiwan learn from Japan and West Germany by strengthening its commercial and industrial associations more generally. Here, then, the trend appears much clearer than in Korea. Government is embedding its transformative capacities in a wider array of industry-related institutions, and in the leading export sectors, industry is gradually developing a capacity for policy input that strong organizational coordination makes possible. In this respect, Taiwan would appear to be following the path of Japan more closely than that of Korea.

This section has discussed the significance of industrial organization, both in principle and as it is instituted in the East Asian setting. The central proposition is that cooperative coordination between state and industry is easier if industry is represented by encompassing organizations like trade associations, rather than partially organized or fragmented among several competing bodies. Where the latter situation prevails, as in Australia, Britain and the United States, intra-industry consensus has been far more difficult to construct and individualized lobbying has tended to over-ride a more collective approach to an industry's problems. A similar situation may also occur if too much economic activity is organized by a handful of giant, highly diversified groups. This, as we saw, is the present danger faced by Korea.

The more general point that emerges from this analysis is that close ties between government and industry are not, in themselves, an explanation for the state's effectiveness. In some contexts, such ties may be more likely to invite rent-seeking than commitment to competitive behaviour. The Latin American case is often cited in this regard. Cooperation seems to work well only if the state is sufficiently insulated, so that it retains a definite capacity for social goal-setting and for coordinating policies and resources to that end. In short, GI requires a state that is, in Evans's terms, paradoxically both distant and close. State connectedness without insulation is likely to breed rent-seeking and distributional coalitions that can smother industrial vitality. By contrast, insulation without connectedness may widen information gaps that encourage policy failure. But states which combine both insulation and connectedness by embedding their autonomy are equipped with greater institutional assets for minimizing these dangers and for achieving policy success.

The Changing Basis of State Capacity

Demise of the East Asian developmental state?

How has the state's capacity changed over time, and in what ways has government–business cooperation evolved as a result? According to the view that has recently come to prevail, the capacity of all three states (particularly that in Korea and Taiwan) has changed considerably, moving from a condition of virtually unqualified strength to one of relative weakness. This articulates the conventional, negative-sum view of power relations that has driven the state capacity debate (the 'strong' state 'wins' if business loses). It is also what many have in mind when proclaiming the death of the developmental state (i.e. if business is strong, the state must be weak).

We can call this the 'grave-digger' or 'irony of state strength' thesis, which reasons that the more effective the state's involvement in the economy, the more it increases the independence and power of private capital, and thus the more the state undermines its own viability. In a twist on the Marxian metaphor, the state, in effect, by being developmentally effective, ends up digging its own grave. Undeniably, private industry has much enhanced its power as a result of successful development in the East Asian Three. None of the major studies, however, concludes that the state's role in coordinating change in such settings is now redundant (cf. Amsden 1989; Wade 1990a; Woo 1991; Evans 1995; Samuels 1994); and while internal struggles weaken Korea's developmental architecture and priorities, there is no compelling evidence that the state's transformative capacity must wither as a result of industrial success.

Moreover, with regard to reports that the developmental state is dead, it is important to be aware of how the term was first applied to capitalist economies. Chalmers Johnson (1982) reserved the term (capitalist) 'developmental state' for a state which was willing and able to pursue a transformative project. How the state went about that project – that is, how the government–industry relationship was structured – was not decisive to the definition. The state might encourage and support the industry's self-governance (as in interwar Japan); it might prefer to act through unilateral, top-down measures (as during the World War II mobilization period); or it might institute a more cooperative approach to decision-making (as since the 1950s). Two things nevertheless emerge with great clarity from Johnson's account. The first is that developmental states are subject to considerable change in the government–industry relationship over time. The heavy-handed, imposing state appears more as an offshoot of military mobilization than of developmentalism, *strictu sensu*. Second, unilateral, coercive policymaking is ultimately the *least* appropriate, and most often disastrous, for developmental progress.

My argument therefore has a good deal more in common with this view than with the gravedigger hypothesis, which posits the inevitable demise or obsolescence of transformative capability. Instead of a shift from more to less state capacity, I propose that: (1) there has been a *transformation* in the *basis* of state capacity (i.e. from autonomy to embedded autonomy, from an insulated state taking many top-down decisions to one which has embedded its autonomy in a range of economic institutions); (2) this transformation of state capacity is most highly developed in Japan and appears unevenly developed in Korea, though it continues to evolve in Taiwan; and (3) as the tasks of the modern industrial economy have changed, so the changes in the basis of state capacity have become *more* rather than less congruent with a transformative project. Some of these points have been established in earlier sections. This and the following section provide further elaboration by way of (1) a clarification of the relation between different types of transformation and of state power, and (2) an analysis of the major forms of GI in the East Asian settings.

Types of economic transformation and state power

One useful way to highlight conditions under which a specific type of state power may be critical to a certain economic outcome is to distinguish between different types of economic transformation and those of state power most appropriate to each. In the recent history of industrialization, we can distinguish, very broadly, three types of economic transformation for which state power has been critical.

Type 1: Revolutionary transformation This type of transformation involves breaking with an antecedent economic system. Examples include the transformation from private property rights to collective ownership, and vice versa, from centralized socialist production to private property-based markets, as is occurring today in the former Soviet Union. Historically, this type of transformation has required breaking the power of the dominant class. In post-1990 Russia, it implies undercutting the power of the Soviet elite, who have effectively 'privatized' state property, yet seek to circumvent reform of property rights (cf. McFaul 1995).

Arguably, in both cases the type of state power required is one whose structure is insulated from, but not embedded in, the dominant economic groups – hence a 'strong' (read autonomous but *not* embedded) state in the sense of despotic-coercive capacity (see e.g. Weiss and Hobson 1995: ch. 3).

Type 2: Structural transformation Here the principal task is the transformation from an agrarian base to an industrial one. In late industrializer countries, such as postwar Taiwan and Korea, the transformative task has entailed shifting the agricultural surplus to subsidize the growth of the industrial sector. But more critically, it has required fundamental land reform in order to destroy the power base of the landed class and liberate important resources.

In principle, this task appears to demand a strong state, as in type 1, detached from the dominant (landed) class and able to impose reforms and redistribute resources. Such a structure may be supplied internally or, as in the Korean case, externally in the form of an occupying force, a point discussed further below.

Type 3: Sectoral (industrial-technological) transformation The third kind of transformation implies a more creative, complex and strategic capacity. It involves the creation of new branches of production, the shift to new products, the adoption of new technologies, and the diffusion of innovation. In effecting transformation of this kind, Japan is the exemplary case. The NICs have also proved increasingly able to meet the transformative challenge, though with some obvious differences among themselves.[25]

Whether driven by a 'catching-up' or a 'keeping-up' logic, sectoral transformation appears less 'radical' than the other two types. But appearance can mislead. In a world reshaped by catch-up strategies, the business of keeping up (or staying ahead) becomes radically redefined. A qualitatively different kind of competition emerges. Competition occurs not just on a wider, international scale, but in the scope of goods produced, in the technologies involved in producing them, and ultimately in national efforts to identify and define technological trajectories. In the context of a highly internationalized economy, the pressures for continuous innovation thus become immense, imposing on the national political economy a kind of *restless rationalization* – a need for constant upgrading and renewal of the industrial portfolio.

This type of *continuous transformation* demands not a 'strong' state in a coercive sense, but a more finely tuned, 'catalytic' state – one that can act as a guiding element in policy networks and in the formation and maintenance of the organizational infrastructure that will provide long-term inducement for firms to invest, upgrade and innovate.[26] So we can see from this distinction that a 'strong' state, understood as one with the 'capacity' to act *against* private interests, is important in one sense only: that is, when the private interests in question are *inimical to*, or in conflict with, a project of economic transformation (and sufficiently strong to block it).

In historical terms, this has usually meant the landed class (*à la* Moore [1977]). In postwar Korea and Taiwan, however, this kind of 'strength' (type 1) was strictly speaking not necessary, because of US intervention. The land reform – which delivered a major blow to the agrarian class – was instituted by the occupying forces (though with the full consent of the Korean and Taiwanese leadership). Thus, state 'strength' in a despotic sense was not needed to effect the requisite change in class relations. A proxy external force, acting in unusual geopolitical circumstances, undertook this role.

The Korean state's export drive similarly required little of type 1 coercive power (statism). Rather than having to act against the vested interests of private industry, the state's turn towards an export-oriented policy reoriented a fledgeling business class to a different source of profits, using handsome inducements. The Taiwanese state too did not have to be strong in a despotic-coercive sense. Like Korea, it benefited from: (1) the US role in enacting land reform; (2) a public sector, based on state appropriation of former Japanese industry, which could be used to create upstream industries; and (3) a fledgeling class of private producers dependent on a state-created infrastructure to secure domestic and export markets. Indeed, most of the local producers emerging from the development of import-substitution industries were amenable to the export-oriented reforms, which effectively benefited most of them.

Conversely, one must note how the lack of such strength (power type 1) in the Philippines and indeed in much of Latin America, which did not experience the luxury of an external force to displace landed power, has continued to beset economic development in those environments (cf. Fishlow 1990).

Similarly, in the post-1990 phase of Russian reform, a weak state has been unable to eliminate the *ancien régime* (i.e. former directors of state property) who have blocked the economic reforms for privatization that would create real markets. McFaul argues that there is a need to demolish the old Soviet enterprise system and create new private property rights, and this means 'to act against the interests of entrenched social groups from the Soviet regime' (1995: 242). In this context, McFaul posits a causal relationship between coercive state power ('despotic' in Mann's sense [1984/1988]) and revolutionary economic transformation.

Here I have indicated how that causal relationship can be extended to other, *non*-revolutionary settings, by distinguishing between different kinds of economic transformation and the different types of state power appropriate to that task. In the early phase of industrialization, when private industry is weak and transformative tasks are largely *structural* (e.g. reforming landownership, shifting the agricultural surplus to industry), the government–business relationship most effective for transformative capacity will most closely resemble statism. But as the task of *sectoral* transformation takes over and becomes more complex – with the gradual move from catching up to keeping up technologically – transformative capacity will involve greater input and cooperation from established industrial groups; in short, a 'catalytic' state.[27]

This argument of course in no way implies that catalytic states will automatically develop, only that transformative capacity will be strengthened rather than diminished to the extent that a relatively insulated state can institutionalize strong industry participation in the policy-making process.

East Asian results: governed interdependence

As indicated in my introduction, the key issue raised by most analyses of state 'intervention' and industrial policy in the East Asian setting is how to make sense of the government–business relationship. The literature is generally disappointing on this issue. On the one hand, it is hard to imagine a serious scholar of Taiwan, Korea or Japan who would deny the *distinctive* nature of the government–business relationship in these countries, especially in comparison with the West (though, ironically, this is the effect of analyses which reject the notion of a 'developmental state', a concept whose original contrastive rationale has long been buried in the ensuing debate (cf. Johnson forthcoming).

On the other hand, with few exceptions, the categories for analysing that relationship have been of the *garden variety*. Most writers have veered between two alternatives: either government 'dominates' or 'leads' business, the two terms often being used interchangeably, as if synonymous (e.g. McKean 1993); or else business dominates the state, a view which has gained favour in recent writing on Japan (e.g. Calder 1993; Callon 1995).

The problem is that there is no space in these sorts of analysis for a catalytic state: the state either succeeds in *imposing* a course of action, or else it meets *resistance* in one form or another. If one agrees with Calder's strong statist (re)definition of 'developmental state', then he is correct to argue that state domination is not a central feature of Japanese political economy. But, as I have argued, this is not the way the concept was originally employed in Johnson's work.

Moreover, why assume that the only alternative to a dominating state is one dominated by the private sector? A major problem with this kind of analysis is the implication that Japanese government–business relations have changed to something approximating the Anglo-American variety. But no attempt is made to theorize that *change* or to indicate how it is supposed to relate to Japan's *continuing* industrial strength, *pace* the constant refrain from the pages of the American business press juxtaposing a weakened industrial Japan with a strongly resurgent America.[28]

One potentially fruitful alternative has been to see bureaucrats and private industrialists in roughly equal partnership, as in the notion of 'reciprocal consent' (Samuels 1987). But even in this case, a compelling study of the energy industry which emphasizes the role of business in negotiating policy outcomes, the underlying thrust of analysis leans towards the business domination view, as embeddedness tends to get the better of autonomy.[29]

Although they are often valuable for their mastery of the detail, a problem with many existing analyses is that they are either static or overly narrow in scope. Frequently, the presentation of conclusions is based on a snapshot view of the government–industry relationship, hence frozen in time. Often this is combined with a narrow selection of case material, interpreted in a highly specific way, to illustrate a favoured hypothesis.[30] Consequently, most general statements about state–economy relations in East Asia posit stark transformations (e.g. from domination to subordination) that are untheorized and poorly evidenced. None appears able to encompass the coexistence of a broad spectrum of cases – ranging from close state–industry cooperation to private-sector initiative to apparent top-down coordination – and their changing importance over time.

A more convincing account of government–business relations and of the industrial policy process in East Asia should be able to make sense of the dynamic picture. In doing so, it should seek to distinguish between prevailing and marginal tendencies, and between those which bolster, as opposed to those which compromise, industrial performance. It was suggested earlier that government–industry relations in East Asia either have changed (Japan) or are undergoing a process of transformation (Korea and Taiwan). The changes in question do not appear to constitute inter-systemic change (i.e. from a state-guided to market-led pattern). Rather they more closely approximate to *intra-systemic* change (involving increasing complexity of tasks and modes of fulfilling them), and hence a growing variety of ways in which government and industry coalesce.

Perhaps the most visible change is one from a situation in which government (the economic bureaucracy) was largely making the big decisions – usually out of necessity, due to a destabilized or underdeveloped business sector – to a situation in which the private sector is increasingly invited *and expected* to take more initiatives, yet within the general guidelines and in keeping with the goals set by the state. The important point to stress is that it is misleading to see this shift as automatically increasing business domination of the policy agenda and the loss of government direction. This *may* eventually happen, particularly in Korea, but those who take this line more generally have not produced convincing evidence.

It is the contention of this chapter that the notion of GI is a more fruitful one for capturing the variety and subtleties of the government–business relationship in East Asia than either of the domination/partnership categories offered in the existing literature. GI, as already intimated, involves a cooperative (though not conflict-free) relationship between government and industry. The precise manner of this cooperation takes a variety of forms and evolves over time, not only as the industrial sector and its leaders grow strong, but also as the tasks of transformation change. In this way, the institutional connectedness of government and industry provides a measure of insurance against harmful or irrelevant decision-making. At the same time, to the extent that the architecture of the state and the nature of the political system continue to insulate policy-makers from short-term interest politics, the ability to derail strategic goal-setting is reduced. Thus, GI highlights the capacity of the state to involve economic power actors in a transformative project, in a way that embraces rather than displaces its goal-setting role.

Finally, it must be emphasized that, in a system of GI, as described for Japan and the NICs, the question of 'who initiates' loses much of its meaning and importance. Both the state and industry can and do take policy initiatives, but this takes place within a negotiated relationship in which the state retains a guiding role, exercising leadership either directly or by delegation to industry. On the other hand, in systems where the government–industry relationship is more distant and erratically organized, the question of 'who initiates' will continue to have some significance.

In the brief space that remains in this chapter, I shall try to illustrate the fruitfulness of this approach by outlining four main forms of GI that can be readily identified in the East Asian political economies. These are: disciplined support, public risk absorption, private-sector governance and public–private innovation alliances.

Forms and Dynamics of Governed Interdependence

An alternative to 'leadership versus followership'

It will assist the logic of the exposition that follows to begin by contrasting my position with that of Robert Wade. Wade (1990a: 28–9, 1990b) introduces the leadership/followership dichotomy in order to distinguish cases in which government has made an important difference to developmental outcomes. In his schema, only leadership – urging or prodding industry to do something that it would otherwise *not* do – counts as making a real difference to investment and production patterns. Thus, for example, if the electronics sector were to propose to government a plan for upgrading the industry, government adoption of the plan would be defined as followership and therefore as not making an important difference to investment and production patterns.[31]

This reasoning runs into two difficulties. One is that it assumes that the pace, scope and success of the upgrading initiative would have been the same had industry acted alone. Such an outcome, while difficult to assess, seems improbable.

A more telling problem for the leadership–followership logic stems from the very nature of the system that it seeks to analyse. Of key importance is the fact that in such settings as the East Asian, *the state has promoted, strengthened and maintained a social infrastructure (a dense organizational structure of industrial networks, cartels, trade associations, and vertical and horizontal councils) to pursue those very leadership strategies on behalf of a given sector*. Does this mean that the state is *following* industry (and therefore making little real difference to its practices and prospects)? Surely in such a context it becomes difficult, perhaps impossible, and certainly not very meaningful to draw conclusions about 'who is following whom'.

As an illustration of this point, consider Mark Tilton's (1996) study of basic industry cartels in Japan. He finds that cartels have played a major role in protecting Japanese industries as well as maintaining stability of supply, and that they exercise an important, independent role in governing the industry. However, the cartels and trade associations are not the whole story. Tilton finds abundant evidence of MITI working hard to organize and maintain industry cartels and enthusiastically supporting high prices. Given MITI's fundamental role in sustaining the cartel structure, Tilton makes a compelling case for viewing the independent actions of cartels as a form of 'delegated industrial policy'. As this example illustrates, there is much about the East Asian political economies which confounds and eludes conventional Anglo-Saxon categories.

These considerations lead me to reject the 'leadership' versus 'followership' terminology which Wade has skilfully applied to the Taiwanese case. While useful for appraising the government–industry relationship in Anglo-American political economies, when applied to the East Asian setting, its value seems less certain. This is because it tends to reinstate the very assumptions (that one side dominates) that the concept of GI is designed to challenge. For the purposes of my argument, *it is quite as significant that the state be able to exercise considerable 'leadership' (guiding business in a certain direction) as it is that the state be able to choose when and whom to 'follow' when industry exercises leadership*. Selectivity reigns in both cases; and both are fundamental to state capacity.

Let us turn, then, to the basic forms of GI. It is important to note that examples of cooperative coordination under state guidance, as manifested in the following forms, can also be found in other settings. The distinctiveness of the East Asian case should be seen in the extent and regularity of their occurrence.

Disciplined support

The first type of GI, referred to here as 'disciplined support', exists where performance conditions (outcomes) apply in exchange for support. This type tends to be strongly associated with the establishment of new industries, and the reorientation of production from domestic to export markets. Here, economic change is *initially* driven by the public sector; private cooperation with public goals is rewarded with generous subsidies; and clear performance conditions, in turn, are attached to public support. For the key problem in allocating state subsidies is how to ensure that the recipients actually do what is expected of them, rather than seek rents. Disciplined support is not simply a guard against rent-seeking behaviour; it is also a way of monitoring and measuring the attainment of policy goals and of establishing public accountability.

In Korea and Japan, especially, where at various times subsidies have played a vital role in driving investment and export behaviour, disciplined support has predominated. During the period of Korea's intensive export drive, for example, the Park administration was famous for the setting of monthly export targets (measured in dollar values), as well as stipulating minimum export items and destinations. Policy loans, trade licences and other generous benefits were always conditional on export performance. Systematic monitoring, through mandatory reporting and regular meetings with the companies involved, accompanied by tough penalties for persistent failure, did much to encourage beneficiary firms to meet policy expectations (cf. Jones and Sakong 1980; Amsden 1989).

Similarly, with regard to protection against imports, East Asian governments have generally made protection conditional, either by specifying limited-duration tariffs and quotas to hasten upgrading and innovation, or by tying protective measures to export obligations. Both Korea and Taiwan pursued such schemes throughout their high-growth era.[32] Japan has also used protection as a creative discipline. In the important electronics industry, companies had to work feverishly to improve productivity and develop technology to meet liberalization schedules. According to JETRO, the government 'always refused to extend liberalization periods, with the specific intention of exhorting domestic manufacturers to pull out all the stops to meet the deadlines' (JETRO 1993: 139).

Disciplinary intervention in Japan has also featured strongly in the creation of world-class industries which could secure market share and minimize long-run costs. Thus, in the steel industry, MITI sought to ensure continuous investment in the most up-to-date equipment by linking a firm's right to build new capacity to its efficiency. 'For any firm to "win" the right to build new capacity,' writes O'Brien (1994: 50), 'it had to show that it had the most modern equipment available.' The effect of this disciplinary system was to force incumbents continually to modernize, introducing state-of-the-art technology.

Upgrading quality standards has been another aim of disciplined support. In Taiwan's early phase of export development, for example, the economic bureaucracy sought to enforce quality standards by making the receipt of official subsidies and licensing of new enterprise conditional upon their fulfilment (Yin 1954). In the mid-1950s, as the Taiwanese government lifted the bans on entry of new firms in ten core industries, it simultaneously applied strict performance conditions to the new plants, which were required to reach minimum standards relating to size and product quality. More recent cases of disciplined support focus on innovation and upgrading rather than exports, as in the case of new product development in Taiwan's electronics industry.

In the NICs, in particular, this first type of GI has tended to predominate in the earlier, most 'authoritarian' phase of postwar industrialization. In this phase, industrial enterprise and the private sector are only weakly established; subsidies accordingly feature as major inducements to entrepreneurship; and control of the financial system is stressed. Other policy instruments – such as the control of industrial licensing, raw materials imports and foreign exchange – typically underpin the disciplined support that prevails in this phase. The establishment of a culture of performance in this initial developmental stage is a means of reducing rent-seeking behaviour in the private sector and enhancing accountability in the public arena.

It is this kind of 'top-down' or centrally driven activity that previous accounts have generally had in mind when evaluating whether or not the state 'led' development. By this they invariably mean that the state was able to *impose* its own direction on the developmental process, *regardless* of private interests. If the argument of this chapter is correct, however, then we need to rethink the nature of state capacity in the settings in question. For the approach taken here implies that 'disciplined support' is inextricably a *cooperative* undertaking. It also means that public resources are used to achieve the most productive outcome, whether to upgrade products, lower prices or expand exports. The relevant contrast is with the Anglo-American version of industrial policy. In this case, the prevailing emphasis on procedures (eligibility) rather than results (performance) means that cooperative coordination is not only absent but unnecessary.[33]

Public risk absorption

The second major type of GI involves public initiatives – usually to establish new or emerging industries – which require the cooperation of the private sector for their success, but which emphasize less the exercise of discipline than the minimization of risk. To solicit the cooperation of the producers involved, the public sector absorbs most or all of the risk, often mediating between producers and end users in the domestic market. The cases of robotics in Japan and textiles in Taiwan are instructive.

In Japan, as in the case of machine tools (Sarathy 1989: 142), MITI played the role of catalyst in developing a robotics industry. Its aim was to quicken the introduction of robots into the production process and to create an indigenous capacity for robot manufacturing. To this end, it mediated between producers and potential end users. To encourage the latter, especially small and medium-sized firms, MITI together with the Japan Development Bank organized a leasing company in 1980 that would enable domestic firms to lease robots under short-term arrangements, and to return them without expense if dissatisfied with their performance. Since this significantly minimized investment risk, firms were increasingly willing to employ robots. Thus, a rapidly expanding market for the producers of robots was effectively guaranteed. The result was a socialization of risk and the establishment of a new industry (Thurow 1985: 238). By 1982 Japan had almost 32,000 robots (compared with just over 7,200 in the United States). By 1990, the industrial-robot population exceeded 275,000, more than twice the number in all other countries combined (OTA 1991: 170).

The establishment of a textile industry in Taiwan followed a similar process in the early 1950s, this time involving provision of state-guaranteed markets in order to encourage the spinning and weaving of yarn rather than the importing of finished cloth. In both cases, the core process is government initiated, but the success of the strategy depends on mutually beneficial exchange.

Private-sector governance

The third type, private-sector governance (PSG), is an unusual kind of state capacity in that it involves 'teasing out' of economic society the capacity for self-governance. It can best be seen as a system of state-informed coordination in which the state acts as coordinator of the 'last resort'.

PSG is marked by the prevalence of private initiative in public policy-making, and can be seen as a form of 'delegated industrial policy' (Tilton 1996), or 'private-interest governance', to use the term of Streeck and Schmitter (1985). PSG is especially well developed in Germany and, for certain tasks, in Japan.

The printed circuit board industry in Japan vividly illustrates this feature of PSG. Through delegation from MITI, the sponsoring ministry, the Japan Printed Circuit Board Association (JPCA) has assumed responsibility for framing and administering public programmes (which specify detailed targets to be reached by the industry, such as those for technology upgrading). As well as wielding considerable enforcement powers over its membership, the JPCA has privileged access to MITI (Sako 1994: 29–31).

Typically, the sector in question is in a state of depression or decline, such as steel, shipbuilding and textiles, and encouraged to coordinate a strategy for survival. These initiatives are often taken at face value as evidence of state weakness and business domination (i.e. the state succumbing to pressure for assistance). Such an assumption, however, misses the point that, generally speaking, such initiatives are either directly or indirectly solicited by the state and are ultimately dependent upon the extent to which they meet publicly defined criteria.

Thus, for example, the Japanese Structurally Depressed Industries Law of 1978 actually *calls for industry to take the initiative* in seeking government support. The law specifies that an industry can become eligible for assistance only if two-thirds of the producers petition MITI, which will then decide whether to grant their request. The ministry is thus able to engender a working agreement among producers whose positions would otherwise differ considerably (Magaziner and Patinkin 1990: 363; Dore 1987: 141–2).

Frequently, the initiatives in question may be privately coordinated, as in cartels for regulating production or promoting export, a prominent feature of all the East Asian economies throughout their fast-growth period. Nowadays, such initiatives tend to be prominent in sectors which are troubled or in decline and in need of restructuring. Thus,

Mark Tilton (1996) found that in periods of decline in the basic materials industries (steel, petrochemicals, cement and aluminium) MITI delegates policy-making as well as implementation to the industrial associations, which then form cartels to control prices, set production levels and coordinate future capacity.

The recent experience of the textile industry in Taiwan provides another illustration of this third type of 'delegated' policy-making. Once Taiwan's premier exporter, but now declining due to price-competition from second-generation NICs, it was the textile industry itself that proposed a strategy to upgrade the sector. The IDB responded positively not because of 'special favours' or crafty lobbying, but because the TTF's proposal could meet the criteria for assistance, and share in the financing of that proposal. In this case, the clinching factor was a (design-intensive) strategy which would increase the value-added component of textile exports.[34]

The Taiwanese machine-tool industry similarly proposed to upgrade its technology by acquiring ailing American companies. The IDB agreed to support the acquisition proposal in return for meeting larger policy goals, which in this case meant that the industry would reinvest a given share of its sales in R&D and environmental protection.

Private initiatives can also fail, as occurred in the case of Korea's petrochemical sector in the mid-1980s. In this case, government encouraged the industry to coordinate a plan for its future and thus avoid the problem of over-capacity. But the industry failed to reach agreement over new investment, output and quotas. The result was a serious crisis of surplus capacity in the late 1980s. It is in such cases that state intervention often becomes necessary to correct business failure. We can see in this case the destabilizing effects of the *absence* of GI.

Such examples can of course be multiplied. They reveal the importance not just of formal state policies, but of strong state backing for informal (or 'delegated') policies which are planned and implemented by trade associations. They provide support for the thesis that the state plays an important role not just in a formal and direct manner, but behind the scenes, giving leadership to firms so that they will more readily cooperate with one another in the making and implementation of policy.[35]

The key point that such examples illustrate is one of an overall context defined by the publicly sanctioned expectation that the sector should internally coordinate a strategy for its future and seek to link that strategy with the larger goals of public policy. In such cases, government has authorized industry to come up with its own plan for survival and, as indicated earlier, this will be more or less difficult, depending upon the degree of sectoral cohesion. (Some sectors, such as consumer electronics, where internal competition is especially intense, can pose major difficulties in this regard.)

Public–private innovation alliances

The final type of cooperative coordination is increasingly associated with policies for acquiring, developing, upgrading and diffusing technology. The importance of a coordinated approach to technology has become especially marked in Taiwan's relatively decentralized industrial structure, and as innovation becomes the major source of further growth. The proliferation of innovation or 'technology alliances' in Taiwan offers a neat illustration.

Led by the state agency, ITRI, these alliances strongly attest to the strengthening of public–private cooperation in the crucial area of technology policy. As of April 1997, ITRI counted more than twenty such alliances (usually averaging twenty to thirty firms each) for high-tech projects ranging from high-definition TV to PowerPC-based computers. Technology alliances combine both disciplined support and risk sharing (as discussed under 'Disciplined support' and 'Public risk absorption' above). Participation is entirely voluntary, but companies do not get a free ride once they join the network, for each is required to contribute a significant share of resources (including capital and costs in kind such as the support of senior engineers). To this extent, such ventures create genuine public–private partnerships, even though they are initiated and coordinated by state agencies in conjunction with the IDB as part of its programme for technology diffusion. Finally, these technology partnerships provide a discipline through the sharing of risks, and an encouragement to participate through access to new technology and new product development.[36]

Among the more interesting forms of innovation alliance which combine risk sharing and disciplined support is the new Targeted Leading Product programme, a project administered by the IDB, within the Ministry of Economic Affairs (MOEA). The programme targets leading products to promote high-tech uptake in Taiwanese firms. Government invests half of total development costs, providing firms with 50 per cent of investment funds as a grant and up to 50 per cent as a loan. Intellectual property rights are equally shared by the MOEA and the firm; but should the firm fail to produce or sell the targeted product within the three-year period following completion of the development plan, it must transfer ownership to MOEA, which then transfers the technology to other firms (San 1995).

As these various forms of GI indicate, so-called 'intervention' has worked more often than not in East Asia because of the intersection of a number of disciplinary mechanisms, which we can summarize as state, market and (industry–government and inter-firm) networks. First, governments have acted to set the larger goals concerning which industries and technologies should be promoted, but they have done this increasingly in conjunction with industry and business organizations, though leaving the major operating details to firms. Second, once these issues have been settled, firms are expected and encouraged to prepare for intense competition, whether with local firms or in export markets. Finally, public–private networks discipline capital and build in public accountability through performance conditions set by the state.

Serving capital or shared project?

Clearly, in such a system, the question of 'who pushes whom around', or 'who compels whom', or 'who decides' (led by a research strategy which takes 'the power of A over B' as its evidentiary cornerstone) becomes less and less relevant over time. In such a system, the attempt to trace out each policy story from beginning (who wanted what at first) to end (who protested, whose initial preferences were most closely accommodated in the final outcome) simply loses its significance. Indeed, when one of the operating principles is to find win–win solutions, it may be inappropriate to seek out who the winner is as a central research strategy. This is a method that appears to be designed for a different sort of system (competitive pluralism) and for limited purposes (explaining 'who wins' rather than state capacity) – but not for a system where business is *expected* to take initiatives in certain areas (as in Japan and Germany).

In a context where the hammering out of policy measures and the constant negotiation over details are the norm not the exception, it is not a question of 'who gets their way in spite of opposition', but rather, from the point of view of the state agency, whether a business proposal fits within the state-defined guidelines; and from the point of view of business, whether a government proposal can be collectively improved and agreed upon.

Clearly a system of GI is highly supportive of industrial vitality and the industrial interests pivotal to that. Some commentators may therefore choose to interpret GI as simply another form in which 'the state' can be seen 'to serve capital', 'to act in the interests of the capitalist economic system', or some such formulation. So be it. Neither in letter nor in spirit, however, does the preceding analysis lend itself to that interpretation, partly because of its *deterministic* overtones: to reiterate, GI cannot exist where the state lacks a sense of its own project. Serving capital was of course a key condition of the development of modern states; it would appear to remain a condition of their continued survival. None the less, as the history of state formation has shown, states most serve their *own* institutional robustness when they serve capital (e.g. C. Tilly 1975). This suggests *interdependence*, not *determinism*.

More tellingly, perhaps, the 'servile state' reading of GI is seriously lacking in analytical finesse. Comparative analysis, after all, demonstrates that there are *many* ways of 'serving' capital and that they are by no means equal in economic and social consequences. Some promote productive capital very well; others rather poorly. Some are conducive to advancing collective well-being over the long haul; others are based on social exclusion. We know, for instance, that the national system of economic management in Brazil also serves capital accumulation. But it falls miserably short of the East Asian capacity to deliver growth with equity, and thus to enhance its citizens' life chances and living standards.[37] Thus, to posit that GI is simply a way of serving capital is hardly illuminating.

But the larger point to highlight is that GI is a *state-informed* system. Such a system does not happen entirely 'by chance' (the importance of historical legacies and situational circumstances notwithstanding). The organization and participation of business is indeed fundamental to its evolution and success; but if a state and its wider political elite are not imbued with the sense of a transformative project, they will not seek to build such capacities or to secure their institutional supports over time.

Conclusion: State 'Power' in East Asia

This chapter has sought to incorporate the notion of government–business cooperation into a theory of state capacity. It has advanced the proposition that a capable state is a key component of international competitiveness. In this new era of international, innovation-driven competition, East Asia's advantage resides in institutions that have enabled and encouraged a coordinated and cooperative approach to economic change. The major theoretical point in this context regards the nature of state power.

Most writers take for granted the assumption that effective states are essentially 'strong' states; such states are able to coerce or impose, and generally have their own way regardless of the will of dominant groups in society. This view is one that so-called statist writers share with their critics. The logic behind that view is such that any contrary instance – for example, the private sector initiating certain measures, or the bureaucracy and business cooperating on policy – is taken as evidence of state 'weakness' or the *lack* of capacity. Consequently, although they disagree about many things, statists and anti-statists alike are united in their view of state capacity as something with a quasi-authoritarian or 'despotic' edge to it. The capable or strong state is ultimately a bossy state.

But if the preceding analysis is accepted, a very different view of state power emerges. In order to appreciate why some countries – e.g. Australia, Britain and the United States – appear to have so little domestic capacity to coordinate industrial change and why East Asian states have so much, we need to distinguish between two notions of state power, 'coercive' and 'infrastructural'.[38] East Asian capacity for coordinating change rests not on greater coercive power (i.e. the capacity of A to impose her or his own wishes over B regardless of B's desires); it rests above all on greater infrastructural, or *negotiated*, powers (the capacity of A to *cooperate* with B *from a position of organizational autonomy* and to coordinate responses to achieve outcomes).

East Asian bureaucracies have on the whole been effective coordinators because they have used their insulation from special-interest constituencies to develop more encompassing networks. By developing formal and informal links with the industrial sector, they have encouraged cooperative responses to economic change and thereby converted their autonomy into organizational capacity.

In practical terms, Japan is the country where such capacities have been developed to the highest degree, even granted the long recession that has dogged Japan in the 1990s and the collapse of several financial institutions in 1997. Taiwan's system has held up well in the 1990s, even during the financial crisis of 1997. Contrary to expectations, Taiwan is looking rather more like Japan than is Korea, thus disproving the idea that an industrial structure based largely on small and medium-sized firms is incompatible with coordination. In contrast, Korea appears the least stable of the three cases. The national system of economic management that underpinned rapid industrial transformation has become more difficult to sustain and now appears in transition. For all its current difficulties, however, it needs to be acknowledged that this system served Korea well for nearly 40 years of uninterrupted growth. Transforming that system to preserve core capacities may prove very difficult. Indeed, the government has for some time been trying to prune the tentacle-like powers of Korea's diversified groups, while at the same time seeking to stimulate greater private involvement and initiative in policy matters. It is the former tactic that results in policies which the *chaebol* see as harmful to their interests (e.g. environmental regulations, fair trading, consumer rights, restriction of ownership concentration), and thus puts government directly at odds with the business groups.

The major problem for the foreseeable future, however, may well be structural rather than political. For extraordinary levels of diversification within the industrial groups have increasingly hampered coordination, to the point where government has sought to streamline *chaebol* operations through a variety of measures, and to stimulate business and organizational initiatives outside the *chaebol* structures.[39] To the extent that these initiatives succeed, Korea in particular and the region more generally will see the strengthening rather than diminution of governed interdependence in the future.

In sum, the notion that the rise of a robust industrial sector must lead to a generalized diminution of state capability in the East Asian setting is an expectation not borne out by either theory or empirical evidence. There is in fact nothing about industrial transformation in Japan, Korea or Taiwan to suggest that state involvement is no longer useful or important. On the contrary, should a significant diminution occur, one should expect more painful adjustment and more erratic and difficult innovation. Evans's analysis of the Korean informatics sector allows him to conclude that while state involvement has perhaps 'become more difficult and politically sensitive', it is 'still central to the process of seeking a more desirable niche in the global division of labour' (1995: 234). The analyses of Amsden (1989) and Wade (1990a) appear to point to the same conclusion: the importance of continued state involvement for industrial vitality.

4

LIMITS OF THE DISTRIBUTIVE STATE: SWEDISH MODEL OR GLOBAL ECONOMY?

> While some nations place high priority on baking more pie
> (that is, on measures promoting productivity and growth),
> others assume that the baking is best guided by the invisible
> hand, which leaves government free to place high priority on
> ensuring a minimum or fair share for everyone (that is, on
> measures promoting economic security and a redistribution
> of income via transfer payments).
>
> *Bruce Scott 1985: 106*

Introduction

If 'developmental capitalism' is an apt label for the high-performance, national-security-oriented polities of North East Asia, 'distributive capitalism' seems a useful way to distinguish the economic-security-oriented small states of northern Europe. Where the goals of industrial growth and income expansion drive public policy in the Asian region, it is income distribution that defines the priorities of the small Scandinavian states. This distinction between national strategies is most clearly reflected in regime goals, though not always in a country's performance outcomes. Thus, for example, while developmentally oriented East Asia has generally produced stronger export capacity, productivity increases and rates of income growth than the distribution-oriented countries, it is not clear that the latter have produced a more equal income distribution than in the production-oriented countries of East Asia (see table 4.1).[1]

The Swedish experience is of considerable interest to my argument. For many years admired for its ability to adjust smoothly to international competition and to ensure full employment and high living standards for

Table 4.1   Patterns of income distribution in selected countries: percentage of national income accrued by each population quintile, selected years

Country	Year	Bottom 20%	Second 20%	Third 20%	Fourth 20%	Top 20%
Sweden	1981	8.0	13.2	17.4	24.5	36.9
Germany	1988	7.0	11.8	17.1	23.9	40.3
Japan	1979	8.7	13.2	17.5	23.1	37.5
Taiwan	1987	8.1	13.5	17.5	22.8	38.0
South Korea	1988	7.4	12.3	16.3	21.8	42.2
United States	1985	4.7	11.0	17.4	25.0	41.9
Brazil	1983	2.4	5.7	10.7	18.6	62.6

Sources: World Bank (1991); Taiwan data from Chan (1993: 95).

all its citizens, the so-called 'Swedish model' was held up for emulation. Nowadays, as Swedish unemployment reaches European levels (rising from less than 2 per cent in the 1970s to more than 9 per cent in the 1990s), as the goal of lowering inflation replaces that of achieving full employment, and as Sweden now embraces membership in the EU, many commentators have begun to talk of the eclipse of the Swedish model. This apparent demise, moreover, is widely believed to support the globalization hypothesis. The alleged unravelling of the Swedish model is now commonly accepted as an important sign that the nation-state, as site of institutional diversity and as agent of economic change, has no further role to play in an era of heightened economic interdependence.

This argument seems congenial to liberals and social democrats alike: to liberals because, in attributing economic disorder to too much domestic social protection (read 'excessive welfare statism'), it vindicates the forces of free-market capitalism; to social democrats because, in attributing economic disorder to external forces, it tends to vindicate the Swedish model. From the evidence reviewed in this chapter, we shall see that neither of these conclusions can be easily sustained. It will show that neither the size of the welfare state as such, nor an increase in the international integration of the Swedish economy, undermined the Swedish model of economic adjustment.

External pressures are now widely regarded as having caused Sweden's economic difficulties and the subsequent changes forced upon the country's distinctive approach to economic management. This chapter presents the case for a different view. It proposes that the unravelling of the Swedish model is the result not of international factors but of internal contradictions which have in fact left Sweden's economy *less* internationally exposed than it was twenty to thirty years ago. This argument emphasizes weaknesses in the transformative capacity of the social democratic state. It suggests that, far from being weakened by the internationalization of Swedish capital or by external competitive pressures, such capacity was severely limited by the nature and dynamics of the Swedish model itself. Above all, Swedish values, institutions and public policies have been oriented preponderantly towards *distributive* goals.

The implication is not that Sweden's welfare state is too 'generous' but rather that Sweden has prioritized a distributive strategy, which has focused on wage and profit levels and differentials. This strategy has been burdened with the dual task of achieving (intensive) growth with equity, a role to which distributively capable states are inherently unsuited. Issues of structural change, innovation and industrial transformation – though intermittently important – have figured at best as a distant, second-order priority, to be invoked in times of economic trouble rather than institutionalized as national strategies. Even the pattern of reactive 'industrial policy', as we shall see, has tended to conform to a distributive, rather than a developmental, logic.

The Swedish problem, then, is not so much its famous system of *public compensation for labour*, affected by economic change, as the absence of *public inducements for industry to pursue qualitative change*. As is well understood, the Swedish system has been quasi-Keynesian with regard to labour, but laissez-faire with regard to industry. In short, there has emerged a serious imbalance resulting from a policy for labour mobility without a corresponding policy for the expansion of productive investment and jobs to receive such labour. Why this bifurcation was maintained and why it mattered are the subject of the analysis that follows.

Distributive State Capacity

Sweden as a distributive state

Along with many of its small north European 'neighbours', Sweden can be described as a distributive regime. Like developmental states, distributive states can be identified according to their national priorities or fundamental goals. Distributive regimes give high priority to the role of government in promoting redistribution of national income. Such regimes tend to deliver an ambitious mix of policies that emphasize income redistribution, welfare entitlements and short-term consumer benefits.[2]

Distributive capacity entails maximizing state responsibility for the socio-economic welfare of the citizenry. Policies of taxation and transfers therefore aim at reducing differences in income. While these have been highly effective redistributive mechanisms in Europe, somewhat counter-intuitively they do not necessarily produce more equitable outcomes than in the more developmentally oriented countries of East Asia (see table 4.1).

What is the 'Swedish model'?

Sweden's approach to national economic management is generally discussed under the heading 'the Swedish model'. A consistent definition, however, remains elusive. Most vary in their inclusiveness. But a key difficulty is that the 'model' itself has been a moving target. As we shall see, it has evolved to be rather different from the model originally conceived.

In its classical form, the Swedish model has three core components.

The Rehn–Meidner programme   At the core of the Swedish system is the Rehn–Meidner programme, named after its two key proponents, Gøsta Rehn and Rudolf Meidner. Developed in the late 1940s and early 1950s, this programme sought to reconcile full employment with low inflation. It included three principal features:

1 a solidaristic wage policy, entailing equal pay for comparable work across firms and industries regardless of profit and productivity levels; these levels were to be determined by the export sector and hence ultimately constrained by the international market;
2 an active labour-market policy able to retrain and move to new employment all those made jobless as a result of the solidaristic wage policy;
3 a restrictive demand (fiscal and monetary) policy to curb inflation and high profits.

The expectation behind this programme was that centralized wage setting negotiated between industry and labour, together with solidaristic wages and a unique mix of labour-market policies, would encourage the shifting of resources to more productive areas of the economy.[3] By making the most internationally competitive firms the pacesetters in wage settlements, a constant 'transformative pressure' would be applied to industry. Inefficient firms would thereby be forced either to upgrade or to exit from the market. Similarly, by compensating labour through retraining and job placement programmes, resistance to change would be minimized.[4]

Social Democracy　The second component of the model relates to the quasi-permanent hold of social democracy on government and the institutionalization of social democratic goals. Since 1932, the Social Democratic Party (SAP) has ruled either alone or in coalitions for all but a dozen years. In no other European OECD country has one party held power for as long as the SAP. Moreover, as a result of the social democrats' dominant political role, the Swedish labour movement also came to acquire a uniquely strong political position. According to Swedish commentators, this longevity of rule has imparted a social-democratic cast to Swedish society as well as an institutional set-up characterized by large, encompassing unions and corporatist policy-making (Henrekson et al. 1993: 51–2).

A universalistic welfare state　A third distinctive feature of the Swedish model is the existence of a generous welfare state focusing chiefly on the delivery of high-quality 'services' (such as health, education and housing) rather than on 'transfers' *per se*. However, it is important to make a distinction between *welfare per se* and *public expenditure*. Much of the latter, as will be evident from later discussion, goes to government consumption (close to 30 per cent of GDP) to support Sweden's very large public sector. The higher quality of welfare services, on the other hand, does not necessarily translate into exceptionally higher expenditure, as we shall see later. Moreover, in spite of some changes at the margin, Swedish levels and patterns of welfare expenditure, as distinct from public spending, have not been significantly affected since the late 1980s, 'globalization' predictions nothwithstanding. Pierson (1996: 171–2) argues that in spite of conditions highly favourable to a radical restructuring of social policy – the extraordinary pressures on the public purse, the emergence of a genuine fiscal crisis, and the advent of a rightward-leaning bourgeois coalition – most changes have occurred at the margins, thus preserving the structure of existing programmes.[5]

Indeed, of the three main features of the Swedish model outlined earlier, it is the first and perhaps most fundamental, the Rehn–Meidner programme, which has undergone the most substantial change. Moreover, as we shall shortly see, this transformation process long pre-dates the recent debates on the demise of the Swedish model.

Strengths of the Swedish approach

Among the advanced countries, Sweden has long appeared at the top of the equality league in a host of areas, including per capita employment, female as compared to male wages, progressiveness of the tax system, generosity of public pensions, public provision of health, education and welfare services, relative absence of poverty, and overall income equality (Glyn 1995: 16). Of these, only the tax system has witnessed significant changes in recent years, with the shift to higher consumption and lower income taxes.[6]

In addition to these distributive outcomes, many observers of the Swedish system also emphasize the benefits of its active labour-market policy (ALMP). The ALMP has been widely viewed as a 'world-class' training programme, absorbing 6–7 per cent of the government budget (i.e. around 2–3 per cent of GNP), which is equivalent to $US5 billion for a workforce of 4.4 million people. Moreover, the 'active' element means that most of the budget (70 per cent) goes to training and placement programmes, and only 30 per cent for unemployment benefits. This compares with a 10:90 ratio in the USA (Magaziner and Patinkin 1990: 353–4). Many observers have therefore concluded that Sweden's labour-market programme has been the main motor of Sweden's restructuring and its low rate of unemployment.

However, in practice, ALMP has followed the French rather than the German model, concentrating more resources on placement than on training. While ALMP has fostered a labour force more amenable to technological change and industrial restructuring, there is scant evidence that it has contributed to economic growth or industrial transformation; some even doubt that it has contributed to employment (Henrekson et al. 1993). Indeed, by all indications, as we shall see in due course, it would appear that the main mechanism of employment since at least the 1970s has been the growth of the public sector.

The Model Unravels: External Pressures?

While the Swedish model is identified with high employment, wage equality, and a generous welfare system, if one excludes the exceptional 1960s, it is clear that it has also gone hand in hand with low investment, low growth and deteriorating manufacturing productivity (Schott 1984; Mjoset 1987; Auer and Riegler 1994; Glyn 1995). In just twenty years (1970–91), Sweden slipped from third to fourteenth place with a GDP per capita 6 per cent below the OECD average. Although other countries have lagged badly (notably the Netherlands, Australia and New Zealand), Sweden's regression has been the most pronounced. This decline has been most obvious from the poor growth of industrial production. Since the 1970s, annual growth rates and industrial production have been a good percentage point below the OECD average. Indeed, many commentators insist that the Swedish industrial crisis began not in the 1990s but in 1976–7. Between 1975 and 1979, among the five Nordic countries, Sweden ranked lowest in growth of GNP, manufacturing production and exports. Its industrial performance was actually one of the weakest in the OECD, recording zero value-added in manufacturing in 1976, −5.7 in 1977, and −2.7 in 1978. By contrast, the OECD average was 8.2, 4.5 and 3.8 respectively (Mjoset 1987: 437).

In spite of some areas of industrial recovery, the problems of low industrial investment and low growth have remained endemic, as earlier highlighted by Kerry Schott (1984). In seeking to explain the relative decline of economic growth in Sweden since the early 1970s, a group of Swedish researchers highlights shrinking investment in productive activities, lagging productivity, a falling share of the economy exposed to international competition, rapid growth of the public sector, and low implementation of R&D outcomes – all of which suggest 'that the incentive structure created by "the Swedish model" made Sweden less successful in adapting to the shocks of the 1970s and 1980s than other OECD countries' (Henrekson et al. 1993: 1).

One important conclusion to be drawn from such studies is that Sweden's economic difficulties are not of recent making. Though probably compounded by macro-economic mismanagement in the 1980s, Sweden's economic weaknesses had surfaced much earlier (Glyn 1995: 19). Yet for decades, Sweden remained highly successful in keeping unemployment well below OECD levels. Even in the period 1973–82, when economic performance deteriorated severely relative to the OECD average, unemployment was maintained at a low level, largely because of a policy of expanding public employment.[7]

In recent years, however, observers of Sweden's difficulties have begun to proclaim the 'end of social democracy', the 'collapse of the Swedish model' and the 'demise of the welfare state'. While such phrases exaggerate, they none the less point to a real shift in Sweden's institutional set-up. The most immediate and visible aspect of this change is the dramatic rise of unemployment – from a low of 1.5 per cent in the 1980s to a high of 9 per cent in the 1990s – and the shift of social priorities from fighting unemployment to beating inflation. To this one must add the withdrawal of employers' support for centralized wage bargaining. These are indeed signs of significant change, if not collapse, at the heart of the Swedish model.

But some clarification is in order at this point. For, as I shall presently indicate, it is not the model in its classic form that has come unstuck, but something else. That 'something else' was rather different from the arrangement that employers and government, with trade union support, helped to establish in the 1950s. Thus while employer defection has certainly weakened the system of centralized wage setting in the 1990s, there were more long-standing pressures that paved the way for that defection. As I shall endeavour to show, these pressures, far from being induced by international economic integration, were overwhelmingly internal to the model itself. Let us first begin with a review of the international system hypotheses.

International system hypotheses

How best to account for this change of fortune in an institutional set-up that was once associated with effective economic performance? International explanations are nowadays the regnant orthodoxy, and the main contest is between different kinds of 'international' or external factor. This turn to the international is in part a response to the perceived tendency of comparativists and area experts over many years to have overlooked the impact of the external environment on domestic institutions. But an equally important force in the current rediscovery of the international is a belief that the mobility of corporate capital is now much easier and more desirable for capital, and more threatening to the nation-state, than at any previous time in history.

Central to this debate is the belief that employers' interests and actions are fundamental to the fate of the Swedish model, that employers are no longer interested in centralized wage setting, and that corporatist institutions therefore no longer function. Let us therefore assume for the moment that the revival of wage-setting institutions is indeed the heart of the matter – that they would not merely revive the Swedish model but engender the necessary industrial transformation. The important issue then becomes why employers are no longer interested in wage-setting institutions.

There have been two main answers to this, both of which highlight *external* opportunities and pressures. In this section, I therefore consider complementary international explanations for the relative decline of the Swedish model.

Mobility of capital

In the first version, it is postulated that growing economic integration has weakened the mutual dependency of the social democratic state and large firms, thus drastically altering the power relations that underpin the Swedish model (Edquist and Lundvall 1993: 292). The employers' waning interest in centralized bargaining, it is claimed, stems from the fact that they now have many more options for investing offshore. In this interpretation, 'globalization' (read 'capital mobility') is responsible for unravelling the Swedish model of coordinated bargaining not only because it gives capital more opportunities for exit, but because it narrowly restricts policy options (cf. Kurzer 1993: 20).

Such arguments can be seen as part of the new 'logic of capitalism' thesis. Its central claim is that national policy models are converging in response to so-called economic globalization, which severely limits what national governments can do for the social and economic well-being of their citizenry (e.g. H. Schwartz 1994; Moses 1994). The following statement typifies this position:

> Despite the fact that Sweden and Norway can be said to have relied on different strategies for meeting social democratic objectives, both strategies have proved ineffective in the new international economic environment. ... A new international economic regime, characterized by increased levels of capital mobility, has made traditional tools for government steering ineffective. ... [A]ll participants are subject to an iron law of policy. (Moses 1994: 140–2, cited in Pierson 1996)

The capital mobility argument has limited explanatory power for at least three reasons. First, the movement of capital is of course a fact of life, but one cannot deduce from this a causal logic. Swedish firms acquired an international orientation very early on in their formation through the establishment of foreign subsidiaries. Substantial increases in employment of the foreign subsidiaries of Swedish corporations occurred well before international integration of capital and investment markets began to deepen, and long before employers would come to repudiate coordinated wage bargaining. In the 1960–78 period, for example, such employment more than doubled, from 12 per cent to 26 per cent.[8] Manufacturing capital may well be more mobile now than in earlier decades, but the causality remains obscure. If Swedish companies were transferring more activities abroad, it needs to be shown that this had more to do with the pull of external opportunities than with push factors in the local environment as the system of wage restraint broke down. Kurzer observes, for example, that 'extremely high wage increases' in 1970–3 and again in the wage contract of 1975–6 pushed unit labour costs of Swedish industry 27 points higher than those of its trading partners. 'Most hurt were engineering employers or large export firms, which felt that the bargaining system had failed to restrain wages. By 1976, the large engineering companies wanted to get out of peak-level bargaining' (Kurzer 1993: 70).

This relates to the second weakness in the capital mobility hypothesis. If Swedish manufacturing firms are increasingly investing their profits abroad rather than at home, as anticipated by the thesis, one cannot deduce from this a zero-sum logic: i.e. that more activities abroad mean the curtailment of domestic involvements. Although financial liberalization has vastly increased the range of investments that domestic firms can make overseas, large direct investment outflows do not necessarily correlate with the *contraction* of domestic manufacturing investment. Glyn points out that in the late 1980s (an unusually investment-intense period in Sweden), large direct investment outflows actually coincided with Sweden's investment recovery, 'which saw the manufacturing capital stock growing at 3.5% per year in 1989, faster than in Europe as a whole' (Glyn 1995: 18). As this kind of counter-evidence suggests, the zero-sum logic inherent in the capital mobility arguments is far from compelling.

Finally, it is assumed that without the exit option, Swedish capital would have invested in new production facilities or value-adding activities rather than in more speculative undertakings. However, according to a number of observers, the typical pattern of foreign investment in the 1980s does not support this assumption. A good deal of Swedish capital went to speculative ventures such as art collections and real estate (Higgins 1996; Glyn 1995). Indeed, the large flows of outward investment, according to Glyn (1995: 15), 'may exaggerate the real internationalisation of production' since much of the FDI from Sweden has involved 'portfolio' purchases of existing assets by conglomerates. Indeed Glyn's conclusions are consistent with the observations of several other analysts, for example Mjoset (1987: 439), who notes that many large Swedish firms in the 1980s displayed product inertia and exploited oligopolistic positions in markets for highly specialized, mature products. Thus, rather than opting for product innovation at home or 'offensive production linkages' abroad, they invested in marketing existing products overseas and in acquiring competing firms. 'Certainly real investment "lost" to the domestic economy cannot be read off from the FDI flows since there is no guarantee that the enterprises concerned would otherwise purchase new fixed assets at home' (Glyn 1995: 15).

On a more general note, consider what the actual size of FDI involves. Indeed, it will help to put this whole argument into perspective to be aware that over the entire 1981–92 period, outward FDI by Swedish corporations, though higher than the European average of 6.2 per cent, amounted to little more than 13 per cent of gross domestic investment (Glyn 1995: table 5).

The question remains as to how important 'external' factors were in Sweden's economic difficulties and consequent dilution of its distinctive model.

The changing structure of production

A more sophisticated variation on the 'international pressure' hypothesis draws attention to the dynamics of international competition and to changes in the structure of Swedish production (cf. Pontusson 1992a). According to this hypothesis, Swedish employers have defected from centralized wage-setting institutions because of the emergence of 'post-Fordist' systems of production, where new skills call for a more differentiated wage structure. Pontusson's analysis posits a link between domestic employer strategies and changing international production requirements as they affected the Swedish economy. In order to introduce structural changes requiring different sorts of skill, he argues, employers sought to use wage systems to sharpen incentives. Pontusson's emphasis on these 'structural' sorts of pressure on and from employers to abandon wage-fixing institutions seems important. However, taking the postwar period as a whole, such pressures to abandon centralized bargaining do occur rather late in the day. It would therefore be analytically premature to leave the matter at this point. For there is a prior, more fundamental transformation at work.

Of central importance is the fact that Sweden's wage-setting institutions had already undergone ineluctable changes in the 1970s (Iversen 1996). As indicated earlier, employers in the key engineering sector had already exited from centralized bargaining by the early 1980s. Pontusson's argument suggests that they were responding to the demands of a 'changing structure of capitalist production' as it impacted on Swedish industry. There is some evidence that changes were indeed afoot. But their sources were not purely external: in particular, skilled labour was in relative short supply as educational levels in the Swedish workforce fell well below those of Sweden's main competitors. The share of the manufacturing labour force completing secondary education in Sweden was only 49.9 per cent, compared with 73.1 per cent in Germany, 79.4 per cent in the US and 67.9 per cent in Japan. These figures lend support to studies of the changing pattern of specialization, which show that at the end of the 1970s the content of imports became more human-capital intensive, and that during the 1980s Sweden's structure of industrial production shifted towards industries with a low intensity of human and physical capital. The study on which this data is based concludes that the rate of return to education fell to levels well below the OECD average and that this was, to a significant degree, an unanticipated consequence of wage levelling, which discouraged higher completion rates of secondary and post-secondary education.[9] In so far as the quality and supply of human capital available for production were thereby reduced, subsequent shifts in the production structure must therefore be related in some measure to the functioning of the Swedish model itself.

We are thus led to a third hypothesis, which places emphasis on both changes and weaknesses within the domestic system of adjustment.

Undermining from Within

If we consider the three 'core' features of the classical model outlined earlier, it is the first, the Rehn–Meidner programme, that has witnessed the most dramatic change in recent years. According to close observers of the Swedish experience, all that remains of the original model is agreement over technical change and ALMP (Edquist and Lundvall 1993: 291).

If one focuses exclusively on the Rehn–Meidner core of the Swedish model, then it would seem that its 'golden age' was already reached by the early 1960s. Shortly after this period, signs of trouble began to appear; these were reflected in a number of changes inconsistent with the model. Such changes included expansionary fiscal and monetary policies, which fuelled inflation; the introduction of regional policies along with rapid growth in transfer payments, which together reduced the incentives for mobility necessary for the model to work; and, in the 1970s a series of laws whose aim was to induce firms not to dismiss workers with low productivity.[10]

Most important of all perhaps were the changes in occupational structure, which had a decisive impact on central bargaining and, with it, on the commitment of employers to that institution. Let us therefore look more closely at the various domestic pressures on Sweden's model of adjustment.

Rise of the sheltered sector

Recall that a central aim of the Rehn–Meidner programme was to squeeze low-productivity firms and industries, forcing them to upgrade or exit from the market, while at the same time, through an active labour-market programme, moving those left unemployed to firms and jobs with high productivity. Government's role in this context was to stabilize the economy, but to avoid direct intervention in the wage-setting process and to maintain a similar distance from industry in the core export sector.

The Rehn–Meidner programme should therefore not be seen as a surrogate for industry policy or for a coordinating mechanism to stimulate and guide industrial transformation. The absence of such a mechanism seems acutely underlined by the problems that surfaced in the Swedish model (Higgins 1996). Most dramatically, growth in the number of manufacturing jobs ceased in the mid-1960s. Industrial production and employment went into relative *and absolute* decline, and the public sector thereby became 'the employer of last resort' (see figure 4.1). The problem was that for those firms which needed to upgrade in order to stay abreast of the competition, there was no coordinating mechanism for assisting industrial renewal and replacement. Firms were simply left to do their own thing; so when firms failed to adjust they simply exited from the market. In the absence of industrial replenishment, the main mechanism for absorbing those released from industry became the expansion of public employment rather than labour-market policy.

Most such expansion took place in the 1960s and 1970s; that is, well before so-called economic globalization tendencies. Between 1973 and 1980, public-sector employment in Sweden grew by an enormous 38.7 per cent, more than doubling the EU rate of 16 (Auer and Riegler 1994: 17). In the period 1960–92, employment fell by *c.*300,000 in the private sector, and rose by over 900,000 in the public. That is, public expansion was more dramatic than private decline, a trend somewhat at odds with the idea of an increasingly 'globalized' economy.

The trends outlined in figure 4.2 add to the picture of an economy increasingly sheltered from the international environment. Using tradables and non-tradables as synonyms for 'competitive' and 'sheltered', respectively, Henrekson and colleagues draw on National Accounts data to plot the secular decline of the competitive sector since 1952 (i.e. the sector exposed to international competition). This decline is especially marked in the 1950s and 1960s. By 1992, the *exposed sector* has almost halved in size, accounting for *a meagre 20 per cent* of the Swedish economy.

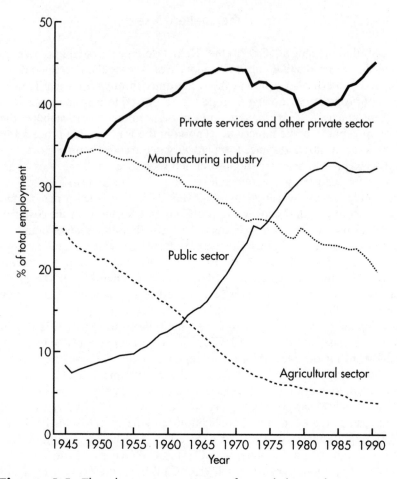

Figure 4.1 The changing structure of Swedish employment, 1945–90

Source: Henrekson et al. (1993)

An 'open' economy?   As this data indicates, the sheltered sector there-fore grew at the expense of the exposed or competitive sector. Changes in occupational structure in turn altered the nature of central wage set-ting. For as wage levels came to be set by protected-sector unions, they were thus less and less sensitive to the international constraints imposed on 'exposed'-sector firms.

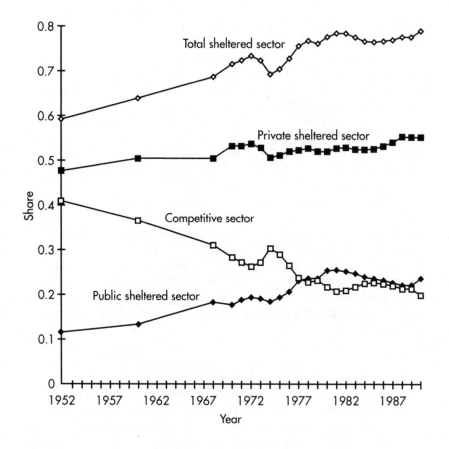

Figure 4.2 The competitive and sheltered sectors of the Swedish economy, 1952–90
Source: Henrekson et al. (1993)

Such trends not only qualify the idea of advancing economic integration; they also pose something of a paradox. For the Swedish economy has usually been associated with the terms 'openness' and 'vulnerability'. Typically, these terms have been invoked to account for Sweden's distinctive blend of social and economic policies (cf. Katzenstein 1985). In most recent debates, such considerations have buttressed arguments to explain the fragility of the Swedish approach to economic adjustment. But, as the preceding data shows, in at least one major respect

Sweden is rather less 'open' than commonly supposed. By the early
1990s, the 'sheltered' sector had grown from some 60 per cent of the
economy in the early 1950s to almost 80 per cent.

How do we reconcile these two apparently antithetical images? It
seems likely that both are true. Measured in terms of employment, the
tradables sector has halved in size, accounting for little more than 20
per cent of total economic activity. The Swedish economy as a whole
has therefore become *less* exposed to international competition. But
within this much-diminished tradables sector, fewer firms are exporting
slightly more of their total production (hence an increase in exports
from 30 to 35 per cent of GNP over the same period). Thus one might
reconcile a moderate increase in the share of Swedish exports as a ratio
of GNP (an index of increased international integration in specific firms
and industries) with a strong contraction of the exposed sector overall
and thus a lessening of competitive pressure (diminished integration).[11]

The most important impact of such changes has been the diminution
of Sweden's outward orientation and the loss of an external discipline.
To appreciate how the main changes in occupational structure occurred
and how they impacted on Swedish institutions, we must look to the
role of each of the major power actors: organized labour, government
and industry.

Pressures on organized labour

In striking contrast to their present stance, Swedish employers had been
strong early advocates of central bargaining. This strong employer
commitment to the institution, however, declined as the Swedish Union
Federation's (LO's) organizational monopoly diminished, as wage
rivalry intensified, and as central bargaining became an instrument of
wage equalization rather than wage restraint.[12]

Crouch develops a powerful argument in which he shows an association between the strength of industry-level unions in the exposed sector
of the economy and the effectiveness of central bargaining institutions.
In particular, his argument highlights the impact on trade union cohesion of major changes in Sweden's employment structure. Specifically, the LO's organizational monopoly had declined notably by the
1970s as a result of significant changes in occupational structure. Figure
4.1 shows a major decline of employment in the manufacturing sector,
from 35 per cent to 20 per cent of the workforce. Inversely related to
this trend is a dramatic rise in public-sector employment, from 8 per
cent to 34 per cent of total employment. The most important changes
therefore concerned the expansion of public-sector employment and

the growing organization of white-collar workers in both private and public sectors. This shift, observes Crouch, 'produced powerful new actors external to the LO–SAF [Swedish Union Federation–Swedish Employers' Association] system and outside its control'. Over some three decades (1960–88), the LO's constituency declined from 75 to 58 per cent of organized labour; the corresponding share of public-sector employees in the union federations rose from 26 to 44 per cent.

As public employment expanded and as manufacturing and trade-related employment shrank, those in the former protected sector of the economy increasingly set the pace for wage increases that were less sensitive to international competitors. Thus, marked changes in the structure of employment meant that wage accords were no longer determined by the 'exposed' sectors more sensitive to international markets, but by labour in the protected sector of the economy, whose numbers soon far exceeded those of their colleagues in export-related areas. This shift from a highly exposed (that part dealing in tradables) to a highly sheltered economy is neatly illustrated in figure 4.2.

There were of course other pressures affecting the system of coordinated wage restraint. One of these was the almost continuous compression of real take-home pay from 1973 to 1985.[13] Another was the intense wage rivalry between manual and non-manual unions that centralized bargaining itself seemed to stimulate. But most decisive for employer support for the system were the changes introduced by the LO itself as it implemented its long-held wage solidarity policy. This move unequivocally turned central bargaining into an instrument of equalization, thereby diminishing employer commitment to it.

The contrast with Austria lends support to this 'internalist' argument. unlike the Swedes, Austrian employers continued to support centralized bargaining throughout the 1980s and early 1990s. As Torben Iversen shows, in Austria the 'crucial elements for change were missing'. Above all, 'the redistributive goal of wage levelling was institutionally subordinated to the goal of collective gain, and pressure for institutional change was therefore dissipated' (1996: 429).

The key point is that by the mid-to-late 1970s centralized bargaining had ceased to function as an institution of wage restraint. The LO's wage solidarity policy had shifted its emphasis on equal pay for equal work to that of equalization across the professions. Moreover, in view of changes in occupational structure – led primarily by public-sector expansion – wage-setting institutions became increasingly driven by the pay demands of labour in the sheltered sector. As such, centralized wage bargaining moved decisively away from the *wage-restraint* component of the model. Thus when employers in 1991 withdrew support for

the institution of centralized bargaining, which they had worked so hard
to establish in the 1950s, they were in fact exiting from a system whose
objectives had much earlier shifted ineluctably from wage compression
to wage equalization.

It would therefore appear that one of the core features of the
Swedish system was already unravelling by the early 1970s. A number
of scholars have therefore argued that the decline of central bargaining
should be dated from that time, not from 1983 or 1990 as many
accounts have suggested (Crouch 1993a; Fulcher 1994: 205).

Accommodationist policies of government

Government also contributed to the demise of the Swedish model, principally by adopting a policy of accommodation, largely based on devaluations and expansion of public employment, both of which had
long-term structural consequences. As employment in value-adding sectors of the economy declined, the aims of labour-market policies
accordingly shifted. Government turned increasingly to public-sector
expansion as a means of holding down unemployment. Expenditures
for public consumption (e.g. wages) rapidly increased, while those for
public investment were reduced (Henrekson et al. 1993: 54; Glyn 1995).

Paradoxically, the Social Democratic government which had overseen the institutionalization of joint central wage negotiations also
helped to undermine them. It contributed, for example, by allowing the
public sector to lead pay negotiations in the early 1970s and thus to
determine the overall wage pattern. Government actions thus 'turned
the classic model of bargaining upside down and helped to alienate
employers from it' (Crouch 1993a: 225).

In an interesting aside, howeve, Crouch suggests that the occupational changes weakening the LO–SAF monopoly need not have
doomed central bargaining. The latter was in fact reinstated by the
bourgeois governments of 1976–82. But it broke down once again in
1983, as soon as the social democrats were returned to government. The
implication of this temporary reprieve is that public–private-sector
cooperation 'could have restored the model', but such cooperation
would have required 'a strong and determined bourgeois government,
and such a government was not available'.[14]

In a further departure from the original conception, economic policy
showed a marked deviation from the Rehn–Meidner model when the
social democrats returned to another nine years in office in 1982. In
addition to accommodating public-sector wage demands, the social
democrats instituted a 17 per cent devaluation of the krona, with the

aim of using high profits as an inducement to industry to invest in production.

Only the high profits in this equation came to pass. While government believed that market forces would stimulate investments and so rejuvenate Swedish manufacturing, the devaluations of the 1980s provided only short-lived benefits. For one thing, they reduced the pressure on firms to upgrade and innovate and allowed those in traditional product areas to amass big profits. By benefiting established labour-intensive industries, the devaluations therefore helped to preserve the existing industrial structure. The substantial reinvestment to upgrade facilities and technology was not forthcoming. Instead, capital was redirected to speculative activities at home and abroad (Higgins 1996: 13–14; Edquist and Lundvall 1993: 295).

Government policy towards industry exacerbated the problem. Massive subsidies to manufacturing firms were extended during severe recessions, particularly in the late 1970s. These were invariably distributed in ad hoc fashion, provided in the form of rescue operations to maintain employment (Pontusson 1992). Short-term job saving, not long-term industry expansion, has been the typical pattern of government support. In the 1976–80 period, massive resources were allocated to support bankrupt firms, as well as ailing shipbuilding and steel companies. This of course left little for adequate funding of R&D, training, or promotion of new products and sectors (Katzenstein 1985: 66–7; Magaziner and Patinkin 1990: 353).

Industry's reluctance to invest

As mentioned earlier, while the Swedish model is identified with high employment, wage solidarity and a generous welfare system, it has also gone hand in hand with relatively low investment, low growth and deteriorating manufacturing productivity. While falling productivity growth has been attributed to the massive expansion of public-sector employment, it was not exclusively caused by a large public sector. In manufacturing, for example, 'total factor productivity ... has grown more slowly than in any other OECD country' (Lindbeck et al. cited in Glyn 1995: 19). The behaviour of large Swedish firms in dominant export sectors in the mid-1970s and again in the early 1980s also played a part. In the most recent period firms were slow to invest in new equipment while maintaining price mark-ups. Their actions in this regard mirrored an earlier pattern. Indeed the persistence of the Swedish industrial crisis of 1976–7, for example, even after real wages and unit labour costs declined, suggests that Swedish business deepened the crisis itself. For it chose to deploy what it gained from devaluations of the krona to repay old loans, rather than to invest (Mjoset 1987: 438, 439).

To these longer-term domestic pressures on the Swedish model one may certainly add the more proximate factor of employer pressure in the export sector, where changes in product markets were demanding more flexibility in the use of wages to attract workers with different skills (Pontusson 1992; Glyn 1995: 18). There is, however, another domestic factor which we have already mentioned and which should not be ignored in this context. This is the shortage of so-called 'human capital skills' in the Swedish workforce, ostensibly an unanticipated consequence of wage levelling. From this perspective, one may argue that external competitive pressures made Sweden's internal weaknesses increasingly likely to collapse. Hence external pressures clearly compounded pre-existing problems. But they were not the originating source.

In a number of important ways, then, the core elements of the Swedish approach to economic adjustment were substantially weakened as early as the 1970s and further watered down throughout the 1980s. Yet, even without this dilution, there is scant evidence that the Swedish model, in either its ideal or applied form, could engender industrial adaptivity or transformative capacity.

A more fundamental argument can therefore be made. In the new global competition, wage-fixing institutions may be much less relevant to the success or otherwise of Swedish economic adjustment. This appears to be the logical conclusion of Mjoset's analysis. Taking issue with Katzenstein, who emphasized the capacity of the Swedish and other corporatist economies to adjust to continuous change, Mjoset (1987: 406–7) argues that such analysis was suited to an earlier era when key pressures were those emanating from a rapidly growing world economy. From the mid-1970s onwards, external pressures have taken on an entirely different character. These now emanate from a world economy beset by low growth and stagflation. In such a context, wage-fixing institutions ostensibly offer relatively little advantage by themselves, for they were designed for a regime shaped primarily by price-driven competition and relatively stable demand.

While Sweden's institutional set-up continues to emphasize the control of costs, the advanced countries have been experiencing a major shift from cost-driven to innovation-led competition (Abernathy et al. 1981; Soskice 1990; Best 1990). This shift, in turn, places a premium less on wage-fixing institutions (centralized or otherwise) than on the public–private infrastructure for managing change at the sectoral and product level. Given this focus, Sweden's political-institutional processes appear increasingly ill adapted to the new transformative tasks (Mjoset 1987: 406; Crouch 1993a: 17).

The following section therefore builds a different argument for the Swedish crisis. It seeks to show that the latter was by and large unavoidable, because the transformative pressures of centralized wage setting could not produce long-term substantive results without a strategy and infrastructure for industrial change. Swedish industry, for all its centralized organization, proved unwilling and unable by itself to implement the continuous changes in products, processes and sectoral composition necessary to meet the new international competition. While emphasis is given to domestic weaknesses, such an explanation is able to accommodate both the fact of international pressure to change and the inability to do so.

The Limits of a Distributive Strategy

What went wrong with the Swedish approach? How is it that something that seemed to work so well in an earlier period seems to many now of limited value? My argument emphasizes the limitations of distributive capacity *in the absence of a transformative complement*. The key problem stems not from the size or generosity of the welfare state *per se*, but from an imbalance in the Swedish system: viz. a policy for labour mobility without a corresponding strategy for upgrading and expanding investment in growth sectors of the economy to receive such labour. The fate of Sweden's industrial production, which, as we have seen, fell both relatively and absolutely throughout the 1970s and 1980s, is one striking indication of the failure to adjust.

What was it about Swedish corporatist institutions that stifled adjustment, while East Asian institutions promoted it? Was it perhaps that the state was too *widely* embedded in economic society, and thus unable to focus its resources and coordinating efforts effectively? In other words, is corporatism with labour an obstacle to transformative capacity, as sometimes suggested?

Quite the contrary, I shall argue. If anything, the state was too *narrowly* embedded in economic society. For while it was strongly based in trade union and labour organizations, it was only weakly connected to Swedish industry. The difficulty would seem to reside not in the lack of industrial organization or in a fragmented business structure, a problem germane to liberal pluralist polities like Britain and the United States. Rather, the problem stems in the first instance from the orientations and practices embedded in Swedish institutions. For these have focused steadfastly on distributionism, to the virtual exclusion of 'developmentalism', on consumption rather than on production, and on full employment rather than on innovation and industrial transformation. The recent reordering of priorities from preventing unemployment to fighting inflation has not altered this focus. The distributive orientation remains in place. Only the social targets of the macro-stabilization policies have changed.

To restate the argument in slightly different terms, it is not corporatism with labour that is the problem, but rather corporatism without industry. This is manifested in at least two ways: a market-led stance towards upgrading and a distributive logic to adjustment.

A market-led stance towards upgrading

As an integral aspect of the model, the market-led orientation of the Swedish state leaves industry ill equipped not only to develop new products and processes rapidly, but also to move quickly out of declining industries and into rising sectors.

This is not to say that the Swedish system lacks innovative capabilities. Sweden ranks among the top countries in R&D expenditure as a proportion of GNP. When this has produced results for Swedish industry, it has been largely in the sphere of process, not product, innovation. In other words, Swedish R&D has been devoted mostly to labour-saving technologies (Edquist and Lundvall 1993: 287–8). But a large portion of R&D does not directly benefit Sweden's domestic industry. Henrekson and colleagues (1993) find that when it comes to R&D outcomes that result in new products, Swedish firms tend to prefer to *license* the results abroad rather than to implement them at home. This may partly account for the Swedish paradox of large R&D spending together with industry's low investment and product innovation.

While world markets for R&D-intensive products are expanding more rapidly than for other products, Sweden's position in R&D-intensive goods, with some notable exceptions, has therefore remained weak. Engineering industry in Sweden has tended to concentrate on producing and exporting traditional low-R&D (i.e. mechanical rather than electronic) goods with limited growth prospects. The slowness of industry in absorbing such products is striking, given Sweden's relatively high R&D investments and high number of US patents per million inhabitants. As already noted, however, much of this expenditure produces results for licensing rather than for product innovation.

A distributive logic to adjustment

Even when the state does 'intervene' in industry, this is typically to prevent decline rather than to promote growth. Government assistance to industry increased substantially in the 1970s (leaping from 8 to 24 per cent of gross capital formation between 1970 and 1976), but the majority of such assistance gave preference to declining over growth sectors (Katzenstein 1985: 66–7).

A significant aspect of Swedish programmes for industry is not their lack of coherence but their focus on short-term benefits for employment and their neglect of long-term prospects for wealth creation. Initiatives to deal with the problems of industry have not been lacking, including a ministry of industry, a technology development board, a council for industrial policy, and the Swedish Development Corporation. Yet none of these initiatives has amounted to a coherent strategy that moves beyond a distributive logic. Katzenstein remarks that even a public investment bank established in 1967, whose mission was to direct pension funds for medium- and long-term financing of promising but risky industrial investments, 'has restricted itself instead to relatively conservative lending policies, increasingly centered around the defense of existing jobs' (1985: 66).[15]

In this respect, Bruce Scott's observations for the United States might apply equally well to Sweden: 'Industrial policy has not so much been incoherent as one more manifestation of a basic distribution-oriented strategy.' To this extent, such policies have had more in common with welfare programmes for the disadvantaged than with industry policy proper (Scott 1985: 134, 137).

Putting Sweden's welfare state into perspective

My argument therefore appears to absolve the welfare state from responsibility for Sweden's crisis. Is this the case?

If one focuses on transfer payments, as shown in figure 4.3, Sweden's spending profile is not particularly high. In 1973 Sweden ranked fourth of seven OECD countries, behind West Germany, France and Austria; in 1987 it still ranked behind Austria and France. Moreover, when measured as a ratio of GDP, expenditure on the social wage (social security, social assistance, transfers to non-profit institutions serving households plus unfunded employee welfare) averaged just over 17 per cent over the 1974–87 period (see table 4.2). This was well outstripped by that of France (21.1 per cent). Sweden's social security outlays thus look less

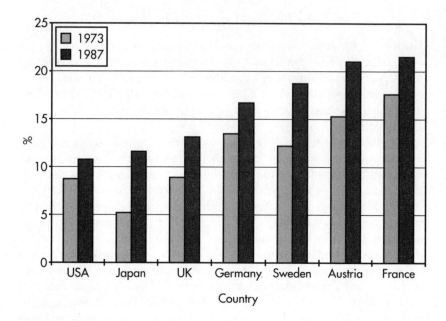

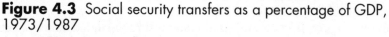

Figure 4.3 Social security transfers as a percentage of GDP, 1973/1987
Source: OECD (various years b)

sumptuous than is popularly believed. Indeed, the generous benefits provided under transfer programmes have always depended on keeping the cohort of recipients small, a condition that has now passed with mounting unemployment (Pierson 1996: 172). While government expenditure in the 1990s has reached about 60 per cent of GDP, just over 30 per cent of this amount is allocated to social welfare proper (health, education, housing, transfers and the like).

But there is no getting around the fact that, in comparative terms, Sweden's outlays on public spending are massive. As a ratio of GDP, these remain the highest in the OECD. Between 1960 and 1990, for example, total outlays grew by 30 per cent, twice the OECD total, reaching 61.4 per cent of GDP in 1990 compared with 43.3 per cent for the OECD. To accommodate that expansion, from 1950 to 1992 real tax receipts grew at almost double the rate of GDP growth (Henrekson et al. 1993: 53). As table 4.2 indicates, Sweden developed a much larger public-employment sector than did countries elsewhere. Accordingly,

Table 4.2 Government expenditures in Sweden and selected countries; annual averages, 1974–87

Country	Total[a]	Consumption[b]	Social wage[c]	Public employment[d]
Sweden	59.4	24.2	17.2	29.9
Norway	49.0	15.8	14.6	21.7
Austria	48.3	17.0	18.9	18.4
France	46.7	11.4	21.1	16.7
Japan	30.9	9.0	9.8	6.5
USA	34.8	12.1	11.0	16.6

[a] Total government outlays as a ratio of GDP.
[b] Final government consumption expenditure (excluding defence) as percentage of GDP.
[c] Transfer payments, unfunded employee welfare, as percentage of GDP.
[d] Government employment as percentage of total employment.
Source: OECD, adapted from Garrett and Lange (1991: 556)

the largest category of public expenditure is not that of 'social wage', but government 'consumption'. This absorbed, on average, a massive 24.2 per cent of Swedish GNP, far ahead of all other countries; and far ahead of expenditure on transfer payments at 17.2 per cent. By contrast, government investment as a ratio of total investment fell by over 9 per cent, a trend found in other countries, though to a lesser degree.

Sweden's welfare state has certainly been put under severe strain by the massive rise in unemployment in the 1990s. Although the welfare state was implicated in the fiscal crisis, it was not the cause of Sweden's economic difficulties or of the breakdown of its economic model.[16]

Rather than focusing on the expansion of social policy as an explanatory factor, one should emphasize the huge expansion in public employment over the same period. This, in turn, may be seen as both a manifestation of and response to weaknesses in the national innovation and industrial system, viz.:

1 the low investment response of industry (Schott 1984);
2 the relative lack of new product development as opposed to process improvement (Edquist and Lundvall 1993);
3 the concentration of government financial support on declining sectors, especially steel and shipbuilding (Katzenstein 1985; Magaziner and Patinkin 1990);
4 the lack of job creation in manufacturing and ancillary sectors.

Weak transformative capacity

The argument of this chapter therefore differs in significant respects from the standard domestic-centred arguments. In their valuable review of domestic factors contributing to the decline of the Swedish growth rate in the 1970s and 1980s, Henrekson and his colleagues, for example, provide an interpretation that locates the root of the problem in the size of political intervention. Thus they argue:

> The rise and subsequent size of political intervention in the Swedish eco-nomy have gradually reduced the efficiency of and return to work, saving and investment decisions. This resulted both from an increasingly distorted incentive structure and from the fact that a growing fraction of economic decisions is taken in the public rather than private sphere, or influenced by an institutional structure with strong non-market elements. (Henrekson et al. 1993: 56)

While this interpretation is undoubtedly true in part (viz. the diminu-tion of educational qualifications in response to wage-levelling policy), a case can be made that it focuses on the more proximate causes rather than on their underlying conditions. The 'size of political intervention' – above all, the expansion of public employment – can more appropri-ately be seen as a *consequence* of the weakness, not strength, of the state's transformative capacity.

One important indicator of weak transformative capacity is the rising import-content in key Swedish exports. In the critically important engi-neering sector, the import content of exports almost doubled over the 1957–80 period, from 24 per cent to a massive 44 per cent (Pontusson 1992: 331). The rising import-content of exports is of course a more general phenomenon. Taken at face value, it can be read as a sign of increasing trade integration. But trade integration hardly explains the breadth and depth of change in the Swedish context. Tellingly, Swedish imports – as indicated earlier – have become more, rather than less, human-capital intensive, paralleling a deterioration in the knowledge- and capital-intensity of Sweden's pattern of specialization. This trend fits the picture of a much-diminished 'exposed' sector, consequent upon the failure of local firms and their suppliers to upgrade, with a cost- rather than innovation-driven corporate sector sourcing more and more abroad rather than locally. One might indeed choose to interpret this shift as evidence of the 'globalization' of Swedish production. But that is merely an obfuscation of the fundamental process at work: namely, the loss or diminution of domestic capacity to produce.

Moreover, if the Swedish state's transformative capacity is weak, this is not because it is *over-embedded in labour*-dominated corporatist institutions. Rather, it is because the state is *under-embedded in industry*. Bureaucratic capability had been built around distributive goals. Accordingly, both industrial intelligence capabilities and policy linkages with industry remain only weakly developed in the Swedish system.[17]

The absence of transformative means was already manifested in Sweden's economic problems in the 1970s. Tellingly, it was the engineering sector and associated trade unions which appeared to understand this most clearly. Together, they prepared reports on the industry, which identified rising sectors with a strong future and urged the state to support these, in contrast to the huge subsidization of declining industries (Magaziner and Patinkin 1990). Such efforts went unheeded as the government maintained its short-term distributive policy of rescuing ailing firms in order to protect jobs.

One can add to these domestic weaknesses in Sweden's adaptive capacity the role of external pressures, namely, changes in the conditions regarding production and the international division of labour. But this restates the problem rather than explaining it; for the key point, surely, is why Sweden's institutional arrangements did not allow industry to adapt more quickly and effectively to these changing conditions. In short, why did it not produce the required increases in investment in human capital, R&D, product development and so forth? As a number of close observers have noted, a corollary of the necessary changes involved is the primacy placed on micro-economic as compared with macro-economic conditions (Mjoset 1987; Pontusson 1992; Henrekson et al. 1993: 56). However, as Crouch (1993a: 17) has indicated, the institutional arrangements known as the Swedish model were largely incapable of acting on micro-economic conditions:

> While corporatist systems may have been effective at the macro-economic crisis management of the 1970s, they have been less successful in the restructuring tasks of the 1980s, which have required action at the level of the firm, not the economy or branch, and which have implied change, rapid adjustment, and job losses.

The Swedish experience of decline is therefore not a simple story of international economic pressures undermining domestic institutional arrangements. A quite central problem is that Swedish governments have fairly consistently maintained a one-sided approach in order to force industrial change. Thus they have sought to control the labour market while leaving the product and capital markets largely to their own devices. But the lack of central coordination and state support in these areas has merely slowed and weakened the adaptive responses of Swedish industry. Hence the Swedish experience gives rise to the paradox of an active labour-market policy without an active industrial policy to create the new wealth and new activities necessary to reabsorb displaced labour.

Explanations of the Swedish Strategy

Why, then, did Sweden adopt a distributive focus to the virtual exclusion of growth sectors? The problem is to explain why Swedish institutions were geared early on to the task of distribution to the virtual exclusion of a transformative role.[18]

Structural vulnerability

Structural explanations have tended to predominate. These draw attention to such factors as Sweden's size and exposure to the world economy, as measured by import–export dependence. Such approaches include Katzenstein's (1985) important argument that the smaller north European states like Sweden cannot adopt a proactive strategy because they must maintain open markets. According to this logic, having a small, internationally vulnerable economy forces Sweden to avoid protectionism and thus to 'live with' change, via a policy of abstention for industry and domestic compensation for the labour force.

There is much to recommend this argument. However, there are at least two strong qualifications which limit its explanatory power. One is that protectionism is neither exhaustive nor integral to a proactive strategy. As the Taiwan case illustrates in the area of high-tech policy (e.g. semiconductors), the creation of such an industry was a complex process that had little to do with protectionism. Indeed, while government agencies employed a battery of nurturing devices, tariffs, quotas and the like were not part of those measures.[19] In short, there are many facets to a transformative strategy and protection is but one of them.

Of more importance perhaps, it is hard to know whether the 'live-with' strategy is the result of structure or some other factor such as the neighbourhood effect or regional diffusion of certain key ideas and practices. In other words, evidence to support the contention that Sweden's economy is peculiarly ill suited to a transformative strategy is not conclusive. After all, in the East Asian region coordinating change is not solely the prerogative of a large state like Japan. Even the small, highly exposed states like Taiwan and Singapore offer interesting adaptations of the Japanese approach.

Institutional incompatibility

An alternative explanation emphasizes institutional incompatibilities. According to this argument, corporatism with labour is incompatible with a strategic industry policy.[20]

The suggestion is that incompatibility arises from the fact that industrial policy is selective whereas corporatism is all-inclusive in its 'targets'. That is to say that the benefits of corporatist policy-making are distributed to all, whereas those of industry policy are more narrowly focused and thus unlikely to be supported in a corporatist system. The distinction is an intriguing one. The question is whether the differences can be so neatly observed. One might well argue the reverse: that central-bargaining, wage-solidarity policy, though inclusive for labour, is highly selective with regard to firms. Those firms which are unable to meet the established wage levels are doomed to shut down if upgrading is not an option available to them.

The Rehn–Meidner programme can thus be seen as an indirect form of *selective* industry policy, at least in principle, in so far as it targets (or discriminates against) inefficient *firms*. While firms are allowed to fail, workers are amply assisted with retraining and job placement. While the LO has therefore little reason to oppose such a policy, the same cannot be said of those members of SAF who are unable to sustain the wage levels set by the more 'efficient' (oligopolistic) firms. This policy has in effect succeeded in driving out the smaller firms while rewarding the largest and most profitable (Kentworthy 1990: 247). Seen in this light, Swedish corporatism has produced selective policies with highly negative impacts on the livelihood of some.[21]

Given that the Rehn–Meidner programme has been highly selective in its impact on firms of different size and market position, the evidence for the institutional incompatibility thesis would therefore appear less than compelling. It can be argued that an industry strategy is much less prone to negative impacts and the problems of unfairness. This is for two reasons. First, it involves the use of transparent criteria, as discussed in chapter 3. Second, such criteria are selective in terms of sectors and technologies, not firms.

Further evidence against the incompatibility hypothesis has emerged in the form of close industry–labour cooperation in seeking to move government in a strategic direction for a particular sector. One case of industry–union collaboration resulted in a study cosponsored by an important industry association, the Federation of Engineering Companies, and the Metalworkers Union. The objectives of their report, which studies four sectors with growth potential, contrasted dramatically with actual government practice of favouring handouts for sectors in decline, especially in the latter part of the 1970s.[22]

Thus the Swedish system apparently lacks neither scope for policy selectivity nor potential for industry–labour collaboration over strategic direction. The problem would therefore appear to be of a different order.

Historical institutionalism

Sweden is less a negotiated polity than a negotiated economy. Historically at least, there has been more negotiation over who has jurisdiction over certain markets than over who participates in certain policy areas. This stems from the historic agreement struck at Saltsjobaden in 1938, which resulted in a fundamental 'class compromise' between the SAF and the trade unions. In essence, this agreement – founded on a common interest in the expansion of the industrial economy – laid the foundation for a modernizing project which would centre on joint industry–trade union regulation of the labour market (governing wages, industrial conflict, training programmes, etc.), to the virtual exclusion of the state. Thus, the Swedish model – as initially conceived – was *also* a means of reducing state involvement in issues centrally concerning labour and industry.

From a comparative East Asian perspective, there were no external pressures of the kind that urged and legitimated a shared project of production-centred growth. In contrast to the geopolitically induced threats to sovereignty and national survival experienced by the Japanese in the nineteenth century and by the Koreans and Taiwanese in the recent postwar period, in Sweden it was the domestic pressures of mass unemployment in the 1930s that did most to shape national fears and public priorities. This founding experience put Sweden on a different path from the East Asian developmental states. But parallels with the latter can be seen in the subsequent evolution of institutional learning that the state's commitment to full employment helped to stimulate. As Goran Therborn (1987: 279) writes on this matter,

> A public commitment to full employment was critically sustained by a post-war pre-crisis experience that a threat to unemployment could be successfully met, and derived historically from a founding experience of the 1930s Depression, that a deep international crisis was not just something which simply had to be accommodated to, but something which could be fought with some success.

The long reign of the Social Democratic Party (SDP) thus saw the insti-tutionalization of a distributive project connected to the goal of full employment, in exchange for which business would require the state to eschew any coordinating role in capital and product markets. Although the social democratic project was amenable to profits, this was mainly from a perspective emphasizing distributive or equity issues. Hence the state would seek to intervene after the fact, to rescue sectors in decline, rather than to promote new areas of growth.[23]

Even the experience of severe economic distress has done little to change fundamental orientations laid down by the historic compromise. 'No broader strategy of industrial adjustment' has developed in Sweden, remarks Katzenstein, 'among other reasons because of the suspicions of the Swedish business community that it might lead to a form of state socialism' (1985: 67).

In sum, it is not that the Swedish state was structurally prevented from assuming a coordinating role in the national system of innovation and investment; but rather that, through an historic class compromise, domestically shaped priorities and subsequent SDP hegemony, the state came to prioritize a distributive project without a corresponding trans-formative orientation.

Conclusion

A key finding of this chapter turns the globalization argument on its head. Sweden's difficulties are not primarily caused by increasing levels of openness, competitive pressure, or regional or international integra-tion. If anything, the Swedish economy is in important respects far *less* open today than three decades ago. This helps to explain why the classi-cal Swedish model of economic adjustment underwent a number of important changes before the employers withdrew support for it. As Katzenstein (1985) famously argued, the model was built for a highly exposed economy. The system of domestic compensation worked when the tradables sector was twice as large. This gave the model an external discipline that was to vanish with occupational change. The data would seem to concur with this reasoning. For it is in the context of *diminish-ing*, not expanding, openness that the core components of the Swedish model have ceased to function.

More specifically, this chapter has argued that the fundamental source of Sweden's difficulties lies not in transnational corporations or globalization or capital mobility, or even in welfare statism. It lies in the inability of Sweden's national system of innovation and economic management to meet the needs of structural change essential to national prosperity. While boasting a handful of highly successful international corporations, Sweden's long-term record of sluggish growth rates, low productivity and shrinking industrial output reflects a failure to invest in new and expanding sectors, at a time when changes in the world economy were challenging the Fordist regime of mass production with its emphasis on cost-reduction strategies. While the Swedish institutional configuration was strongly skewed towards the latter for labour-intensive industries, concentrating on wage restraint, on process improvements and on labour-saving technologies, it failed to induce a shift towards more skill- and knowledge-intensive production, in new and expanding sectors. The main obstacle was not industry or labour, but the adoption of a distributive strategy (most notably, wage equality) that for a limited period provided some measure of transformative pressure (i.e. a motive to change), but without a corresponding means to ensure transformative results.

With the exception of its famous labour-market programmes, the Swedish approach to industrial adjustment has operated almost exclusively at the macro-economic level, relying heavily on demand-management techniques (in the form of increased public expenditure). The main exception to classical Keynesianism has been an active labour-market policy, which sought to encourage labour mobility (and, to a lesser degree, retraining) as industry shed jobs in certain sectors. But whether aimed at stimulating demand or at manipulating supply (as in the case of the 1980s currency devaluations), the Swedish system has very clearly bypassed what is arguably the most critical task: that of stimulating industrial investment in growth sectors of the economy.

The critical problem in the Swedish system is not so much the fact of distribution (what Peter Katzenstein has called 'domestic compensation') as the absence of a developmental complement to balance distributive goals. In short the one-sidedness of the formula, particularly marked in Sweden, produced an institutional complex promoting a strategy of employment and distribution without a corresponding focus on stimulating industrial growth. Neither structural constraints nor institutional incompatibilities are sufficient to explain this laissez-faire approach to industrial competition. For this is one of the legacies of the class compromise at the heart of the Swedish model.

The Swedish case illustrates the point that a strong business community by itself is not sufficient to ensure industrial transformation. Swedish industry, with its large corporations and encompassing industry associations, has a strong organizational infrastructure, yet has proved unable to upgrade the industrial portfolio without institutionalized public–

private coordination. State support, in turn, has remained oriented in the direction of short-term domestic protection rather than long-term industrial transformation. Contrary to expectations this imbalance, I have argued, stems from an under-embeddedness of the Swedish state (with its ample linkages to organized labour, but little institutionalized connection to industry). The contrast with Germany is instructive. For in that setting, as chapter 5 will seek to show, one finds an 'over-embeddedness' of the state leading to wide delegation of public policy – with a consequent robustness of coordinating capacity, though in highly circumscribed areas.

To set this chapter in relation to those which precede and follow, it can be said that from the perspective of economic vitality, industrial performance or international competitiveness, the most important differences among coordinated market economies stem from their transformative capabilities. From a performance perspective, differences in transformative capacity far outweigh in importance inter-state differences in distributive capability. One important implication of this argument is that where states have the capacity to pursue a transformative strategy, the adoption of a distributive project is likely to complement rather than compete with the former. This is a theme we shall encounter in the following chapter, which sets the German developmental experience in relation to that of Japan.

5

DUALISTIC STATES: GERMANY IN THE JAPANESE MIRROR

Introduction

In the preceding chapters, we have seen the two principal types of state capacity that have a bearing on a nation's prosperity and industrial competitiveness. The first type, exemplified in the East Asian context, emphasizes the socialization of producer risk. The expectation in return for state support is one that falls on the business sector: it is that business expand, upgrade and innovate in order to provide increasingly high-value-added jobs that raise the nation's living standard. The second type of state capacity, more typical of corporatist Scandinavia and of Sweden in particular, gives primacy to the socialization of costs to employees, which result from economic change. In exchange for universal social protection, it is expected that employees be adaptable to change and moderate wage demands. And in exchange for wage moderation, business is expected to acquiesce to the social protection package. In this system, distributive capacity could, in principle, boost national competitiveness to the extent that it acted on the cost structure of the nation's industry, restraining wages in exchange for a 'social wage'. But 'cost containment' is a minimalist strategy for national competitiveness. While Sweden's national institutional framework served that goal reasonably well in the 1950s and 1960s, the heyday of the Swedish model, it has served poorly industry's longer-term need to compete through innovation and rapid adaptation to the external environment.

What would happen, then, if a state were to combine both types of capacity, promoting both equity on the one hand and industrial growth and transformation on the other? This is the issue that concerns us here. Would the one counteract and enfeeble the power of the other? For many, they have seemed mutually exclusive. This is evidenced not only in the presupposition that growth and equity are necessary trade-offs in the advanced democracies, but also in the extent to which many analysts predict the demise of East Asia's developmental states as democratization and distributive politics mature.

This chapter proposes a different view. Developmental and distributive capacities are indeed an uncommon combination. Yet, as I will seek to show, it is precisely that combination which distinguishes the industrial economies of Germany and Japan. Moreover, it is this uncommon dualism, I propose, which has underpinned an equally uncommon industrial vitality and competitiveness over the long postwar period in Germany and Japan. One might emphasize that there is more to development than developmental or transformative state capacity. In the case of the East Asian developmental states, the very manner of their emergence and consolidation was bound up with extensive redistribution – exemplified by the postwar land reforms in Korea and Taiwan (and the destruction of personal wealth through war in Korea and Japan). In that sense at least, developmentalism and distribution have gone hand in hand. Indeed, both have been much more sustained in Taiwan and Japan, where growth, political change and social cohesion have taken a smoother path than in Korea, where income inequality has recently widened.[1]

The task of this chapter, then, is to show how the world's two leading industrial nations balance two different types of capacity which, in combination, have enhanced national competitiveness to an unusual degree. Such a proposition is contentious: few would associate Germany with developmentalism, and perhaps even fewer would associate Japan with distributive policies. Nevertheless, we shall see how Germany measures up as a 'developmental society' (rather than a full-blown developmental state) while Japan takes on certain attributes of a 'welfare society' (rather than a welfare state). Thus, much of the chapter is devoted to establishing the importance of these attributes respectively for each country. Since Japan has already figured in an earlier chapter, most of the discussion will necessarily focus on Germany, highlighting both the institutional similarities with Japan that have made Germany a leading industrial nation, and the differences which throw light on its current problems.

More generally, this chapter seeks to develop the proposition that Germany and Japan have emerged as the world's leading industrial nations with prospering citizenries because they have 'invented' an especially powerful type of institutional capacity. This capacity is at once developmental and distributive. Both countries have found a way of combining a politics of productivity with that of social solidarity. This capacity for coordinating industrial growth without sacrificing equity has made for an unusually dynamic type of political economy. There are, however, different types of cost and benefit in each system. Germany trades off somewhat less transformative capacity for less employment and more social security payments; while Japan trades off extensive transformation of its exposed sector for protection of its sheltered (non-tradables) sector, resulting in more employment and fewer transfers, but at the cost both of redistribution from competitive sectors and of considerable market closure towards foreigners.

While Japan is widely perceived to be primarily 'developmental' in orientation, this chapter will emphasize another side to the state's transformative capacity: namely, its distributive character. By contrast, where Germany is typically portrayed as interventionist in social policy but market-led in economic change, I will highlight the developmental side to state capacity. The proposition, in short, is that the long-term industrial competitiveness of Germany and Japan is strongly related to their *combined* developmental and distributive capacities, which are institutionalized in public-sector and private, state-informed organizations.

It is proposed to develop this argument by concentrating on a different aspect for each of the two cases. In this chapter, which focuses principally on Germany, the key question is: in what ways, if any, can the German state be seen to possess a 'developmental' (i.e. transformative) capability? An influential interpretation of the German case is that of a 'free-market' economy. Has Germany's industrial development been merely market-led, as economists tend to claim? Or has there been considerable coordination of the economy by German institutions, including its political institutions? Because state capacity in this sense is controversial in the German setting, I shall give it most attention.

By contrast, when turning to Japan in the final section, these concerns must be reversed. For it is in reference to that country that most commentators see developmentalism in its purest form; that is to say, divorced from the distributive commitments of the corporatist democracies and welfare states of Europe. There is, in short, little doubt about Japan's developmental commitment. Japan is of course the *locus classicus* of the 'developmental state', as discussed in chapter 3, and as originally conceptualized by Chalmers Johnson (1982) in his magisterial study of the Japanese bureaucracy. Rather, the key question for analysis in the Japanese setting concerns the state's 'distributive' capabilities.

The German Case: How 'Developmental' is the State?

The German case is of particular interest to the larger argument of this book, namely, that strong (read 'transformatively capable') states are able to shape not only the national economy, but also the very process of internationalization itself. The importance of the German case stems in part from of its lengthy membership and central position in what is now called the European Union. Has European integration forced Germany, as many now believe, to relinquish any real capacity to shape industrial outcomes? We must assess this possibility in the light of our definition of state capacity, which in the sphere of industrial strategy entails resource coordination, selective intervention and disciplined support. Decentralization adds another element that has informed mainstream perceptions of the German state. For even apart from its involvement in the EU, the German state has often been perceived as inherently weak because of its federal structure and the variety of social partners with which it must negotiate on various aspects of public policy. Thus we must also ponder the transformative implications of this more decentralized quality of the German state.

The basic argument is that Germany's industrial strength owes much to the capabilities of a developmental state which – like that of Japan and the NICs – has emphasized production- rather than consumption-based objectives, and to a state-informed system of private coordination which has ensured constant industrial upgrading. As in Japan, the transformative capacity of the German state has rested on robust institutions which allow for close cooperation with organized industry. By the same token, Germany's developmental orientation has been tempered and complemented by a strong 'distributive' thrust to state activity since German industrialization in the nineteenth century. The German system has recently been tested by the rise of more powerfully coordinated systems, especially that of Japan; this has given rise to perceptions of a competitiveness problem and to a more elaborate set of domestic linkages (government–industry relations) which more closely parallel those of Japan.

Five propositions

This argument is elaborated in terms of five propositions, outlined as follows.

1   *The German pattern of late industrialization bears the hallmarks of a developmental state, the legacies of which have made an important impact on the postwar institutions.*

2   *In the postwar period, in response to geopolitical pressures, the state's transformative capacity was partially submerged rather than dismantled as a result of reforms.* Rather than be seen as actively orchestrating outcomes, the policy-making authorities sought to stand 'behind

the scenes', promoting and privileging one particular set of domestic linkages for coordinating change, a form of GI emphasizing private-sector coordination.

3   *PSG, a congenial alternative to state activism, became the principal means through which the German state was able to effect its developmental goals. PSG, however, is far from being 'state free'; it is by and large a state-sponsored and state-informed system of coordination.* Strong contemporary parallels in the Japanese setting can be found with MITI's encouragement of, and delegation of policy to, cartels in the basic materials industries.

4   *PSG in Germany has worked to favour the status quo rather than new industries and technologies as in Japan; in an increasingly integrated environment, this has contributed to a competitiveness problem and to the closure of new employment and wealth-creating opportunities.* The particular form of GI at the centre of the postwar German model, PSG, has worked very effectively to establish German industry in world export markets for capital-intensive, customized, and highly engineered quality goods in which innovation has been presumed within an already established technological paradigm. But PSG has proved a much weaker system for anticipating and coordinating structural transformation, and thus in establishing Germany's presence in relatively new, promising or high-risk areas of technology. This began to matter even before the collapse of the Berlin wall as Germany began to be challenged by Japan and, to some extent, by the NICs entering its traditional markets, and even to be outflanked by them in certain high-tech sectors (e.g. micro-electronics).

5   *The German state retains an ability to deepen and strengthen its transformative capabilities by expanding the forms of its linkages with domestic industry.* In response to the limitations of PSG, there are signs of renewed state activism in two areas, technology policy and industrial financing. While these changes do not add up to Japan's more encompassing, strategic type of approach, they are none-the-less indicative of a degree of transformative capacity that the German state can command in the 1990s.

The State in the Rise of German Industrial Power

This section addresses the question: how does Germany compare with Japan as a 'developmental' (production-oriented) state with a transformative project? Emphasis is placed on the state's impact on the German pattern of late industrialization and the consequences for the post-war political economy.[2]

Germany's developmentalism in historical perspective

As a late industrializer like Japan, Germany's developmental pattern was in many respects a deliberate, 'catch-up' affair, in which public support for economic institutions was imbued with a strong sense of what Samuels (1994) earlier described for Japan as 'techno-nationalism'. Industrial power and military strength went hand in hand, harnessing the energies of capital in the service of the state. As Johnson notes (1995: 47), the fast-follower strategy gave rise to developmental-authoritarian regimes in both Bismarckian Germany and Meiji Japan. This involved social goal setting, forced saving, mercantilism and bureaucratism (i.e. using the elite state bureaucrats to set the goals for society, while at the same time respecting private property and harnessing market mechanisms).

In the sixty years or so prior to the interwar period, the state centred on Berlin bore many of the characteristic hallmarks of the late developer. Like Japan, the German state sponsored not only the development of industry but its organization, promoting cartel-like structures for the implementation of public policy and legally mandating membership in certain kinds of association.

In this period, the state was omnipresent in German industrialization. Most generally, the state's involvement spanned agrarian reforms and the establishment of related government banks, as well as tariff protection and a generous programme of social insurance. Not least, the state played a crucial role in setting up vital infrastructure and ancillary industries – such as the railways. These were vital for their backward and forward linkages: backward to the banks, forward to the development of the capital goods sector (R. Tilly 1989; Wever and Allen 1993).

But the state was also more directly involved in nurturing heavy industry and the key technologies in heavy engineering and toolmaking linked to the development of its military capability. As Wever and Allen (1993: 186) write, the German state, in an effort to compete with more industrially advanced Britain and the United States, 'rapidly mobilized vast amounts of capital [through publicly created financial institutions] which it concentrated in large firms in heavy industry'.

Evidence of the state's catalytic role in early industrialization can be seen especially in the way the public sector fostered industrial financing capabilities via a distinctive system of savings and lending institutions. The powerful role of private banking in supporting German trade and industrialization is well known. Somewhat less well understood is the critical role of the state in establishing Germany's celebrated system of industrial credit. As a number of studies show very clearly, the state encouraged the activities of the so-called universal credit banks in a number of ways.[3] It did so, first, as a major client. The large credit banks (a catch-all category for all privately owned banks) were willing to engage in risky investment finance due to the predominantly elite character of their business operations – many of which involved lending to the state.

Secondly, the state acted as underwriter of banking activities. By the 1880s, it was the Reichsbank, a government institution, which dominated the payments system with over 200 branches and which provided the credit banks with unlimited access to its discounting facilities, providing guaranteed liquidity. In striking contrast with market-led Britain, where the Bank of England tended to resort to credit rationing, the German banks could 'lend to the hilt' when necessary 'because the Reichsbank provided extremely liberal rediscounting facilities' (R. Tilly 1989: 148). Thus, the Reichsbank contributed to the 'German system' of industrial credit by enabling the universal banks to hold 'more risky portfolios than would have otherwise been the case'. Reviewing the evidence on nineteenth-century German development, Richard Tilly (1989: 150) concludes that 'in order to explain the evolution of banking structures and institutions in countries like Germany, one must devote considerable attention to political forces and institutions'.

The transition to industrial finance

This tradition of state involvement in the financial system has had a significant impact on postwar banking. One direct legacy is a strong public banking sector. The latter, with 52 per cent of the total, today accounts for the majority of banking assets. This compares with only 9 per cent for the large private banks – the Big Three commercial banks, Deutsche Bank, Dresdner Bank and Commerzbank – which have none the less attracted so much more attention. Most important of all is the public savings bank (*Sparkassen*) sector, with almost 40 per cent of total banking assets. Moreover, if importance is measured simply in terms of lending to manufacturing, it is again the public savings sector which, with some 30 per cent of all outstanding loans, accounts for the lion's share, compared with less than one quarter for the Big Three banks, and 17 per cent for the cooperative banking sector (Vitols 1995: 27, 46).

Another distinctive legacy of state support in banking is the German preference for long-term investment credit. What is perhaps less well understood is that long-term lending itself has been a hallmark of the public banking sector. Almost 90 per cent of bank credit to manufacturing in the decade after World War II (and, indeed, in the nineteenth century) was overwhelmingly short-term. Only since 1950 has long-term bank lending (loans of four years or more) to manufacturing increased in importance, exceeding 50 per cent of total lending in 1990 (Wever and Allen 1993: 186; Vitols 1995).

How was this postwar transition from a commercial credit model to the industrial finance model achieved? Fundamentally, the state systematically and directly set about promoting a savings and lending strategy. To expand the long-term lending capacity of ordinary banks, the state provided inducements for long-term deposits, one of which was the exemption of the latter from reserve requirements. This means that 'at no cost to themselves, banks can offer a 1 per cent higher interest rate on long-term than on short-term deposits' (Vitols 1995: 35). Through a series of tax laws in 1948, 1949 and 1950, significant tax incentives were also created to encourage long-term savings. By providing inducements for long-term savings, giving banks privileged access to long-term deposits, and diffusing long-term lending skills throughout the banking sector, the state thus coordinated a major move towards an industrial finance model of banking. Thus, from 1950 to 1993, long-term loans to non-bank institutions grew from 45 per cent to 77 per cent of total loans (Vitols 1995: 26).

Legacies of late industrialization

More generally, the German pattern of industrialization had three main consequences for postwar development.[4] A system characterized by 'producer economics', 'growth with equity' and 'organized capitalism' is a stylized way of describing the impact of late industrialization on the German model as it evolved before 1945. In view of the strength and effectiveness of all three institutional patterns, it was not surprising that the thinking associated with these arrangements would continue to shape economic strategy beyond the Third Reich. That strategy emphasized producer-oriented incentives rather than privileging short-term consumption; it deepened and extended social protection; and it consolidated a highly organized, corporatist society in which government, labour and the banks participated in the coordination of German development. Let us examine these briefly in turn.

Producer economics In a system of producer economics, as opposed to consumer economics, emphasis is placed on increasing investment and savings rather than consumption as the linchpin of economic strategy. As in Japan, policy-makers were convinced (partly by the success of earlier public policies) that investment rather than consumption was vital to the rejuvenation of the economy. The importance of producer economics in postwar Germany can be seen in a host of ways, including a strong export orientation and an undervalued currency (as occurred for both the Deutschmark and the yen for most of the Bretton Woods era), and above all in the strong support for industrial investment and for private savings, and the tardy development of consumer credit in postwar Germany – all of which are hallmarks of the developmental states of East Asia.

During the 1950s and early 1960s, German policy-makers pursued a high-investment, low-consumption strategy, boosting exports of capital goods to revitalize the economy.[5] In addition to the use of tax policy to stimulate investment-led growth, government also set about increasing the domestic savings rate in the 1950s.[6] In this respect, the Germans were like the Japanese, providing subsidies to individuals who accrued savings, thus curbing the consumption of consumer goods as well as providing the banks with a major source of investment. As Allen (1989: 287) observes, 'Compared to the United States where consumer credit card interest has long received tax breaks, credit cards themselves – except for the wealthy – were virtually unknown in West Germany until the 1980s.'

Growth with equity The success of Bismarck's social legislation similarly persuaded later generations of politicians and officials that a well-developed welfare state was not only highly compatible with, but also conducive to, rapid economic growth. As the comparative data on welfare spending indicates, Germany's distributive efforts in the postwar period have placed it among the leading group of large democracies (cf. Allen 1989: 266; Mitchell 1990: 17–18). Of greater significance, Germany, like Japan, has one of the more equal income distributions in the OECD (see table 4.1 in chapter 4). Elaboration of these aspects of distributive capacity must, however, be postponed until Germany's developmental features have been more amply analysed.

Organized (cooperative) capitalism A long-entrenched pattern of industrial organization left many postwar German officials, politicians, economists and business people with a view of the private economy that conflicted with some of the most fundamental tenets of 'free-market' economics. In a discussion of the weakness of Keynesianism in postwar Germany, Allen (1989: 268) has argued that the organization of German capitalism made for a level of cooperation within the private sector that seemed to exclude the kind of state action that Keynesianism emphasized. Yet, as we shall see, the very same business structures made for a closer relationship between industry and the state than can be countenanced in the neoliberal model, as well as the building of consultative forums that institutionalize collaboration. In a similar vein, there has been much more tolerance of cartels in Germany than in Britain or America, a point I return to shortly.

Perhaps the defining feature of organized capitalism is the existence of numerous 'para-public' institutions: trade associations, chambers of commerce, cooperative savings banks, research institutions and so on (for an overview, see Katzenstein [1989]). These are organizations which straddle the public and private spheres, powerfully enhancing the activities of individual firms and industrial sectors. German firms, for example, generally turn for information, services and even financial aid to such peak associations as the Federation of German Industries, the German Chambers of Commerce, and the Confederation of German Employers Associations (Wever and Allen 1993: 186).

But it is not only firms which rely on these para-public organizations. They are integral to the state's capacity to implement its objectives. If these peak-level bodies are able to organize their members and to shape public policy, this is because the state has granted such organizations substantial power and responsibility to perform such a role. As such, '[t]hey are more than [private] interest groups being explicitly chartered by the state to perform important public functions' (Wever and Allen 1993: 186; Coleman 1990).

The question addressed in this section could easily justify a lengthy study in its own right. The evidence, while not conclusive, is certainly highly suggestive of a state with considerable transformative capacity, at least right up to 1945. What happened thereafter? In the following discussion we shall see how geopolitical and domestic pressures combined to favour a more delegated system of industrial policy and of 'private-sector' coordination in the postwar period.

Geopolitical Submergence of Transformative Capacity

As in Japan, so in Germany, the role of external pressures exerted a decisive influence on domestic policy and institutions after World War II. But the nature of those external pressures remained distinctive in each case, and the respective responses were correspondingly different.

Whereas in Japan the politics of economic vulnerability over-rode the pressures of Cold War politics for economic liberalism, galvanizing business support for state guidance, in Germany, the politics of state atonement absorbed and processed those pressures. As the state was restructured and its role redefined in the immediate aftermath of the war, its transformative capabilities became partially submerged.

One of the most dramatic changes in this regard was the loss of Prussian leadership to East Germany, a loss which had repercussions for the innovation system. Keck (1993: 146) argues that 'the old innovation system had been driven by the dynamism of the Prussian bureaucracy that because of Prussia's preponderance could force other federal states to follow suit'. After World War II that role fell to new institutions, which were set up by the government to coordinate federal and regional efforts in technology and science. But these institutions, such as the *Wissenschaftsrat*, took some time 'to assume their responsibilities and catered only to parts of the innovation system'.

To the territorial change one must add the dismantling of Nazi administrative structures and the creation of strong regional governments. While the imperial period and the Third Reich have in common a powerful central state, this power was the target of allied policies immediately after 1945. With two reforms – one aimed at the centralized state built up under Nazism, the other at the giant industrial combines – the allied powers thus sought to break up the institutions associated with German militarism. The outcome was a more thoroughgoing, decentralized federal system dividing Germany into eleven *Länder* or regional parliaments, with considerable authority over such things as education, the environment and industry in their locality. But the net result of these reforms was far from a debilitated state incapable of economic guidance. Two observations are relevant in this regard.

First, federal reforms did not produce the decentralized pluralism typical of other federal systems. A strong state tradition has been maintained, argues Dyson (1980: 218). Thus, federal organs like the *Bundesrat*, the upper house whose members are appointed by the *Länder*, act as an integrating force. Rather than promoting pluralist competition, as is generally the case in federated states, the *Bundesrat* conceives its institutional purpose as defending the idea of a *Bundesstaat* (federal state). This means that it seeks to integrate territorial interests rather than to act as narrow defender of the rights of the *Länder* (Coleman 1990).

Second, in critical moments throughout the postwar period, the federal state has demonstrated a willingness and ability to provide strategic economic guidance. One example highlighted by Abelshauser (1983) is the policy reversal soon after the Korean War, which re-established the place of cooperative capitalism and the role of corporatist organization in governing the industrial economy, thus overturning free-market policies. Credit and import controls were reimposed to shore up the external balance, and government delegated to business associations the powers of raw material distribution and credit allocation. The significance of this reversal lies not in whether or not the controls were permanent, but rather in its illustration of the fact that policy-makers possessed both the developmental priorities and the social infrastructure (corporatist organization) to bring them about. As we know, the corporatist organization of the economy was not dismantled. It became the basis of Germany's system of industrial coordination.

Neoliberal rhetoric nothwithstanding, West German governments were clear about the kinds of investment that they wanted to encourage, and went about that task systematically from the early 1950s onwards. In this period, their aim was to reconstruct and modernize the basic materials industries such as coal, iron and steel, as well as energy and railways. What is especially interesting in this case is the way Ludwig Erhard, Germany's first economics minister, and chancellor 1963–6, sought to conceal the fact that the operation was a state-sponsored initiative. Thus, Abromeit (1990: 66) observes, the DM1 billion channelled under the Investment Assistance Act of 1952 from the consumer goods industries, by means of a compulsory bond, was presented as a market-driven initiative, 'as if the bonds had been issued by the benefiting firms'.

The government's management of funding from the Marshall Plan provides another example of state activism dressed up in market clothing. Funds from the Marshall Plan were used in a highly selective way, as the Ministry of Economics (the *Bundeswirtschaftsministerium* [BWM]) in those early years sought to direct investment towards the basic materials and capital goods industries, sponsoring mergers and cartels in the process. Again, in this instance, Abromeit (1990: 66) argues that the government sought to maintain some pretence of a 'free-market economy' by placing the allocation of funds officially in the hands of the Reconstruction Loan Corporation, which was organized on the same lines as a commercial bank.[7] In fact, as recent evidence comes to light on Germany's management of Marshall aid, the notion of a developmentally capable state promoting production in a selective and disciplinary way seems ever more real. For while other European governments treated the Marshall funding as finite, the German government kept on replenishing the funds by requiring firms to repay on easy terms (*cf. La Repubblica* [1997], May).

Going 'behind the scenes'

Much subsequent debate on Germany's political economy has been about the extent to which the economy was market-led or corporatist and state-guided in the early postwar period (cf. Sally 1995). But this debate often downplays some of the more intriguing and subtle changes that offer a different perspective on the state's capacity.

Most important, the state's transformative role after 1945 is not so much downgraded as moved behind the scenes. Accordingly, its capacity for guiding industrial change does not so much wither as take a back seat. What appears new in this period is not the structure of corporatist economic organizations, or their role in sharing public authority, which pre-dates the state centrism of the Third Reich (Crouch 1993b: 84), but the redefinition of the state's structure and role. The new state centred on Bonn appears not only to have suffered partial dismemberment and territorial fragmentation; it also appears riven with jurisdictional conflict between free traders (with their stronghold in the BWM) and economic nationalists (located both in the Foreign Office and in the Ministry of Finance, the *Bundesfinanzministerium* [BFM]).[8] The official compromise after the mid-1950s, which leaves trade policy to the Foreign Office and domestic economic policy to the BWM, is one that leaves the postwar German state without a pilot agency of the kind provided in Japan by MITI. This suits the international and domestic political temper of the times. Make no mistake, however; this is not an era of state retreat. Quite the contrary: throughout the 1950s and again from the mid-1960s state agencies pursued an active policy of targeting and subsidizing strategic sectors of industry, including aeronautics, coal, computers and nuclear energy (cf. Kreile 1978: 199).

Rather, what stands out is the effort of the state to stand 'behind the scenes' and to delegate coordination powers more widely. This is not hard to do, since many of the structures – regions, business organizations, the banking system – are already in place. The federal government adds to these a number of innovative intermediary institutions – such as the critically important Fraunhofer Institutes, established with central funding in 1949 to promote technological upgrading – which together constitute the national system of innovation. Through the trade associations, producer cartels, credit banks, research institutes and similar institutions, the state delegates industrial policy for much of the postwar period. Consequently, the German system has many coordination mechanisms able to provide for incremental improvements, but no central coordinating intelligence aimed at permanently shifting the production profile up scale. The resulting innovation system, in short, has a strong emphasis on small improvements to the existing structure, rather than on structural change itself. I shall consider in due course whether in new circumstances this emphasis may have become a point of weakness. For the moment, we need to ask what lies behind this distancing process of the state.

The geopolitics of state denial

Why should the state centred on Bonn take pains to be seen to 'stand behind the scenes', as it were, to the point where it seeks officially to deny having any industrial policy?[9] The answer, I suggest, lies partly in an unusual combination of geopolitical pressures: the effect of the nation's war role and military defeat, the search for acceptance in the new Europe, and the economic correctness of the Cold War. It is also in part a response to domestic fears that intervention would reintroduce authoritarian ways, but these concerns in any event tend to gain meaning and strength from the wider international context.

Defeat in 1945 galvanized a national effort to excel in economic terms and thus to regain international recognition. Both the tragic actions of the Nazi era and the strong postwar influence of the US gave force to the idea within the German leadership that the nation could only regain stature by showing that Germans were capable of being the best students of democracy and economic liberalism. As many studies have argued, the first pillar of the German model was therefore what came to be known as 'ordered liberalism', an ideology particularly vaunted by the Freiburg School, which synthesized Catholic and free-market thought.

> In this *weltanschauung* ... there is no real political democracy without [economic] liberalism, for the planned economy is historically marked by totalitarian regimes. All forms of interventionism are therefore discredited *a priori*, and ... the role of the state must be as limited as possible. (Godet 1989: 351)

Cold War thinking equated state guidance with the 'planned' economy of the USSR, and thus with non-liberal, pro-socialist regimes. From the West German side of the Cold War fault line, it was thus difficult to sustain a Japan-style system. Noting the resolve of Ludwig Erhard and his colleagues to avoid active economic policy wherever possible and to put greater reliance on market mechanisms so soon after the war, Christopher Allen (1989: 270) explains that many German economists believed that state intervention and reflation could quickly lead to a system of centralized planning and totalitarian politics. In their eyes, even Keynesianism seemed to lean too far in this direction.

For much of this period we therefore see a substantially toned-down version of the state's developmentalism as the government–industry relationship takes the form primarily of PSG. And it is this apparently less actively 'up-front' state which most commentators have in mind when seeking to classify the German system as 'private-interest' coordinated (cf. Streeck and Schmitter 1985). But even here, the story is rather more complex, as we shall see.

Private-sector Governance: a State-informed System of Coordination

This section argues that the system of PSG, through which the German state's developmentalism has been delegated and restrained since 1945, is not simply a product of private-sector initiative. It is by and large a state-sponsored and state-informed system of coordination. While PSG has allowed the state to stand back from the task of guiding or orchestrating industrial change, its position in the wings has been vital to the operation and maintenance of that system.

The distinction between public and private is of central importance in understanding the German system. In the European late developers, like Germany, business associations are not unambiguously part of civil society, a distinction so central to the pluralist tradition for whom these entities are bottom-up lobbyists. Two tendencies complicate the relationship between business associations and the state. One is the tendency of associations to draw upon the state for their organizational subsistence. The other is the tendency of the state to grant them considerable public status and responsibilities (Streeck 1983: 266).

This pattern of coordination has been called 'private interest governance', *Ordnungspolitik* or the 'politics of industrial order', concepts intended to indicate that the state supports an organizational infrastructure which removes the need for direct state controls and strong regulatory interventions of the kind one finds in market-led economies like the United States (cf. Wever and Allen 1993: 185). Private interest governance exists when self-governance of an industry association or trade organization becomes legally mandated (Streeck and Schmitter 1985; Hollingsworth et al. 1994: 276). But this offers only a partial understanding of the German system of coordination. What I have called 'private-sector governance' goes quite beyond that. PSG can also be unofficial, even illegal, as when a sector of industry is given the task of organizing price or capacity cartels, as in Japan (Tilton 1996).

PSG can be seen as a system of public–private industrial coordination which, in Germany, has taken two main forms. One entails delegation of some aspects of policy to private institutions, in particular the private banks, which form an equity relationship with individual firms, thus maintaining a strong stake in their long-term viability. As we shall see, however, the importance of this pattern of industrial governance has diminished since about the late 1970s. Another involves joint coordination of the national innovation system involving the state and organized groups (business and labour) in the management of industrial issues (e.g. training, technology, restructuring, reindustrialization of the east and so on).

The national innovation system is made up of semi-public institutions in the public continental law tradition, such as the Federation of German Industry (BDI), the Federation of German Chambers of Industry and Commerce, and specific trade or industry associations which administer and monitor public policies, as well as a host of state-sponsored agencies and institutions.[10] The latter include the state-sponsored training and technical colleges (managed by trade unions and employers), whose task is to ensure high-quality transmission of technical and engineering skills to German industry, and the state- and industry-funded technology institutes, whose task it is to improve and develop technologies and diffuse them to industry. Together these organizations constitute the national system of innovation, a system of public–private coordination of the industrial economy for the constant upgrading of skills and technologies in the German environment.

As used in chapter 3 with reference to East Asia, and again here with reference to Germany, PSG is a concept that for our purposes highlights two important features of the German system. One is a structure of organized or cooperative capitalism in which industry, government and organized labour collaborate over relevant matters of public policy, with industry and labour doing much of the implementation. The other draws attention to the state-informed nature of the system, the different aspects of which I shall indicate shortly.

With regard to the first point, Colin Crouch (1993a: 84, 87) argues that imperial Germany was not just a 'state-led' society (though continuity with the centrism of Nazi Germany is often assumed). When the Prussian state built a united Germany, it inherited and adapted a range of corporatist and representative structures. The idea of sharing political authority over economic issues was central to these institutions. In contrast with the more centralist France, the German model 'incorporated the idea of representative organisations of trade interests' (Crouch 1993b: 84). The chambers of commerce (*Kammer*) and other forms of business association thus came to play an intermediary role linking bureaucracy and business to each other.

It is through such intermediary organizations that German officials have implemented most of their industrial programmes.[11] Conversely, it is through the state's sponsorship that industry has come to play a strong coordinating role. This is neatly illustrated in the historical example of the important German Engineering Association, which in the nineteenth century 'lobbied to have the state's authority devolved to its own committees for resolving technical disputes'. The author of this statement (Ziegler 1995: 355) adds that the 'salaried engineers at Siemens and other large companies adopted the civil servant [to whom the term *Beamter* applied] as their model, thus coming to be known as *Privatbeamter*, "private civil servants"'.

As this example indicates, the system of PSG is based in part on organizations legally mandated to carry out functions that in Anglo-Saxon systems are the preserve of the central administration (Coleman 1990: 236). Consequently, in such settings as Germany and France, associational membership for all business firms is compulsory, a statement that can be generalized to the East Asian NICs and Japan.

From this perspective, German associational strength turns out to be closely related to the projects and resources of the state. As in many other late industrializing countries, comprehensive business associations in Germany were created in response to the urgings of government. For instance, the immediate predecessor of the BDI, the Reichsverband der Deutschen Industrie, took shape under the direct tutelage of a government seeking assistance in dealing with the end of World War I (Braunthal 1963: 9).

Coordinating innovation

The so-called national innovation system is another, perhaps the most important, example of the state's role in PSG.[12] Its management has often been described in terms of a self-governing system of organized groups (*Selbstverwaltung*). But neither 'statism' nor pure 'self-government' captures precisely either the origin or the operation and maintenance of such a system. PSG, in short, involves more than the private sector. In view of the nature of the linkages between state and industry, it would appear that PSG in Germany most closely resembles one of the four forms of governed interdependence analysed in chapter 3. As discussed in the East Asian setting, PSG occurs when organized business is expected not merely to implement proposals but often to initiate them. As shown in chapter 3, this typically occurs in matters relating to industrial adjustment where established sectors are affected by recession or declining demand. In such matters, the state sets the goals but readily delegates responsibility (through crisis cartels, for example), or shares it with the relevant private-sector organizations in administering programmes. Stark contrasts which juxtapose statism with self-government miss the duality of such systems. Indeed, in recent years a new vocabulary has emerged in an effort to capture this duality, in the notion of an 'indirect-specific' approach to industrial innovation in Germany. We shall presently return to this in more detail.

Here I seek to detail not all aspects of the innovation system, but only those bearing on my central argument that a key pillar of this system, though ostensibly managed by the private sector, is provided by the state and its agencies. Administrative responsibility for coordinating the national innovation system has been the subject of some contestation. Since the late 1970s, this role has once again been assumed by the Federal Ministry for Research and Technology (BMFT), which administers more than half of the federal R&D budget. Even so, the role of pilot agency is hard to sustain with three other agencies jostling for some jurisdiction, however minor, in this important area, a situation that has obtained for much of the postwar period.[13]

Official technology policy, understood as measures designed to support and guide the direction of technical change, came into being at federal level only in the late 1960s (at state level in the 1980s). But prior to that period, efforts were focused primarily on building a system (the so-called 'diffusion' model of innovation) which concentrates on 'doing things better rather than doing things first' (Burton and Hansen 1993: 39). In this respect the effectiveness of federal agencies has been widely acknowledged, in spite of the failure of some large projects in nuclear technology in the 1980s (cf. Ziegler 1995).

Two major aspects of the innovation system which are state maintained include training and technology diffusion. Area training centres are operated and funded in part by chambers of industry and commerce which advise firms on training and vocational education for employees. However, these forms of PSG depend for their maintenance on federal support. The government maintains these activities not only by legally requiring firms to join such chambers, but also by financing about half of the training centres' costs (Burton and Hansen 1993: 44).

The technology diffusion system is similarly sustained by a range of para-public, state-sponsored organizations, including industrial research cooperatives, industry groups, chambers of industry and commerce, trade associations, and regional technology transfer and innovation centres such as the Fraunhofer Institutes (FI). The latter, with annual funding of c.$US400 million shared equally by government and industry, is the pre-eminent organization for applied research in Germany. It is the typically hybrid institution of Germany's system of PSG, administered by industry, academia and government.

Producer cartels: running parallel with Japan?

Cartels are the quintessential form through which German industry has been seen to exercise self-governance. The historian Maschke (1969: 257–8) attributes the great growth of German cartels in place before World War I, unique in the Western world, wholly to the private initiative of entrepreneurs. If this is correct, it raises the obvious question of what was so special about German firms as to create such an outcome. Whatever the origins of organized capitalism prior to World War I, there is considerable evidence after that point that cartelization was rapidly increased where it served either the war economy or the developmental-mercantilist goals of the state. In interwar Germany under the National Socialist regime, which used cartels to guide and plan the economy, cartelization spread rapidly, at its height reaching around 3,000 (Maschke 1969: 257–9).

In spite of the efforts of both the allied government and German neoliberals to break up industrial combinations through legislation, the law eventually passed in 1957 to prohibit cartels contained far-reaching exceptions. Neoliberal rhetoric notwithstanding, there has long been official support for *abgestimmtes Verhalten*, concerted behaviour in the form of cartels. Right through Germany's high-growth period, firms cooperated to avoid product and price competition, a practice which found support in the Federal Supreme Court, which ruled against the Federal Cartel Authority's right to sanction such agreements (Abromeit 1990: 63). Even as late as the 1980s, Wyn Grant and his colleagues (1988: 84) studying the chemical industry found in their interviews with Ministry of Economics officials strong support for adjustment cartels, even when it was clear that such structures readily blur the boundaries between capacity and price control.

In many ways reminiscent of the Japanese industry–government arrangement, the cartel has provided a powerful instrument for delegating industrial policy. In a highly competitive international environment where, for various reasons, certain forms of state activism are likely to provoke criticism, the cartel arrangement is a highly congenial one that allows the state to stay in the background. In times of crisis management, these structures become especially important. As Abromeit (1990: 73) puts it,

> Typical of West German dealings on matters of structural adjustment is a type of arrangement that has been termed the 'informal crisis cartel' which allows the state to stay in the background and to avoid direct and open involvement.

We can perhaps better appreciate the import of this statement by way of a Japanese example. Mark Tilton's (1996) valuable study of Japanese cartels in the basic materials sector shows how trade associations run cartels on behalf of both industry and the state. Through producer cartels, Japan is able to retain high domestic prices in declining sectors (i.e. in most basic materials, such as steel, petrochemicals and cement) without significantly increasing imports. This is done through a public policy which supports long-term relational contracting, a form of non-tariff barrier whereby the buyer pays a price high enough to keep the supplier in business. Until recently, cartels were given strong official support by the state because MITI values secure domestic supply of basic materials more than efficiency in depressed sectors. In petrochemicals, where product differentiation renders cartelization difficult, official cartels began in 1983, combining private-sector implementation with government oversight. The official version, however, was represented purely as a capacity cartel, not a price cartel; in reality there was an elaborate, unofficial, price-fixing scheme. In order to avoid international criticism, therefore, government eliminated the last official cartel in 1986 and delegated implementation entirely to the private sector. MITI is thus able to continue to use the organizational infrastructure of the corporate sector to pursue strategic industry policy by the back door. For this reason, Tilton (1996) characterizes the self-organization of these sectors as a form of 'delegated industrial policy'.

Much more systematic research on postwar German cartels might reveal many similar patterns to those Tilton has found in Japan. German cartels, like the Japanese, can be seen as an attempt to deal with adjustment problems by means of self-organization. But it would be misleading to regard such arrangements as 'state-free'. On the contrary, they are highly dependent on the state's help in providing sanctions and compulsory membership in order to function.

The material presented in this section has indicated how the state, for quite context-specific reasons, has set up institutions, funding and private–public-sector interaction in a way that tends to generate the appearance of a passive state able and willing only to react to pressures rather than to provide some strategic capacity. This may in part account for the often ambiguous evidence and conflicting accounts of the government–industry relationship in postwar Germany (for references see Sally [1995]). While such accounts often counterpose a passive state with a self-organized business community, we have seen that the system of PSG does not preclude state involvement; it presupposes it. In this sense, the capacity of the German state is deeply embedded in the system of PSG.

Postwar Developmentalism: Innovation Without Change

This section outlines the strengths and weaknesses of the German system of coordination in place for most of the postwar period. It argues that the strengths of PSG as a model of coordination depend on a stable technological paradigm: a low-risk technological environment and an ability to compete via incremental innovation and by, generally, 'sticking to one's knitting'. This presupposes a fairly stable market, which German industry found in the relatively protected environment of the EU. Thus, the German model has been cushioned rather than tested until recently, with the rise of new competitors like Japan operating under a more comprehensive model of coordination with a multifaceted system of governed interdependence. In response to this competitive challenge, and to the perceived limitations of PSG, we see signs of a more active state, adopting a more transformative role in close cooperation with industry.

Strengths and weaknesses of the German model

PSG is highly effective for certain kinds of task. In the German context, it is particularly suited as a means of sustaining innovation within a known technology, when the risks are low, the market stable, and the industry already well established. It is also an effective means of regulating shrinkage in a declining sector. This form of GI has therefore worked well when the task at hand has been that of 'rationalization' (downsizing), as in the textile industry, or when the industries are well established, relying on slow, incremental innovations within an existing technological trajectory, such as heavy engineering.

However, the German form of GI – whereby the state creates,

finances and maintains the innovation infrastructure but delegates much of its management to so-called 'private-sector' organizations – has limited strategic capacity. It is therefore both *slower to respond* to changes in the external environment and *more restricted* in the kinds of change it can make. In Japan, by contrast, industrial strategy has been key to the corporate sector's capacity to upgrade so extensively and so rapidly. In sector after sector, Japanese industry has moved up scale, relentlessly widening the sphere of high-value-added jobs in manufacturing, and consolidating its position as high-end supplier to other countries, including even high-tech leader the USA (cf. Magaziner and Patinkin 1990). Authors often draw attention to corporate-level factors, such as differences in production methods, as the heart of the issue. These no doubt matter to some degree. But this begs a more fundamental question. Why is it that Japan's corporate sector has been able to move relentlessly up the technological scale, while Germany's has pursued 'business as usual' on the assumption that no challenge was in sight?

This, surely, is the problem that needs to be addressed. It is very hard to answer without some understanding of the differences in the larger institutional environment in which these firms operate. Much has been made of the organized nature of German capitalism, with its peak bodies and private banking sector exercising corporate governance. But for all this organizational infrastructure, German industry itself does not appear to possess much indigenous strategic capacity. If it did, it would surely have noted (even anticipated) the challenge from Japan and the East Asian NICs and acted to meet that challenge rather sooner than has been the case. In this respect, the German system of PSG is no match for the more comprehensive forms of governed interdependence, such as disciplined support and public–private risk sharing, that have underpinned both the relentless production improvements and the new industry creation in East Asia, as discussed in chapter 3.

Institutional strengths as fetters? Engineering and banking

A common way of summarizing the strengths and weaknesses of the German system is to say that it is strong on incremental change within existing sectors and technologies, but weak on structural change leading to the establishment of *new* fields of production. The system of PSG, however, has another limitation. It constrains the ability to respond to challenges to the *existing* production system. Such weaknesses are revealed above all by Japan and the NICs' assault on Germany's 'high-end' market niche: that is to say, not only by Germany's marginal presence in the knowledge-intensive industries.

The problem for Germany then is twofold, as succinctly outlined by Burton and Hansen (1993: 47). In the first instance, it is 'how to counter the growing manufacturing sophistication of foreign competitors'. Germany's 'high quality at high cost' approach is being undermined by the 'high quality at low cost' of Asian producers, notably Japan. So there is a direct challenge to German prowess in its traditional area of strength. The second challenge stems from the fact that

> Germany may not be able to continue looking to traditional manufacturing industries for economic growth, unless it devotes considerable attention and resources to newer cross-cutting technologies such as semiconductors and information technology that apply to a range of industrial sectors. (Burton and Hansen 1993: 47)

Both challenges, it is argued below, highlight the limitations inherent in the model of PSG. How can these limitations be attributed to the PSG system? Two components of the model deserve highlighting in this respect. One is the role of the engineer, symbol of Germany's much-prized vocational system and centrepiece of its social and economic fabric. The other is the role of the banks. Let us take each in turn.

With regard to Germany's weakness in the new knowledge-intensive industries, many writers point out that Germany is predisposed to 'diffusion-oriented' rather than 'mission-oriented' policies for promoting technological change. By this is meant that change is incremental rather than structural, taking place within an existing technological paradigm. Ziegler (1995) argues that this orientation is due to the distribution of technical expertise, which, in Germany, is concentrated not within a group of state-created technical elites (as in France, Japan or Taiwan), or among non-state experts closely tied to the state (as in the US military-industrial network), but within professional, industry-based groups. Presumably, a more equitable distribution of technical knowledge between industry and government would allow for a more comprehensive co-ordination system and therefore a greater emphasis on movement into emerging and frontier fields. But what is to prevent the German government from simply recruiting more engineers into its agencies, as has been done with considerable effectiveness in Japan, Taiwan and Korea? This is a question Ziegler does not address. Recent directions in technology policy, as we shall see, would suggest that the *choice* between making things better or making things first is somewhat less rigid than anticipated.[14]

There is, however, another aspect of the centrality of the engineer in *Modell Deutschland* which may explain one of its currently identified problems, namely a slowness to respond to the 'high-quality, low-cost' challenge from competitors in its traditional market niche. The suggestion is that as a result of the craft system which elevates the importance of the engineer, key German products are often 'over-engineered' (Vitols 1995: 7). As a result of such over-engineering, they are accordingly over-priced, relative to competitors' products. In short, the German innovation strategy is technology driven rather than market driven. By contrast, Japanese competitors identify the market and then the technological capability needed to penetrate that market (Freeman 1987; Fransman 1990; Samuels 1994). They are thus able to produce high-quality goods without over-engineering, hence at a lower cost. The PSG system, however, stymies rapid response to the Japanese challenge. It is restrained at least in part by the fact that the engineering profession continues to occupy a key role in management, and hence in coordinating the innovation system. The attempt to introduce new production methods which would lower costs has therefore been met with 'jurisdictional battles' (Herrigel 1994). Cost cutting would thus appear to be less a matter of 'cheapening labour' (a low-wage strategy) than of redefining the role of the engineer in the production system. This contrast is important because it allows one to see that the problem of 'reducing costs' in the German system is not reducible to a 'cheap-labour' strategy, with which it is often confused in discussions about the threat of competition from East Asia, capital mobility and similar matters.

Germany's vaunted system of industrial banking is another component of PSG which, somewhat unexpectedly, has limited rather than expanded technological opportunities. At first glance, this statement seems counter-intuitive, for the German banks are frequently cited as the cornerstone of the nation's industrial success. As one writer puts it,

> it is indeed difficult to over-rate [the role] of the German banks ... They are not only 'Hausbank' and source of credit for their clients, but usually also own a considerable share of the latters' equity [and] are represented on their clients' supervisory boards [which] puts them in a position to influence their clients' policies ... [They also receive] privileged information on a range of industries, which allows the banks to do what the West German state never would or could do, namely to influence the direction of industry's development; in other words to embark on schemes of 'active industrial policy'. (Abromeit 1990: 79)[15]

The author of this statement is of course articulating the mainstream interpretation of postwar German development. I have been presenting evidence for a more complex view of the postwar experience. Excellent recent studies of the role of the banking system provide further evidence for scepticism towards the conventional view (cf. Deeg 1994, 1997; Vitols 1995, 1997).

What needs to be stated about the role of the banks is that they have been highly effective up to a point, that is to say within the relatively low-risk framework in which they have operated. As the author of the previous statement herself observes, the banks have been 'risk-averse', encouraging firms to stick to well-trodden paths. Thus the banks, '[b]eing rather risk-averse ... appear to have taken some care not to meddle [*sic*] too much in the development of new technologies' (*ibid.*).

In retrospect, as the external environment has altered, this questionable virtue has become a definite limitation. For all their merits in overseeing industrial upgrading, the banks have failed to provide German industry with a transformative capacity, a central coordinating intelligence supervising a permanent and sustained shift from old and mature technologies towards new ones.

The bank–industry linkages which worked so well to coordinate the upgrading of existing sectors in the 1960s and 1970s have proved unable to meet the task of financing more risky new technologies, thus inhibiting the formation of new firms in the new information technology (IT) industries. German banks have typically taken conservative commercial decisions, allocating resources to existing, 'tried and tested' fields of technology. Thus whatever other important functions the banks have performed, they have been slow to provide the crucial institutional 'sharing of risk' necessary to spawn new industries.[16] That function, in Japan, has been institutionalized to an important degree by MITI's use of the Fiscal Investment and Loan Plan (FILP), whose main source of funding comes from the postal savings system. Administered by the Ministry of Finance in close collaboration with MITI, the FILP secures long-term funds at low cost for key industries. It provides moderate-sized grants for firms investing in new technologies, in order to signal to banks that this is an area of collectively supported risk, hence worth funding. Amounting to some 15–20 per cent of the nation's gross fixed capital formation throughout the postwar years, the FILP has thus provided a vital means of public–private risk sharing. In Taiwan, as discussed in chapter 3, it is the state-sponsored agencies like ITRI that have assumed this pivotal role, pushing industry in new directions through extensive risk sharing, technology alliances, and the creation of in-house innovations which are then spun off as fully fledged private enterprises. In Germany, as we shall see, the main response to the technological conservatism of industry and the financial conservatism of the banks has come from the federal government with the constitution of a technology ministry.

The German experience, then, exemplifies the way in which institutional strengths may become fetters as the external environment changes. A lively debate has ensued in recent years on precisely this topic, focusing on the problem of German competitiveness (cf. Casper and Vitols 1997; Vitols 1997; Audretsch 1995). Does Germany have a competitiveness problem? If so, how serious is it and what if anything can be done about it?

A competitiveness problem?

The perception of a competitiveness problem has emerged with force in the 1990s. In 1990, Germany led the world in the export of manufactured goods, exporting $386 billion worth of goods, compared with $US282 billion for Japan and $287 billion for the United States. Today, however, there is broad concern that Germany is facing a 'competitiveness crisis'. One problem is that Germany excels at innovation in traditional industries such as machine tools and chemicals, but has been tardy to enter the critical sector of micro-electronics. Thus, for example, while Siemens has a strong presence in European office machinery markets, its position in computers 'is virtually nonexistent outside the German government market' (Ferguson and Morris 1995: 233).

Another problem is the loss of market share in existing fields. As one of the world's top three machinery producers, Germany surpassed Britain by 1960 to become second after the USA, then ceded second place to Japan in 1969. Herrigel (1989: 189) characterizes the problem well. Up until 1980 or so, Japan's larger size and rate of growth were at the expense of US, not German, markets. While West Germany specialized in markets in advanced industrialized countries (which absorbed just under 70 per cent of its machinery exports), Japan's machinery exports went largely to developing countries (61.1 per cent, compared with Germany's 25 per cent). Indeed, Japan's machinery exports were sold primarily in Asian markets (45 per cent), compared with just under 12 per cent of Germany's products. And while West Germany sent 53.3 per cent of its output to Western Europe, the Japanese sent only 14 per cent. Japanese growth has therefore occurred very largely in markets in which the presence of West Germans has been marginal. Since 1980, however, this situation has changed as Japan has begun to make inroads into German markets.[17]

At the same time, there is broad agreement that Germany has created a highly dynamic economy in the postwar period – i.e. one able to sustain a high standard of living with generally moderate levels of unemployment, meeting its own relatively ambitious goals of short working hours and high environmental standards. As Aiginger (1995) has shown, Germany is competitive on a number of indicators, including its trade balance,[18] share of foreign markets, and per capita GNP growth which exceeds the EU average. On other macro-indicators such as inflation and unemployment, Germany generally fares better than the rest of the EU. It also has what Aiginger describes as 'a higher social standard' (e.g. shorter working hours), as well as 'a higher environmental standard' than most other European countries. It is, however, a high-cost country, with the highest unit labour costs within the EU.[19] This of course must be set against the fact that Germany is also a high-productivity country. One might add here that the 'high-wage' factor is not clearly attributable to higher welfare state expenditure; it is at least in part due to Bundesbank policies which have strengthened the Deutschmark. For these reasons, Aiginger (1995) concludes that German fears about competitiveness relate more to the future, as costs are increasing faster than productivity, and are exacerbated by social goals set more ambitiously than in most other countries.

The significance of high-tech

Perhaps, then, one should not overplay the importance of high-tech. Experts agree that the key to national prosperity is value-added activity, and this appears to correlate more strongly with level of investment per employee than with level of technology (Scott 1985: 98). Yet these things are often hard to disentangle. Consider the case of Japan, which controls high-end supply not only in the Asian region but also in many sectors in the United States. Japan has strategically positioned itself at the top end of the value chain in a host of product areas. In most cases this is also at the high end of technology: the most expensive components with the highest levels of value-added tend also to be the most technologically sophisticated. In positioning itself thus, Japan has effectively established in East Asia a regional hierarchy of production with itself at the apex (Bernard and Ravenhill 1995). There is thus considerable force to the view that country capability in high-tech is increasingly important for the future control of the nation's production. By way of contrast, should Germany not establish a strong base in the new IT industries, it will effectively abrogate to others the supply of crucial components for the very industries in which it has traditionally specialized.

There are, then, reasons for policy concern even if Germany maintains a large trade surplus. While no single industry can make or break an economy as a whole, none the less because of their so-called linkage effects and spillover effects, certain industries or activities may contribute more than others to national competitiveness over the long run. The electronics sector – broadly defined to include the semiconductor industry, the telecommunications industry, the computer industry and at least segments of the consumer electronics industry – appears to fall into this category. (Hart and Tyson 1989: 133)

Domestic institutions and international economy

The key question is whether, as a result of new external circumstances, German competitiveness and thus the institutional arrangements supporting it can be sustained. From the perspective of the new convergence theory, the German system is succumbing to the logic of global capitalism. But if we leave to one side this kind of deductive reasoning, which interprets everything in terms of some supposed logic of 'globalization', then an alternative hypothesis presents itself. In this hypothesis, it is the interaction of domestic institutions and international economic relations which shapes the outcome in question. The changing international environment has increasingly highlighted not the advantages but the limitations of the German system. Most generally, Germany has institutionalized certain strengths to the point where they have become fetters hindering rapid adaptation to change. The 'strengths' have been conventionally described as the capacity for incremental innovation in existing technologies, an emphasis on refinement or improvement of existing processes for which markets are assured (Herrigel 1994: 37; Audretsch 1995: 14).

My argument thus is that the German model is not being undermined by *globalization* (whether conceived as trade liberalization, capital mobility, cheap-labour competition or some other such process). Rather it is succumbing to the pressures of *transformative capacity*: that is to say, to a competitive challenge from systems with more strategic state capacity, institutionalized in a wider variety of public–private modalities. The key change affecting German industry, therefore, is not a market-led process of globalization but the emergence of new competitors whose rise is underpinned by a more encompassing system of economic management, one with accordingly greater transformative capability. This system provides firms not only with organizational infrastructure, but with risk-sharing inducements and technical and economic information often beyond the research capabilities of firms themselves. The challenge to the German model above all is one posed by a more flexible and comprehensive system of coordination, which has spearheaded the East Asian drive not only into new technologies but also into Germany's traditional markets.

Set against this new environment, Germany's recent problems of competitiveness – described by Audretsch (1995: 14) as an 'innovation crisis' – would appear to stem in good part from the preponderance of one particular form of coordination in the post-World War II period, which has left industry unprepared to undertake the rapid shifts both in production processes and in industrial structure that would ensure its continuing vitality.

Reconstituting Transformative Capacity

In this section, it is proposed that the German state has recently sought to respond to the limitations of the existing model of coordination by strengthening its own capabilities. It has done so by expanding the forms of its linkages with domestic industry, emphasizing public–private risk-sharing strategies for nurturing new industries and technologies, and guiding investment in the industrial restructuring of the east.

In at least two areas, then, there are signs of a reassertive state. One is the promotion of new industries and technologies, especially since the late 1970s, with the state coordinating the players, mobilizing the resources, targeting the sectors, and delegating the implementation to non-state agencies. The other is the financing of industrialization in east Germany, as the house-banks withdraw from high-risk investment. While these changes do not amount to the strategic capacity that continues to characterize the Japanese bureaucracy (see chapter 7), they are none the less evidence of a state able and willing to move from 'behind the scenes' as the occasion warrants. To this extent, they provide us with an indication of the degree of transformative capacity that the German state can command in the 1990s.

The new context of state activism

In order to understand the emergence of this more active, 'visible' state, the details of which must await discussion, three significant changes are relevant. The first, mentioned earlier, concerns the perception of failing competitiveness, sparked initially by the second oil shock of 1979, after which export markets of the prized machine-tool sector began to be ceded to foreign competitors. In more recent times, the ensuing crisis of confidence has led to a search for new institutions and to a reassertiveness on the part of the federal state in technology policy.

Changing role of the banks   The second change relates to the commercial banks' traditional role in firm financing and thus in industrial investment. This is now much diminished, declining substantially over the past two decades, both as large firms have become more financially independent and as the banks have become increasingly market-oriented in their lending strategies.[20]

In a careful study of the German financial system, Deeg (1997) shows that contrary to the traditional and still-dominant view of the German banks, their capacity for 'private' industrial policy – whether to promote new activities or simply to reorganize ailing firms – is significantly more circumscribed than in the past. Indeed, 'their ability to coordinate firm collaboration for the purposes of sectoral transformation has virtually vanished' (1997: 54).

Large non-financial firms are now much less financially dependent on the big banks, having substantial reserves of their own, mainly in the form of pension funds. From 1978 to 1989, for example, the bank debts of such firms declined from 13.7 per cent to 7.6 per cent of balance-sheet liabilities. By the same token, the major commercial banks in west Germany have followed more risk-averse policies at least since the early 1980s, reducing their equity holdings in individual firms.[21] Accordingly, the bank–firm relationship is now characterized less by equity-holding-based cooperation than by market criteria according to which banks provide sophisticated financial services for fees.

These changes, moreover, cannot sensibly be attributed to the global integration of financial markets. This is because they began in the late 1970s at the latest; they are thus better explained by the growth in financial and managerial autonomy of large non-financial companies.

Of considerable significance for my argument is the finding that because of this demise in bank-led industry policy, there has been a corresponding increase in pressure for state industrial policy since the 1970s, both in the west and more recently in the east (Deeg 1997: 55). Evidence of such a response can certainly be found in a range of new policies for industrial adjustment, innovation, and the creation of new high-tech industries (such as biotechnology and micro-electronics), as we shall see in further detail below.

Integration of the East   The final change relevant to increased state activism is the fall of the Berlin Wall. The way the federal government has gone about integrating the east can be seen as a major test of state capacity. As is well known, this has had little in common with the market-led 'shock therapy' adopted in many parts of Eastern Europe. For the federal government has become an active coordinator of industrial development, setting up special-purpose banks which channel massive financial resources to firms in the east.

In 1991, the state allocated to eastern firms interest-subsidized loans amounting to more than 50 per cent of bank lending to the enterprise sector. Total investment subsidies (including tax incentives) for eastern firms amounted to DM150 billion by the end of 1992. To put the significance of the state's developmental role in perspective, compare this with the DM165 billion representing total business investment in the east for 1991 and 1992. Most of the investment grants and subsidized loans are directed to the creation of a small and medium-sized enterprise sector and industrial upgrading to prevent decline.

It is of particular interest to the larger argument of this book to observe how the opening of capital markets has had quite the contrary effect on the state's economic role to that predicted by globalization. Banks obviously operate under new circumstances compared with the relatively isolated domestic markets of the 1950s, when longer-term lending strategies were possible. This has impacted on their behaviour in so far as bank activity in the east of Germany in the 1990s contrasts quite strikingly with that in the west in the 1950s. But the nature of competition in the 1990s has had a somewhat paradoxical effect. For while it tends to preclude banks from pursuing 1950s-type policies, nurturing and investing in the long-term future of the firm, by the same token this has obliged the state to expand greatly its role in guiding industrial change. The state has thus been 'obliged to contribute a significantly greater amount of public funds and "public power" to restructuring the eastern economy than initially planned' (Deeg 1997: 71).

Making industrial policy more 'visible'?

In 1985, Peter Katzenstein wrote that '[t]he secret of West Germany's industrial policy is its invisibility' (p. 68), thus alluding to a clear division of labour between public and private sectors, whereby the banks coordinate industrial restructuring and protect key firms against foreign takeovers. Yet Katzenstein is also fully aware of the irony of this invisibility – the action 'behind the scenes', as I have argued, which has supported the liberal illusion of a state without developmental goals or industrial policy. Even while writing about 'invisibility', however, Katzenstein could not help noting the important instances of 'targeted' interventions – in nuclear energy, aircraft and computers (to which must be added micro-electronics, machinery and telecommunications) – which have augmented industrial capabilities (Esser and Fach 1989: 109).

Others would want to add to this list of not so invisible activities the central developmental role of the Federal research and technology ministry since the first oil shock in 1973, which made possible the rapid upgrading of the critically important capital goods sector (Ziegler 1994: 7).[22] Even the defence against foreign acquisition of majority shareholdings in major industries has prompted the state to shed its invisible garments, stepping out directly to coordinate activities to preserve domestic ownership.[23] Thus, in 1975 legislation formalized the national consensus by securing protection of core German automobile companies against foreign takeovers, a protectionism that has come to apply more generally, via the regulation of mergers and public procurement policies. As Ernst Horn (1987) explains,

> The regulation of mergers has been used, in effect, to discriminate against foreign investment (e.g. when GKN tried to take over Fichtel and Sachs or BP tried to acquire a major share in Preussag) and the Deutsche Bank was applauded for taking over 25 per cent of the equity capital of Daimler-Benz to prevent the shares falling into the hands of newly oil-rich countries. In public procurement (civilian and military hardware, the railways, the post office, state-owned public utilities) there is a strong preference for the domestic product, particularly in cases where technology policy wishes to demonstrate its success in the market-place. (cited in S. Reich 1990: 193)

Whether or not the state is becoming more 'visible' is open to some interpretation. What seems quite clear, yet contrary to expectations, is that the state is becoming more not less 'active'. What is the basis for this claim? An important piece of evidence highlights an increasing propensity for *industrial targeting*. Compared with the 1950s and 1960s, the state's policies for industry have become more not less *selective* in allocation of subsidies (Horn 1987: 54; Hart 1986: 169). The first of such changes occurred in the wake of the oil price shock of 1973 with the formation of the Ministry of Research and Technology in 1972 (formerly the Ministry for Nuclear Energy). The new programmes, which were aimed at upgrading production technologies, involved a shift from non-selective tax rebates on the purchase of investment goods used in R&D (the major form of subsidy in earlier decades) to the use of direct grants for promoting automated production technologies. The second policy shift occurred in response to critiques of this 'direct' approach from the neoliberal policy and business community. It resulted in a decisive shift in the mid-1980s towards so-called 'indirect-specific' measures (Kentworthy 1990: 252–3; Ziegler 1994: 7).[24] This somewhat contorted terminology simply means that most innovation policies are 'specific' in that they direct funds to precisely defined activities. The state selects the sectors and technologies it wants to promote (i.e. sets the developmental goals), but not the particular firms which will benefit. The latter is an implementation task for the trade associations and the special external non-governmental agencies.

Behind the curious vocabulary, it appears that the Germans have come to do what the East Asian developmental bureaucracies have long been doing in a variety of ways: that is to say, targeting the sectors, products and technologies (rather than firms) to be promoted, upgraded, restructured or whatever (albeit after due consultation with relevant bodies and experts), and then assigning implementation to the trade associations or other para-public agencies. One can call this 'indirect-specific'; however, it is not a peculiarly German approach. Nor is it, in neoliberal terms, a 'minimization' of state involvement. It is simply a different way of the state being involved. Above all, it reveals the goal-setting willingness and capacity of core state agencies, and the strong embedding of their powers in domestic linkages which allow for smooth implementation. In this respect, the so-called 'indirect-specific' approach looks very close to the highly governed, yet interdependent nature of industrial policy in the East Asian setting (analysed in chapter 3): neither a purely top-down nor a purely bottom-up process, but a creative fusion of the two.

Such policies are certainly quite removed from state *dirigisme*, where the state acts over and above the private sector. Like Japan's, German industry is also served by a 'network of well-organized and articulate business associations' which have strong information-providing and planning capacities (Kreile 1978: 201). These organizations – which include the powerful Iron and Steel Association and the German Machine Builders Association, grouped under the BDI or the German Diet of Industry and Commerce (DIHT) – provide the institutional basis for bureaucrats and business to cooperate on policy-making. Whether the policies concern credit allocation in the east or technology promotion in the west, their formulation and execution entail considerable collaboration between state agencies and the industrial and financial community. Indeed, under German administrative procedure all target groups are accorded the same rights to consultation during the drafting of legislation. Thus, in the Technology Ministry's advisory boards, individual firms, industry associations and trade unions are represented regardless of the party in power.[25] Thus to the extent that such domestic linkages are vital to the functioning of the German model, the latter would seem to have a secure future, even if in modified form (cf. Deeg 1997).

Perhaps the most recent piece of evidence of increased state activism is the creation of *a pilot agency*. Precisely in order to spearhead German innovation and the drive into new industries, the education and technology portfolios were merged into one ministry in 1995. This was accompanied by the establishment of a 'technology council', composed of industrialists, scientists, bureaucrats and political leaders, whose task was to formulate proposals for nurturing new high-tech industries. While neoliberal fears are no doubt exaggerated, these moves have prompted criticism from *The Economist*, anxious that a 'super-ministry' like MITI may be in the making.[26]

Parallels with Japan's transformative capacity?

Parallels with Japan's transformative project can thus be seen in the manner in which the state has sought to spearhead technological change. Its technology policy has three major features which lend themselves to such comparison. It is state-guided, in that certain technologies or sectors are targeted for promotion; it is participatory, in so far as industry and other relevant bodies collaborate in the design and implementation of programmes; and it contains a strong disciplinary element, in so far as the subsidies are provided on a risk-sharing basis, whereby industry and state each contributes around half of the total resources.[27]

Relative state insulation in the industrial policy-making process is another feature prompting comparison with Japan. Through the use of deliberation committees and the complex consultation process that precedes presentation of proposals before the *Bundestag*, policy-making in Germany tends to be more distanced from the short time-horizons of pluralist politics. Neither cabinet nor Parliament has effective control of government policy. Instead, this role tends to be assumed by senior civil servants representing the various ministries in inter-ministerial committees (Kreile 1978). Such officials, as indicated earlier, consult key economic groups at the drafting stage of projects, clearing proposals with the relevant industry and trade associations (including where relevant, the banks and trade unions) long before they become known to *Bundestag* deputies (Katzenstein 1978a: 20). Representatives from such groups also participate in an advisory capacity in inter-ministerial committees. This compares with the Japanese case, whereby trade and industry projects are hammered out and approved in deliberation committees long before they reach the Diet (cf. Johnson 1982, 1984a; Okimoto 1989).

Some caveats

Such comparisons should not be overplayed. The German system of industrial innovation has no think-tank function equivalent to that provided by MITI; nor does it appear to offer unequivocal support for an 'up-front' transformative state. While the financial linkages between banks and companies typical of West Germany in the 1950s and 1960s have been just as important in the Japanese political economy, such linkages have not substituted for other vital forms of coordination supplied by MITI in that setting. Moreover, according to most experts, the banks have wielded more economic power in Germany than the bureaucracy. This too is a significant difference from the Japanese case, especially for its transformative impact. As Reich has observed of the German banks, unlike civil servants and politicians they are not politically accountable for their major decisions. Thus, in the task of industrial adjustment and firm restructuring 'the Dresdner Bank', for example, 'never assumed the same public responsibilities for West German economic development that the Sumitomo Bank assumed for Japanese development. Unlike the Sumitomo Bank, the Dresdner Bank was not an agent of government policy' (R. Reich 1988: 346).

None the less, the federal state has stepped in to bridge the gaps in the system of private-sector coordination, at times taking on the transformative role it played in pre-war industrialization. Contrary to expectations, its industrial policy has become increasingly *less* 'invisible'. Its developmental orientation has surfaced and resurfaced in a number of ways in the postwar period, including its coordination of the nation's technology effort, a targeted anticipatory approach to policy, the creation of a pilot agency, and a disciplined approach to state support via risk sharing and other performance-oriented programmes. I set out in this chapter to probe a much-neglected topic, namely, the extent and importance of the state's role in the nation's high-performance economy, especially in the postwar phase of industrial growth. The material presented in these pages suggests one might reasonably conclude that Germany's industrial success, both past and present, has been closely linked to the developmental-transformative capacities of the state.

Dual Capabilities and National Prosperity

Germany's distributive capacity

In contrast to 'developmentalism', the 'distributive' features of the German system are relatively uncontroversial. Moreover, unlike in Japan, we do not need to look in unconventional places to find them. Since Germany has an ample welfare state, distributive efforts can be measured in fairly conventional ways, and therefore need not detain us long. Germany is well known as an important provider of collective welfare. Whether evaluated in terms of state spending on health and education or on social security transfer payments, its postwar commitments have been well above the rich-country average (on transfer payments, see figure 4.3 in chapter 4). As table 5.1 shows, in 1993 the central government spent around 24 per cent of the country's GDP on welfare services and transfers, a sum which is only 8 points lower than Sweden's welfare effort, yet twice as large as that of the US. The German welfare system is none the less different in character from that of Sweden, as famously argued by Esping-Andersen in his *Three Worlds of Welfare Capitalism* (1990), being 'geared toward transfer payments rather than public services, and toward redistribution over the life cycle rather than across income groups'.[28] A strong emphasis on education and further training, on less hierarchical pay structures than the Anglo-American norm, and on transfer payments for those excluded from the labour market has also helped to produce an income distribution that, as mentioned above, is one of the more equal among the OECD countries (see table 4.1 in chapter 4). West German citizens, moreover, have recently sustained a substantial tax surcharge, the so-called solidarity tax, in order to fund the process of unification, demonstrating the considerable ability of the central government to extract resources from society for redistribution to different groups. In all these ways it would appear that Germany's distributive capacity ranks high among the developed countries'.

Table 5.1 Total government expenditure on welfare as percentage of GDP (excluding defence), 1993

Country	Total central government expenditure on welfare and social security transfers as % of GDP
USA	12.1
Australia	15.6
Japan	14.0
France	32.3
Germany	24.0
Sweden	31.5
UK	21.1

Sources: IMF (1995a, 1995b).

This social protection orientation has coloured German development since Bismarck's social policy innovations in the nineteenth century. Far from thwarting development, social protection has been integral to Germany's industrial rise and prosperity. Indeed, it would be misleading to conclude that Germany's current 'competitiveness problem' is a function of the distributive side of German experience. When linked to a transformative project, social protection – so-called social solidarity – would appear to be the friend rather than the enemy of developmentalism. This conclusion, we will see, is also borne out for Japan.

The central proposition can be phrased more boldly: far from being at odds with industrial vitality, distribution is for the most part complementary to a dynamic economy. Japan and Germany, arguably the two most industrially dynamic economies in the world, may be seen as exemplary in this regard. While the developmental-distributive combination may seem clearer for Germany, where generous welfare provisions have gone hand in hand with a strong industrial economy, it remains to be shown for Japan, where the welfare state in its classical Western guise remains more basic in its provisioning and expenditure levels (table 5.1).

My argument about the importance of combination has two parts. The first, elaborated in the latter part of chapter 4, questioned the proposition that (Sweden's) industrial dynamism was undermined by an expanding welfare state. Rather, it was proposed that the causal sequencing be reversed: the expansion of public spending should be seen as a manifestation of, and response to, weaknesses in the industrial system. In particular, the market-led approach to industrial adjustment and the low investment response of industry, leading in turn to a shrinkage of employment in manufacturing and ancillary sectors, contributed in Sweden to a massive rise in public consumption expenditure. The latter of course should be treated quite separately from expenditure on the classical welfare state, comprising services and transfer payments.

The second part of my argument concerns the 'dualism' of Germany and Japan's political economies. Strong parallels, I shall suggest, exist between Japan and Germany in the way they have successfully combined developmental and distributive commitments. However, whereas Germany can at times more properly be seen as a 'developmental society' rather than a 'developmental state', by virtue of embedding so much of its coordination capacity in a para-public organizational infrastructure, by contrast Japan's distributive capacities justify more readily the characterization of 'welfare society' rather than 'welfare state', due to the way the state has sought to embed social protection measures in *economic* institutions, and to protect livelihoods, jobs and ways of life (e.g. farmers, small business and so on), thus moderating the size of transfer payments.

The power of dual capabilities

At this point in the argument, it is useful to reflect on how developmental and distributive capacities combined may work to complement rather than hinder industrial performance. At the outset, it is important to note that 'distributive' outcomes involve more than simple 'welfare benefits'. Perhaps more important than outright transfers *per se*, as we shall see in the Japanese context, they include measures that promote greater equality of income distribution, such as those aimed at keeping people in jobs (rather than on social security) or supporting the retraining and relocation of workers in declining industries, or initiatives sustaining self-employment and so forth. Some active labour-market measures can also be seen in this light, in so far as their main focus is on employment preservation rather than economic transformation as such.

The economic importance of distributive capacity has been amply analysed in such classic accounts as that of Katzenstein for the small states of Europe (1985) and that of Calder for Japan (1988). Both studies have highlighted one of the major contributions of the politics of social protection in the way it assists the process of adjustment. By socializing the costs of economic change, such measures avoid the creation of an underclass of 'losers' versus 'winners'; they thus not only enhance social solidarity, but promote industrial peace by producing a workforce more adaptable to change. One must of course bear in mind that the kind of change to which people are being adapted is an issue of some importance. For as we saw in chapter 4, in the Swedish setting the main structural changes in question were from private- to public-sector employment, rather than significant upgrading of skills and technologies leading to expansion of employment in high-valued-added areas.

One further way in which equity can contribute to growth has been highlighted by Alice Amsden, reflecting on the experience of late industrializers like Korea and Taiwan. Tempering developmental objectives with the solidarity goals of equity makes more difficult the amassing of huge concentrations of wealth which can be used to oppose state power. This has implications for state capacity. To the extent that public policies make the distribution of income more equal – whether through land reforms, mass education, or industrial policies fostering rapid growth of production-related employment – the quality of the state's transformative potential is also thereby enhanced. In this context, state coordination of the economy has been amply documented. Amsden speculates that a more equal income distribution

> raises the probability of industrial success for a host of reasons related to class struggle and, hence, worker motivation, the expected returns to investments in education, cost-push inflation, the effectiveness of currency devaluations, and other micro- and macroeconomic variables. (1992: 73)

Against such an argument, many of course would claim that solidarity can only be bought at the price of economic dynamism. In this view, European solidarity is commonly contrasted with the rising inegalitarianism of Britain and America, where the market-led economy, weak domestic capacity and high income inequality are seen to be restoring competitiveness. *The Economist* (1994: [5 November], 19) writes that '[i]t is no coincidence' that the biggest increases in income inequalities have taken place precisely in the relatively uncoordinated market economies (most notably in America, Britain and New Zealand) where free-market economic policies are the most zealously pursued. Income inequalities in America and Britain are now apparently larger than at any time since the 1930s, and high relative to other rich countries: the top 20 per cent of American households, for example, received eleven times more income than the bottom 20 per cent in 1992, up from a multiple of 7.5 in 1969. Moreover, because of the drop in real income since the late 1970s, the poor have grown poor absolutely.

Many now believe that the free-market policies that have produced rising poverty and inequality have also allowed Britain and America to achieve lower rates of unemployment than the European average. This has given rise to the plausible claim both inside and outside the EU that the neoliberal approach emphasizing deregulated markets and low wages provides the most viable solution to current economic woes.

But there is reason to doubt this proposition. First, the kinds of job and level of remuneration that underpin higher employment creation in Britain and America suggest that the neoliberal trade-off between growth and equity is being bought at a price that may mortgage the future. In return for short-term gains in employment, these socially unambitious economies may well be creating long-term deficits not only in social solidarity, but in higher-quality, value-adding jobs and skills, without which future prosperity and social well-being will prove increasingly difficult to secure in international competition.

Second, there is evidence of the continuing strength and viability of highly coordinated market economies like Japan and Germany. This lends credibility to the growth-with-equity formula. Recent economic difficulties in Germany and Japan have undoubtedly contributed to the sense that capitalist diversity is doomed, and that convergence on the neoliberal model is increasingly likely.[29] But it is important not to confuse an important adjustment phase with long-term decline. Commentators have been too hasty in writing off the Japanese economy – as if forgetting several previous crises deftly managed from Tokyo. Signs that Japan is once again on the rise are as easy to find as those indicating continued recession. As one of several recent press reports acknowledges, 'After five years of halting growth, and despite only cosmetic changes to its heavily regulated institutions, Japan's economy has finally turned the corner, Japanese officials and many executives say.'[30]

Some suggestive evidence for this statement includes a 2.5 per cent growth rate for the year ending March 1997, among the highest in the industrialized world; a trade surplus which in the first quarter of 1997 achieved the second-largest rise on record, of 164 per cent; and strong increases in profits for automobile manufacturers, who altogether captured a further 2 per cent of the US car market. Moreover, according to MOF officials, the highly unpopular increases in taxes on consumption, income and health care of $US77.6 billion have thus far not had the depressive effects that many economists had predicted. It may take several years more for Japan's banking system to be restored to health, as a result of the financial bubble. But Japan's recent financial crisis should not be generalized to the industrial economy. The banks' bad debts were caused by massive speculation in local and foreign real estate at often wildly inflated prices, an aftermath of the Plaza Accord of 1985, which drove up the yen with respect to the dollar (cf. Fallows 1994).

Contrary to expectations in some quarters, then, a resurgent Japan is not an unlikely outcome of the quiet restructuring and institutional consolidation of the early-to-mid-1990s. It is surely no coincidence that the world's most industrially vibrant economy is also one of the most egalitarian societies, as we shall shortly see.

One might venture an analysis along parallel lines for Germany, another highly coordinated market economy where recent economic difficulties have led analysts similarly to predict the demise of an industrial giant, ostensibly laid waste by uncompetitive institutional arrangements. Although regulated labour markets, high wages, a relatively egalitarian income distribution and social welfare are being posited as the enemy of economic advancement in the new international competition, there is surprisingly little evidence for this claim. Germany's worsening unemployment rate, averaging 7.7 per cent between 1990 and 1995 (compared with 8.4 and 6.2 per cent respectively in Britain and the US), remains for most commentators the single most important indicator of the weakness of the German model. But a good part of Germany's unemployment is a recent phenomenon. It rose sharply as four million jobs were lost in the east during the first two years of reunification. It must therefore be set against the huge costs and burdens imposed by this process, a uniquely German problem which has been managed with remarkably little economic or social discord.

At the same time, the massive cost involved in trying to pull the *neue Länder* to a much higher economic level and thus avoid their becoming a permanently depressed region 'has provoked panic in the German business class, which now clamours for the short-term orientation and reduced social burdens of the Anglo-American model' (Crouch forthcoming: 7).

This is not to deny that the classical welfare state is now in need of a significant overhaul. On the contrary, it seems that profound changes in the structure of labour markets and in the life-cycle circumstances of workforce participants demand a rather different welfare system from the one which defined the 'golden age' of capitalism (Esping-Andersen 1996; Rhodes 1996). Neither the calls for dismantling the welfare state nor those for its preservation tackle this issue with any finesse. Reconfiguring the welfare system to make it more compatible with such social and structural changes, in an internationally competitive environment, is one task. But the other is to join that *distributive* task to the *transformative* one of strengthening the national innovation system (cf. Rhodes 1996). In short, distributionism requires developmentalism, and vice versa, if each is to be robust.

This is not to absolve *Modell Deutschland* of any shortcomings. Rather this is to say that if the model is in as good shape as it is, this is in part because it can dispose of a level of transformative capacity greater than most other European countries'; and if it is not in even better shape this is not because of the superiority of neoliberal competitors, but because it has increasingly had to confront head-to-head competition with even more highly coordinated market economies – above all, with *high-wage, egalitarian* Japan. Making less 'overengineered', hence 'less costly', products may be one necessary change in production strategy for Germany; but, to reiterate, such a change should *not* be confused with a 'cheap-labour' strategy.

For these reasons it seems necessary to reject the notion that Japan's and Germany's recent economic difficulties have undermined the viability of the dualistic state. Still among the most industrially vibrant countries, Japan and Germany are also among the most equal societies, with income ratios of the richest 20 per cent to the poorest 20 per cent of between 4.3 and 5.7. Growth with equity, (see table 4.1 in chapter 4) and developmental and distributive capacities combined, would appear to offer a robust alternative to the socially and economically unambitious model of neoliberal political economy.[31] But we are moving ahead too fast. The question that needs to be posed is: how 'distributive' is the Japanese state?

How 'Distributive' is the Japanese State?

While an enormous amount has been written on Japan's industrial policies and developmental commitment generally, there has been very little attention paid to those aspects of Japanese policy more aptly characterized as 'distributive' in orientation. Moreover, Eurocentrism has often blinded us to the possibility that distributive capacity may be reflected in activities other than the state's formal welfare spending effort. In the case of Japan, to concentrate on the latter may well be to look in the wrong place. For Japan moderates the costs of economic change via redistributive 'social protection' policies for its agricultural producers, small business, declining sectors and recession-affected industries. This is the subject of the following analysis.

The Japanese case suggests that there are more ways than one to distribute the fruits of growth and to 'socialize the costs of change' that might otherwise destabilize industrial order. Nationally centralized welfare programmes are of course one such way, which Western countries have typically favoured. But a focus on aggregate public expenditures as a way of measuring and comparing the 'distributive effort' has two major limitations. First is the assumption that 'more is better', a point neatly refuted by Mitchell (1990: 4). Higher levels of expenditure may reflect the existence of less social well-being, as would occur when large payouts would be needed to meet high rates of unemployment. Second, a focus on aggregate welfare expenditures may be completely misleading as a guide to the state's most important measures for distributing the costs of change more evenly throughout society. This is indeed the case, as we shall see, for Japan.

Distributive politics and state power

In democratic polities it is anticipated that distributive politics will prevail and accordingly the state will be relatively porous and responsive to organized interests. In the Japanese setting, scholars who have drawn attention to the presence of distributive policies have usually done so with a view to challenging the developmental state interpretation.

Calder (1988), for instance, documents a range of compensatory distributive policies designed for groups in six non-traded or non-export sectors of the economy: agriculture, small business, defence, regional policy, land use and welfare. What Calder and others conclude from this is that Japan is 'an easily penetrated state' (McKean 1993: 83).

Okimoto (1989) offers a rather different explanation of the same data, which is attentive to intra-state differences. These are the sectors, he observes, which come under the jurisdiction of ministries other than MITI: those governing non-tradables, which have narrower responsibilities and are therefore more vulnerable to particularistic appeals.

Indeed, one might venture the more general statement that the Japanese state is neither 'completely insulated' nor 'easily penetrated'. It is rather a dualistic polity, one that is able to combine a judicious blend of developmental and distributive orientations, more or less consistently in different sectors, as changing economic circumstances warrant.

Japan is probably best known for its corporate welfare system. Japanese companies have long been involved in welfare provision for their employees, a practice initiated by government enterprise and encouraged by the state (Weiss 1993). By contrast, official welfare programmes have been tardier to develop, though these have become increasingly important in the postwar period, offering basic guarantees for health care, retirement and service needs.[32] However, these rather well-known and amply analysed features will not concern us here. Instead, I shall sketch four main patterns of social protection, whether promoted by the governing party (LDP) or the industrial bureaucrats, where resources are distributed to the potential losers in economic competition. These include: (1) agricultural policy, (2) sunset industry policy (structural adjustment), (3) employment support and (4) small business policy.

Some of these programmes – as in (2) and (3) – are administered by MITI and may be viewed as a direct adjunct to its industry policies. The others have traditionally emanated from party politics rather than the bureaucracy. But even in these two cases – e.g. subsidization of rice farmers, restricted retail licensing and special financial arrangements to protect small business – support has become institutionalized.

Agricultural policy: the rice farmers   Throughout the postwar period, the Basic Food Law has protected the price of rice and ensured a subsidy to Japan's rice farmers. This policy has been shaped by both international and domestic considerations. In common with most nations, Japan has aspired to national self-sufficiency in its staple food supplies. The experience of near starvation in World War II when food supplies were blocked by the allied powers has been a powerful catalyst for agricultural protection. Accordingly, in agricultural policy (as indeed in basic materials), objectives of national security have prevailed over those of economic competitiveness (cf. Hirono 1988: 251).

At the same time, agricultural protection has assured the strong support of farming communities for the LDP. Subsidization of rice producers may not be 'rational' in strictly economic terms. Agricultural pricing policies have had serious repercussions on the national economy in the form of high land prices. But politically and socially they have made a good deal of sense. As Hirono (1988: 251) has argued, in spite of its distorting effects on resource allocation, agricultural protection has had a very positive impact on income maintenance of the farm sector, 'contributing to a fairer distribution of income at the national level'.

Sunset industry policy: Adjustment support for declining sectors Among the advanced countries, Japan stands out for its unusually strong support to smooth the adjustment of declining industries. It has sometimes been remarked that MITI spends more on sunset than on sunrise industries, the so-called ' "structurally depressed" industries which are not expected to recover from recessions' (OTA 1991: 250). Commenting positively on this aspect of Japanese policy, the American Office of Technology Assessment writes that

> Industrial adjustment – contracting the size of an industry and shifting workers, managers, and capital from one industry to another – is difficult, time-consuming, and expensive in any country. ... Countries differ in the extent to which those costs are borne by workers and owners of enterprises, as opposed to the public sector. ... Japan's government takes more responsibility for adjustment, and bears more of the cost, than do most developed nations. One reason is the value Japan places on employment security. (*ibid.*)

It is possible to see this aspect of Japan's industry policy as having a 'nation-building' function, as argued by Williams (1994). By socializing the costs of economic change – in the manner Sweden has done through social and labour-market policies – Japanese policy serves to enhance the sense of community and to protect those who would otherwise bear the major brunt of international competition. While Katzenstein's (1985) emphasis on Japan's *pre-emptive* capacity is productive, it nevertheless underplays these other aspects of state policy. The Japanese state seeks not only to pre-empt the costs of change through its developmental policies, but also to absorb and socialize such costs through its distributive programmes.

While money spent on declining industries may contribute little to the overall competitiveness of industry, the social advantages cannot be dismissed lightly. As one study puts it, such expenditure 'contributes to a stable business environment, prevents cutthroat competition and large-scale chaotic layoffs, and helps keep Japan's unemployment rate extraordinarily low' (OTA 1991: 251). One might venture that this dual capacity is the key to Japan's unusual internal cohesion and wider strength in the international economic arena.

Employment support Japan has some of the world's strongest employment-maintenance programmes. As early as 1963, 'the revision of the Unemployment Insurance Law granted financial support for training technical workers, subsidized housing to encourage workers to move to new jobs, and expanded employment programs for workers aged 45 or over' (Garon and Mochizuki 1993: 160). The innovative 1974 Employment Insurance Law, by which the state subsidized employers to maintain workers on their payroll, was introduced in response to the first oil crisis. Several such initiatives to protect employment have followed, such as the 1977 Temporary Measures for Workers Displaced from Specific Depressed Areas, and the Temporary Relief Law for Workers Displaced from Specific Depressed Industries (Garon and Mochizuki 1993: 161, 163).[33]

The value that Japan places on steady employment is evident in a number of national institutional arrangements and public provisions, not least in the practice of 'life-time' employment, an institution that is strongly supported by the state. While labour turnover and mobility are much lower in large undertakings than in the female-dominated small-firm sector, where the distinctive life-cycle features of Japanese women tend to apply, there is nevertheless a strong social expectation that firms, regardless of size, should seek to retain their employees through the hard times. Though employment security has no legal foundation, it is an expectation of the community that has been built up over the years through judicial practice and government policy. Indeed, government policies have repeatedly buttressed this expectation with solid financial support to companies, large and small, in times of marked economic downturn, most notably in the 1970s following the two oil shocks (Weiss 1993).

With the first oil shock of 1973, government's attempt to keep unemployment low while managing inflation and restructuring industry also gave rise to a 'Japan-style incomes policy', as the major trade unions supported such efforts. Union influence expanded in the 1970s with the formation of the Industry and Labour Conference, the central forum for tripartite consultation on wage determination. Thus an evolving pattern of 'negotiation among government, business, and organized labor' became ever more explicit 'in response to a shared sense of economic crisis' (Garon and Mochizuki 1993: 161–3). It was in this new climate marked by a national sense of crisis that organized labour acquired a more important role in national policy-making, winning some of the world's strongest employment-maintenance programmes as a result.

The point is not that unions in Japan have matched the public policy-shaping abilities of unions in countries like (West) Germany or Sweden, where power-sharing arrangements have long been established. Rather, the point is that even in the country of enterprise unionism, organized labour has avoided political exclusion. Employment protection has thus become a norm. Even since the collapse of the so-called bubble economy in the early 1990s 'firms have basically still adhered to long-term employment practices' (Sato 1997: 18).

Policies for small business   From the 1880s onwards, Japan's industrialization saw state sponsorship of both heavy industry for domestic and military strength, and small-scale textile production for export earnings (Rosovsky 1961: 55ff). Throughout the Meiji period and beyond, the Ministry of Agriculture and Commerce pursued policies to support smaller firms, whether in agriculture or in industry. In the period since 1945, as electoral reforms strengthened opportunities for Diet member influence, it has been the politicians rather than MITI's officials who have been most attentive to small business, especially outside the manufacturing sector. The result has been an extensive array of programmes dedicated to the upgrading, maintenance and financial support of this substantial sector (cf. Calder 1988; Friedman 1988).

As a result of these and similar measures, Japan has maintained one of the lowest unemployment records in the OECD throughout the postwar period. The 1996 figure, at 3.4 per cent, was the highest recorded in forty-five years. In distributive terms, Japan's egalitarianism is also remarkable. Only 2 per cent of Japanese households now have annual incomes of less than $US16,000; and only 2 per cent of incomes reach $US160,000 or more. This places the great majority in the middle, with around half of all Japanese households earning between $US35,000 and $US75,000 a year. The public effort to eliminate large economic disparities can be seen in ways great and small. According to a recent report,

> Only 1 per cent of the population is on welfare. Public schools in every part of the country look alike, because the government guarantees parity right down to the books in the library. ... Corporate titans have relatively modest incomes – the average chief executive earns about $300,000 a year – resulting from a purposeful effort to prevent a gigantic divide between entry-level workers and the company president.[34]

Japan as 'welfare society' and Germany as 'developmental society'

Japan's distributive capacities would seem to justify the characterization of 'welfare society' rather than 'welfare state'.[35] Such a characterization does not mean that the state plays no part in social welfare. On the contrary, the state has a pivotal role. But to concentrate on the size of the welfare effort or social security expenditure is to miss a more significant source of distributionism. The Japanese state seeks to ensure a strong measure of income support and income equality, with an emphasis on security of employment and measures to minimize the displacement of those threatened by market forces. Its overall efforts directed to subsidization of the rice farmers, to financial and infrastructural support for small business, to employment maintenance programmes in times of acute crisis, and in particular to the institutionalized measures for sunset industries are all far more indicative of the Japanese state's 'distributive' effort than the provision of social security payments *per se*.

Similarly, when we turn to Germany, the notion of a 'developmental society' rather than a fully fledged 'developmental state' seems appropriate. This does not mean that the state is absent from the developmental effort or without developmental capabilities. On the contrary, the state remains central to the German story. But to look only at the extent of postwar changes in industrial structure, or at the state's degree of activism in already well-established industries for evidence of developmental capacity, is also to look in the wrong places. The German state has sought to ensure the nation's industrial leadership through the creation of an organizational infrastructure, a system of para-public institutions that it has worked hard to maintain and extend.

Conclusion

The unusual industrial dynamism of Germany and Japan has been sustained by the existence, in each case, of institutions endowed with considerable transformative capacity. In both cases, such arrangements involve GI; that is, state-sponsored forms of public–private cooperation. The key difference, however, is that Japan's developmental orientation has been institutionalized in a greater *variety* of state-sponsored forms (state–industry relationships), which are in turn suited to a greater range of transformative tasks. Consequently, steady and far-reaching structural change has been paramount in the Japanese setting, but more marginal in Germany.

By contrast, in Germany, struggles within the federal state after World War II saw the entrustment of at least two crucial transformative tasks, investment and innovation, to the initiative of sub-national and non-state institutions – banks, trade associations, regional governments, etc., in which the central government's role as a coordinating intelligence with transformative capability was significantly diluted. The state delegated the task of industrial change to sub-national institutions in an endeavour to 'remain in the background'. This was partly the result of internal ideological struggles within the state; it was also in good part geopolitical, in so far as Cold War allegiances of the time made it likely that any departure from free-market policies would be viewed as a goal scored for communism. Whatever the precise mix of factors, the resulting institutional framework enabled highly effective (corporate) governance, as long as coordination took place within a well-established technological paradigm. It permitted 'incremental' innovation and imparted a robustness to German industry second to none. But there was also a high price. Under this system of semi-devolved coordination, structural change was virtually foreclosed. German industry remained stuck within the existing technological trajectory. The banks remained risk-averse, unable and unwilling to stimulate investment in new areas of technology. Thus the idea of 'shifting the industrial structure' from sunset to sunrise industries has, until recently, had little resonance in postwar Germany.

The core issue for Germany in the 1990s is whether its institutional arrangements are adequate to the sorts of task undertaken by the much more powerfully coordinated system in Japan. The question is whether the state's transformative role will be revitalized and made more visible in guiding industrial change. This chapter has argued that there are at least two signs that a reconstituted transformative state may be the outcome. One is the renewed activism of the federal state in east German development since unification, consequent upon the banking system's diminishing role as financier and coordinator of German industrial investment. The other is the emergence of federal programmes targeting high-tech sectors, plus the constitution of a pilot agency in the newly merged Education and Technology Ministry, in an endeavour to close the innovation gaps created by the system of private-sector coordination.

In sum, recent weaknesses in that system, shown up by changed international circumstances, have brought a more overtly active state to the fore once again, in an endeavour to deal with both the competitiveness challenge from East Asia and the integration challenge of eastern Germany. Whether as sponsor of investment in the east, or as promoter of new technology and industry creation in the industrial heartlands, central government is beginning to appear more as key catalyst of industrial change, in spite of European unification.

This chapter has also suggested strong parallels between Japan and Germany in the way they have successfully combined developmental and distributive commitments. However, whereas Germany can at times more properly be seen as a 'developmental society' rather than a 'developmental state' (by virtue of embedding so much of its coordination capacity in PSG), Japan's distributive capacities justify more readily the characterization of 'welfare society' rather than 'welfare state'. This is due to the way the state has sought to embed social protection measures in economic institutions and to protect livelihoods, jobs and ways of life (e.g. farmers, small business, etc.), thus moderating the size of transfer payments.

Germany and Japan are unusual forms of capitalism in that they have each, in different ways, combined a powerful emphasis on growth-oriented policies with a relatively strong distributive politics. The late industrialization pattern of strong state plus guided market has, in recent times, been capped by democratic political institutions. But rather than eroding the growth ethic, this has added a participation ethic, thus avoiding the pitfalls of the Swedish imbalance (as we saw in chapter 4). Important differences and limitations of each national approach notwithstanding, I believe that this dualistic capacity of the state to coordinate growth and to oversee the distribution of its fruits is a strength, not a weakness, in an age of interdependence.

If the thrust of this analysis is essentially correct, then at least two lessons can be drawn from the comparison of Germany and Japan. First, solidarity is more appropriately viewed as the complement of wealth creation, not its enemy. Solidarity creates the conditions in which economies can be renovated, old skills discarded and new skills acquired. The experience of Germany and Japan suggests that the countries which have sustained an uncommonly robust industrial performance in the postwar era are those which have sought to combine, not choose between, developmental and distributive goals. This has clear implications for social democracies like Sweden, which have pursued high social standards independently of a strategy for national innovation and wealth creation. What then of the implications for the neoliberal alternative?

The revival of growth in the US in the 1990s and the strong job creation witnessed in both Britain and the US in recent years have done much to instil confidence in the superior power of neoliberal recipes to produce prosperity. One of course can make the important point that non-standardized, national accounting criteria reduce unemployment differentials to statistical artifacts, as evidenced in OECD standardized comparisons (cf. Carlin and Soskice 1997). But that does not undermine the basic fact that the non-coordinated market economies are looking much more vibrant, of late, in the job-creation department. Just why this is occurring and what is leading the apparent (but hard-to-measure) 'boom' in the United States are issues still to be resolved. However, one thing seems to be emerging with some clarity. If the measure of a prosperous economy and society is the degree to which *more* people are enjoying *higher* standards of living, then one must surely conclude from the evidence presented earlier that the neoliberal model is not yet meeting this basic criterion. Similarly, if one thinks of the fruits of growth as improvements in the general level of skills, wages, and higher value-adding jobs, even here, with the important exception of the IT boom in the US, the picture is far from rosy.[36] The neoliberal tree is certainly yielding some juicy fruit, but the evidence that it is destined to nourish more than a wealthy minority remains to be discovered.

One final lesson emerges from the comparison of Germany and Japan. Simply put: there is more than one way of instituting solidarity and thus pursuing equity measures; when it comes to growth and wealth creation, however, some strategies may prove more effective than others in an increasingly interdependent world economy. To phrase the point in a different way, major differences in performance among the coordinated market economies like Sweden, Germany and Japan would appear to emerge not from their 'distributive' features but from their 'developmental' capabilities. Keeping people in jobs while ensuring continuous upgrading of skills in high-value-added production and the shift of technology towards ever more knowledge-intensive areas is a stylized way of describing the Japanese strategy. Subsidizing those ejected from the market while opting for improvements to the existing structure of skills and technology is a more fitting way of differentiating the German approach. In a highly integrated world economy, however, these approaches may not prove equivalent in the long-run task of wealth and employment creation.

Thus a major implication of my argument is that if *Modell Deutschland* has an important limitation, *vis-à-vis* strong competitors like Japan, this would seem to derive not from its well-institutionalized distributive efforts, but from its more narrowly channelled developmental effort: the extent to which its postwar system of economic coordination has relied preponderantly on one particular form of GI. While PSG has enabled considerable upgrading of German industry, the changing circumstances of international competition have begun to highlight its limitations rather than advantages. If Japanese industry has been more successful in anticipating change, this is in large part because of MITI's central coordinating role. The increasingly high-tech industries in which Japan has excelled in international markets over the last fifteen years have generally been targeted by MITI for public support. In the German setting, however, for geopolitical–ideological reasons, this kind of strategic intervention has not been institutionalized to the same degree.

This does not mean that Germany should seek to become like Japan.[37] The relative strengths of the German model are perhaps most clearly evident in the international political realm, where German power is perceived as less threatening than that of Japan and its leadership is potentially more acceptable. Being strongly embedded in the multinational environment of the EU, Germany appears to have moderated its economic nationalism over the years, and at the same time to have developed a less overt system of centrally coordinated capitalism. For these reasons, argues Chalmers Johnson (1995), Germany has not seemed as economically threatening as Japan to liberal economic orders like the United States, even though its capitalist institutions diverge substantially from Anglo-American orthodoxy. Maintaining a lower level of state 'visibility', but not necessarily of state 'involvement' (rather as the Japanese are now attempting in the face of international criticism), may therefore be the key to the German system's wider acceptability.

My argument to this point has been that states with strong developmental orientations and domestic linkages have generally been able to exploit a greater degree of capacity to rationalize their industrial economies. Where this has occurred, as in Germany, Japan and the NICs, the effects of economic integration have not clearly diminished the state's role in the economy, but rather in certain cases augmented it.

This implies that the state's career as active centre is far from over. As the analyses of Sweden, Germany and East Asia have sought to show, it is not simply the character of the state as such, but the way it informs, shapes and links up with domestic institutions, that has great import for national economic outcomes. In particular, the extent to which domestic institutions provide for a central coordinating mechanism is critical to an understanding of the impact of pressures emanating from an integrated world economy. Is economic globalization an all-encompassing tendency as portrayed with considerable certainty in the literature; and if economic integration is indeed advancing, what does this imply for the future of state capacity? Will state capability and the capitalist diversity associated with it be boiled away in some kind of global hot pot? It is to these questions that we now turn in the final chapters of this book.

6

THE LIMITS OF GLOBALIZATION

Introduction

Having reached the closing chapters of the book, we are now in a position to review and assess the globalization thesis in more general terms. With varying degrees of boldness, its proponents posit the disintegration of national economies and the demise of the state's domestic power.[1] This chapter and the following lend support to the small but growing number of sceptics who question these claims. Chapter 6 argues that the novelty, magnitude and patterning of change in the world economy are insufficient to support the idea of a transnational or global market place in which locational and institutional constraints no longer matter. The changes are consistent, however, with a highly internationalized economy in which economic integration is being advanced not only by corporations but (as chapter 7 will argue) by national governments. In these concluding chapters I therefore seek not only to emphasize the empirical limits and counter-tendencies to global integration, but to elucidate theoretically what much of the literature has hitherto ignored: the adaptability of states, their differential capacity, and the enhanced importance of state power in the new international environment.

Globalization entered the popular lexicon as the new buzz word for the 1990s. While the term itself tends to be vaguely defined and used with widely varying meanings, enthusiasm for using the language of globalization has itself become a global phenomenon, infecting all levels of society, from poets to prime ministers.

According to the new orthodoxy, we are now entering a new phase in world history in which cross-border flows in goods and services, investment, finance and technology are creating a seamless world market where the law of one price will prevail. What we are witnessing, say the proponents of globalism, is no less than the demise of the nation-state as a power actor, the end of 'national capitalisms' with their characteristic welfare systems and industrial policies, and ultimately world-wide convergence on one kind of economic system: Anglo-American-style free-market capitalism.

Like all orthodoxies which attract a majority following, this one is not without substance. The sheer volume of cross-border flows, of products, people, capital and above all of money, is hard to ignore. The real question, however, turns on the meaning of these flows: in what way are they unprecedented and therefore posing novel challenges? Are they of necessity producing global convergence, ironing out national institutional differences? And to what extent does globalization impose uniform responses to change, rendering states powerless to pursue their own national objectives?

Providing definitive answers to these complex questions will demand far more systematic research than has been done to date. The aim of this chapter is necessarily limited in scope. It seeks simply to provide some empirical assessment of the economic trends which are purportedly driving integration. To pave the way for that analysis we begin with some conceptual clarification.

What Does 'Globalization' Mean?

It must be said that enthusiasm for the idea of globalization has not been matched by clarity in the way the term has been applied. 'What does globalization mean?', asked *The Economist* in its 1992 'Survey of the World Economy'. The term, it went on to assure the reader, 'can happily accommodate all manner of things', including 'expanding international trade, the growth of multinational businesses, the rise in international joint ventures and increasing interdependence through capital flows' (1992: 5).

While *The Economist* here alludes to possible *indicators* or measures of globalization, it does not provide any insight into the nature of the beast itself. Indeed, for many enthusiasts of the global idea, 'global' and 'international' are interchangeable. One writer observes with regard to the concept of the 'global' corporation that '[i]t has been preceded in the last 30 years by a string of synonyms such as: international, interterritorial, multinational, transnational, and world-wide' (Hu 1992: 120). Yet these terms are not at all synonymous. More to the point, the language of globalization implies tendencies quite different from those captured by the language of internationalization. To use the language of globalization is fundamentally to claim that the nation-state is no longer important either as an actor or as a site of economic accumulation. The existence of a 'global' economy – in the sense intended by global neo-classicists like Ohmae (1990) – is synonymous with 'transnationalism'. It implies an open market place free of institutional or locational constraints; hence the displacement of **'national'** (and therefore **'international'**) networks by **'transnational'** networks of economic interaction.

The distinction is neatly clarified in a recent study, which notes that

> there is a vast difference between a strictly *global* economy and a highly *internationalized* economy in which most companies trade from their bases in distinct national economies. In the former national policies are futile, since economic outcomes are determined wholly by world market forces and by the internal decisions of transnational companies. In the latter national policies remain viable, indeed they are essential in order to preserve the distinct styles and strengths of the national economic base and the companies that trade from it. (Hirst and Thompson 1996: 185)

From this perspective, one could easily envisage a world economy with very high levels of international trade and investment. But that would not necessarily make it a *globalized* economy, in the sense defined above, because nation-states could still retain an important role in governing domestic economic activity.

The real issue, then, is whether the kind of world economy in the making is a 'transnational' one, in which displacement of national and international networks of interaction is occurring, or instead a highly internationalized one, in which the state retains a pivotal, if changing, role. To return to Michael Mann's metaphor (see chapter 1), the question is whether society is 'uncaging'.[2]

Globalization hypotheses

While I have thus far alluded only to the 'strong globalization' hypothesis, there are in fact at least three hypotheses that can be identified in the literature:

1 strong globalization; state power erosion;[3]
2 strong globalization; state power unchanged;[4]
3 weak globalization (strong internationalization); state power reduced in scope.[5]

Evidence surveyed in the following section provides strong grounds for rejecting the first and second propositions in favour of the 'weak globalization' thesis. However, there is no compelling evidence for that part of the third proposition which claims that the state's role is now generally reduced to that of legitimating decisions initiated and implemented elsewhere. I would therefore propose a fourth hypothesis that stresses instead the differential capacities of states and how the world economy, far from eliminating such differences, is more likely to underscore and intensify further their salience for national prosperity. This fourth proposition is expressed as follows:

4 weak globalization (strong internationalization); state power adaptability and differentiation emphasized.

The remainder of this chapter focuses on the first part of this proposition, the limits to globalization. The second part will be the concern of the final chapter.

The case for globalization rests on claims about the novelty and magnitude of change in the world economy, as well as the extent of worldwide economic integration. I therefore consider the extent to which the patterns of world trade, finance, investment and production point to a clear globalization tendency.

The Question of Novelty

How unprecedented are international flows?

There is plenty of evidence that the world economy is much more interconnected today than it was in the 1960s or 1970s. The trade figures provide a glimpse of what lies behind the new globalism. The ratio of exports to GDP more than doubled in the period 1960–90 (from 9.5 per cent to 20.5 per cent). World merchandise trade has clearly outpaced production, growing on average one and a half times faster than world GDP in just twenty-five years from 1965. There is then some substance to the idea that foreign markets have increased in importance relative to domestic ones, hence producing a greater openness and interdependence of the international system (Wade 1996a: 2).

The question is whether the current levels of openness and interdependence are unprecedented. Researchers with short time-horizons have created that impression by measuring changes that have taken place largely since the 1970s. But as several studies have shown, the world in the 1970s, even in the 1980s, was in a number of ways far less internationalized through trade, investment and capital flows than it was in the period prior to World War I.

Table 6.1   Exports as a percentage of GDP, 1913–92

Current prices	1913[a]	1950	1960–73	1974–90	1980–90	1991–2
USA	(6)	4.4	5.2	8.4	8.5	10.6
Europe	(25)	19.5	19.3	25.8	28.7	26.4
Japan	(20)	12.6	9.8	12.6	12.7	10.3
OECD	(16)	9.9	12.4	17.3	18.4	17.9

[a] 1913 figures are estimates.
Source: Glyn (1995).

Greater international openness through trade in the earlier period is suggested by the finding that, for a range of industrialized nations, the ratios of export trade to GDP were consistently higher in 1913 than they were in 1973. As table 6.1 shows, even as late as 1991–2, OECD shares of exports in GDP (17.9 per cent) barely exceeded those estimated for 1913 (16 per cent).

Even with regard to capital exports, it appears from a number of studies that the international economy was much more open in the pre-1914 era than at any subsequent time. As with trade, the ratios of capital flows relative to output were much higher during the gold standard period than even in the 1980s. While no doubt one can point to distinctive aspects of each period, it seems hard to disagree with Hirst and Thompson's conclusion that 'the present period is by no means unprecedented' (1996: 31).[6]

The Question of Magnitude

How big are the changes?

Claims about the rapid growth in globalization of trade, production and investment rest on data that should not be taken at face value. While the figures for *trade* are somewhat more reliable than those for investment, distortions enter in at least two ways that existing accounts often ignore. One is the rising incidence of *intra-firm trade*, where the practice of transfer pricing notoriously inflates the real value of the transactions between parent and subsidiary, with a view to understating the corporation's taxable profits. This practice can often lead to over-estimation of the real value of traded goods. One may well argue that this is a primary example of transnational capital outflanking the extractive powers of the nation-state. But tax-avoiding and tax-evading practices, such as transfer-pricing, are as old as the nation-state itself. They are by no means exclusive to, or necessarily more threatening when practised by, transnational capital.

The second concerns the phenomenon of *entrepôt trading*. This has increased markedly (particularly for geopolitical reasons) in the Asian region, for example, where Singapore and Hong Kong function as staging posts for the re-export of goods to third parties. The re-export nature of these economies is reflected in their high export to GDP ratios (141 per cent for Hong Kong and 185 per cent for Singapore in 1991).

But the real problem with the trade figures is that they tell us almost nothing about *changes in trade patterns*. These would provide a far more realistic indicator of 'globalization'. For the question is one not simply of how much is traded, but of how many trade how much with one another. For the most part, most OECD countries continue to have only two to three significant trading partners. The main exceptions are the smaller countries; but even here, trade partners have been established over a long period, reflecting ties of geography, empire and culture.

If we bear these points in mind, what then do the figures indicate from the vantage point of the late 1990s? The main finding is clear. The postwar trend towards greater trade integration, especially marked since the 1960s, has been weakening. While world trade has grown much faster than output, this growth has actually been slowing over the 1980s and 1990s, the ratio declining from 1.65 in 1965–80 to 1.34 in 1980–90. Moreover, as Wade (1996a: 66) has argued, there are not only cyclical but also structural reasons for expecting that slow-down to continue. Structurally, a gradual shift away from manufacturing within the OECD will mean less rather than more trade integration as the share of less trade-intensive services rises.

When we turn to *investment*, the picture gets more complicated. One of the biggest misconceptions is that *manufacturing production* is becoming increasingly globalized, rather than say, regionalized (a different story, as we see below), as multinational corporations (MNCs) relocate parts of their production process offshore. This conclusion appears to derive from the way FDI figures are used: as proxies for the so-called 'globalization of production'. The new transnationalism measures globalization predominantly (if not only) by the rising level of FDI.

But using FDI figures in this manner poses three major problems which have not yet received the discussion they deserve.

The preponderance of non-manufacturing in FDI   First, most FDI is
for *non-manufacturing*. Indeed, a major proportion of world FDI is
directed towards technically 'non-productive' assets or speculative ventures (golf courses, real estate, hotels, department stores and so on).
FDI figures for Japan are especially revealing in this regard. For even
the leading industrial investor nation in Asia – whose FDI is driving the
industrial integration of the region – *puts almost two-thirds of its world
FDI (61.3 per cent) into non-manufacturing*. These are 1995 figures, representing an increase of 16 percent over the previous year.

Anecdotal evidence, however, is frequently deployed to suggest that
the true level of manufacturing investment by foreign firms may be
understated. The reasoning here is that foreign investors often borrow
locally, raising funds on the local market (e.g. Japanese investors in
Thailand borrowing from Japanese banks operating in Thailand).
Because such investments leave no trace in official statistics, the latter
must under-estimate the true level of foreign investment. But while
such practices raise questions about the aggregate *level* of FDI, they do
not obviously challenge the basic point about FDI *composition*. For one
might very easily deploy the same anecdotal evidence to highlight
the point that locally raised funds tend to find their way into *non-
manufacturing* ventures, particularly into construction, real-estate
markets and financial services. Thus while official FDI understates the
true figure because of MNC borrowing in local markets, this would
most probably affect its *non-manufacturing* component. A rising level
of FDI in such assets would clearly increase the level of 'foreign ownership'. But it is hard to see how this has much to do with advancement of
the 'globalization of production'.

*The preponderance of mergers and acquisitions in manufacturing
FDI*   The second problem is that a high proportion of world manufacturing FDI is directed towards the acquisition of *existing* assets, rather
than the construction of new facilities. Why should this matter? It matters because globalism claims increasingly tight integration through the
proliferation of production networks. But mergers and acquisitions
(M&A) investment is often of the 'arm's-length' variety. This makes it
much closer in character to the 'portfolio' type of investment (though
less short-term in character), and it therefore has little significance for
the internationalization of production. The large outward flows from
Sweden and the UK since about the late 1980s, as discussed in chapter
4, were mainly for 'portfolio' purchases of this kind, involving mergers
and acquisitions of existing assets (Glyn 1995: 15). Indeed, since the
1980s, cross-border M&A expenditure has grown at the expense of

'new establishment' investment. In the United States, as the fall of the dollar has made American companies available to foreigners at bargain rates, the expansion of M&A activity has been dramatic, rising from 67 per cent to 80 per cent over the course of the 1980s (Hirst and Thompson 1996: 72). By 1990, new businesses accounted for only 14 per cent of all foreign acquisitions in the United States (Fallows 1994: 481). The description of much of this activity as 'paper entrepreneurship' reflects its speculative character rather than the generation of new value-added activity. Given the coincidence of heightened M&A activity in industrialized countries with relatively poor industrial performance through the 1980s, one might well conclude that such investment trends are the sign less of a growing global economy than of an embattled productive system.

A more realistic indication of the extent to which the 'national' economy is being outflanked by transnational linkages can be gained by measuring inflows and outflows of FDI as a percentage of gross domestic investment. By this standard, the rates of FDI are actually quite modest. In most cases, gross *domestic* investment exceeds total FDI – both outbound and inbound – by more than 90 per cent (cf. Glyn 1995: table 5).

The preponderance of portfolio investment over FDI   One final point worth underlining is that overall FDI has steadily been dwarfed by 'portfolio' investment (various arm's-length investments including bonds and mutual funds). In the ten years up to 1991–2, portfolio flows rose 28 per cent to account for half of all long-term capital transfers from the thirteen major OECD countries. Over the same period, total FDI declined from 21 per cent to 18 per cent of total long-term transfers. From the point of view of both sustainable world growth and the effectiveness of domestic policy, it could be argued that this is far from a desirable trend.[7]

Strong inter-regional contrasts in investment patterns – between East Asia and Latin America – are instructive in this regard. In sharp contrast to the Latin American pattern, FDI in the East Asian region remains the dominant form of external finance and inward flows of portfolio capital are relatively small as a result of tight state controls. It has been argued that this emphasis on direct investment contributes to the region's greater industrial vitality and macro-economic stability. For, compared with portfolio investment, FDI is more likely to be linked to investment that facilitates exports as well as the importation of technology and know-how. Moreover, being more difficult to withdraw at short notice, FDI is more conducive to a stable policy environment. In contrast, large flows of portfolio capital have the potential to destabilize domestic policy, as seen in the Mexican crisis precipitated by the non-renewal of bonds. FDI of course is not always export- or technology-intensive. Studies of intra-regional differences in East Asia have shown that the type of FDI depends largely on state policies and the capacity to pursue developmental objectives.[8]

While one must recognize that joint ventures and various forms of technology and production partnership between firms from different countries also complicate the picture, their existence does not change the basic argument. While such partnerships may complicate ownership patterns, there is little evidence to suggest that their existence erodes the institutional basis for a national political economy. On the contrary, there is clear evidence, even for Europe, that at least some states, namely Germany and France, take an active role in controlling access to partnerships with local firms (Jenkins 1991). Moreover, inter-corporate linkages have by and large tended to follow trade patterns, whereby most trading nations have but two to three main trading partners (usually determined by history and geography). While this pattern may change in the future, it is not as currently constituted one that is implied by a 'globalized' production base.

In sum, globalization proponents have overstated the magnitude of change, and hence the degree to which production is being transnationalized. For all the talk of huge global investment flows, three stubborn facts remain. First, as a proportion of long-term capital flows, FDI has been declining, not growing, over the past decade; and, second, most long-term capital transfers are of the 'arm's-length' portfolio variety. Finally, of the direct form of foreign investment, a major part goes towards non-manufacturing investment and to the acquisition of existing rather than new assets – all of which have minimal significance for the transnationalization of production.

There is, then, a need to insist on certain basic distinctions in the data on 'investment stocks and flows'. This is important because the literature makes much of the transnationalization of production as the driving mechanism of economic integration, and draws on aggregate FDI figures in support of that hypothesis. I have shown why FDI figures cannot be seen as automatically extending economic linkages, especially in those areas of multinational economic activity that might have a direct bearing on state policies. For this reason one might want to question the conclusion of Barbara Stallings and Wolfgang Streeck that one can read off from the FDI figures the 'degree of economic linkage' among countries and thus 'provide strong support for the globalist hypothesis' (1995: 78).

So much for the magnitude of change in international flows. But the case against globalization does not rest here. I turn next to evidence concerning how the changes are *distributed*.

The Question of Distribution

How 'global' are trade and investment patterns?

Up to this point, my aim has been to show that the novelty and the magnitude of change have been overplayed. I have not sought to deny the existence of a more integrated world economy, a fact which I broadly recognize. My concern here is to draw attention to the way trade and investment are distributed. In one of the most balanced and succinct assessments of economic globalization to date, Robert Wade (1996a) shows three trends inconsistent with a globalization tendency.[9]

The national bases of production First, even if we accept that national economies are increasingly integrated through trade and investment flows, it nevertheless remains the case that in all but the smallest economies, trade constitutes quite a small share of GDP, with exports accounting for 12 per cent or less of GDP in Japan, the US and a single Europe. This means that in the main industrialized economies around 90 per cent of production is still undertaken for the domestic market. Thus, the national bases of production seem as pronounced as ever.

North–South divisions A second important pattern runs counter to the idea of a globalizing tendency. Whereas globalization predicts more even diffusion between North and South, world trade, production and investment remain highly concentrated in the wealthy northern countries of the OECD. Over the 1970–89 period, the North's share of trade grew from 81 per cent to 84 per cent (though the decline of the South's share in world exports masks their changing composition in the South, with largely negative growth of primary product exports, and a rising share of manufactured exports). Investment has followed a similar pattern, with around 90 per cent going to the North over the same period.

Regionalization Finally, this predominantly Northern trade and investment is itself becoming more geographically concentrated in intra-regional patterns. Intra-European trade, for example, now accounts for some 62 per cent of Europe's total export trade. But the importance of intra-regional trade now extends well beyond Europe, where most trade is among member states of the EU. Intra-regional trade is now the dominant trend in Asia (China, the Association of South East Asian Nations [ASEAN], Japan and the NICs), as the region has steadily enhanced its importance as export market and production site for Japan and the NICs. Intra-Asian trade in the period 1986–92 rose from 32.4 per cent to 47.7 per cent of total exports, thus reversing the traditional dominance of trade with the US (Kwan 1994: 4–5; Y. Chu 1995: 230). In short, trade within Asia has been growing more rapidly than trade between Asia and the US.

A similar story can be told for investment. Especially since the 1985 Plaza Accord, which drove up the value of the yen (and indeed of the NIC currencies), economic interdependence among Asian economies has increased through investment and production networks as well as trade. Japan has now replaced the United States as Asia's primary source of FDI (Kwan 1994: 4–5). In 1980, Japan's cumulative investment in the rest of Asia was worth little more than half as much as America's, at $US9.8 billion. By 1990, it was worth around 30 per cent more, at $US41.8 billion (Fallows 1994: 265). Korea and Taiwan are similarly large investors in the region, with investments in China exceeding those of Japan. This increase in foreign investment has at the same time boosted intra-regional trade.

Within the American region (the United States, Canada and Mexico), the trend is also towards increased reliance on intra-regional trade – from 68 per cent to 79 per cent of total US–Japan and US–EU trade over the twelve-year period. While the United States, Europe and Japan are not simply regional traders, current trade patterns suggest that intra-regional trade is increasingly important for the Big Three. Overall, trade within the three regions has grown to overshadow trade among triad members (US–Japan, US–EU, Japan–EU). Exports within North America, Asia and Europe rose from 31 per cent of total world exports in 1980 to 43 per cent in 1992 (Stallings and Streeck 1995: 73).

In contrast to the EU experience, trade and investment within Asia have not been driven by supra-national agencies. Yet it would be wrong to conclude that integration has proceeded spontaneously, or in the absence of any institutional framework. Asian integration appears to have been a more orchestrated affair than some commentators suggest. As we shall see later, dramatic revaluation and deepening trade surpluses with the United States have combined to underpin the publicly coordinated diversion of Japan's lower value-added production to the region. Japan has thus succeeded in shifting some of its huge trade surplus with the United States (particularly in consumer electronic goods) to the South East Asian countries; while the latter, in turn, now run larger surpluses with the United States. To a considerable degree, then, the process of integration in the Asian region has assumed an hierarchical shape, with the Japanese system and its high-end components at the top (Bernard and Ravenhill 1995). To the extent that the region's production is becoming integrated, the process is therefore not purely market-led as anticipated by globalists; rather, it is being coordinated by a transformative state tightly enmeshed with its corporate sector. To this extent, regionalism in Asia is being advanced by the most domestically robust states, a point I shall return to in chapter 7.

The Question of Mobility

How complete is financial integration?

We come now to the core of the globalization tendency: finance. Central to the global hypothesis is the claim that capital mobility has undermined the capacity for national economic policy-making and thus rendered irrelevant cross-country institutional differences. Capital mobility has two aspects, one involving transnational finance, the other referring to the behaviour of MNCs. Concentrating for the moment on the first aspect, I ask: how 'global' is finance, and does it matter?

Of the three aspects of internationalization, it is the huge growth in cross-border financial flows that does most to distance the world economy of today from its earlier incarnation. Since formal removal of the gold standard in 1971, and subsequent liberalization of exchange controls, international capital flows have reached truly spectacular levels. It is this change which has given most life to the idea and reality of 'globalization'.

Nevertheless, one can note three important trends that qualify or contradict globalist predictions even in money markets:

1 *The cost of money has not converged.* The first point concerns the actual degree of financial integration. If this were indeed advanced, one would expect to find much more price uniformity, with firms drawing as readily on foreign as on domestic finance. While studies disagree on whether real interest rates in different national markets continue to diverge, the price differential for both loan and equity capital remains considerable (Wade 1996a: 75). It should also be noted that even in the major industrial economies (e.g. Germany), governments continue to shape net price differentials in borrowed funds by instituting particular tax regimes designed to favour certain kinds of investment (see chapter 5).

2 *Large differences in savings and investment rates persist.* Whereas globalization predicts equalization, big differences in savings rates and investment rates persist. Among the industrialized countries, differences in savings rates have become more rather than less pronounced since the late 1970s, while investment rates continue to diverge, as shown in figures 6.1 and 6.2. In 1992, for example, the ratio of savings to GDP in eleven countries ranged from 0.5 to 25 per cent. In the lowest band (0.5–2.0 per cent) sat the US, UK, Australia and Sweden; Germany and Austria occupied the middle band (10–15 per cent); and in the highest band (20–25 per cent) were Japan, Taiwan and Korea. The differentials in national investment rates tend to parallel those for savings. In 1992, investment as a percentage of GDP ranged from *c.*15 to 36 per cent, with the US, UK, Australia and Sweden in the lowest band (15–19 per cent), Germany, Austria and Taiwan in the middle (22–25 per cent), and Japan and Korea in the highest (31–36 per cent).

3 *Rather than drawing freely on other countries' savings, the bulk of domestic investment in the OECD is still mainly financed out of domestic savings.* Thus domestic savings and investment rates remain tightly linked. This strong correlation between savings and investment rates has been interpreted to mean that countries do not draw freely on other countries' savings. Recent data, however, indicate a fall in the OECD savings–investment correlation from 75 per cent in the mid-1970s to 60 per cent in the 1980s. This leads Wade (1996a: 74) to conclude that financial markets have become more integrated, even if the mobility of capital is somewhat less than anticipated. However, this conclusion may be misleading. The decline in the savings–investment correlation may be an artifact of the enormous drop in national savings in a large economy like that of the United States (see figure 6.1b). The US is now more dependent upon the savings of other countries (especially Japan) than at any time in the postwar period.

In a suggestive comment about the 'dualism' of financial markets, Mann (1996) notes that relative immobility applies especially to company shares, which tend to be fixed to specific national stock markets. This contrasts dramatically with other parts of the financial market (e.g. the bond, currency and futures markets) which are genuinely 'transnational', thus suggesting a clear division rather than integration in the operation of financial markets.

One might venture that this dualism of financial markets reflects not an expanding neoliberal frontier, but a growing mismatch between the 'symbol' economy of (borderless) finance and the 'real' (national)

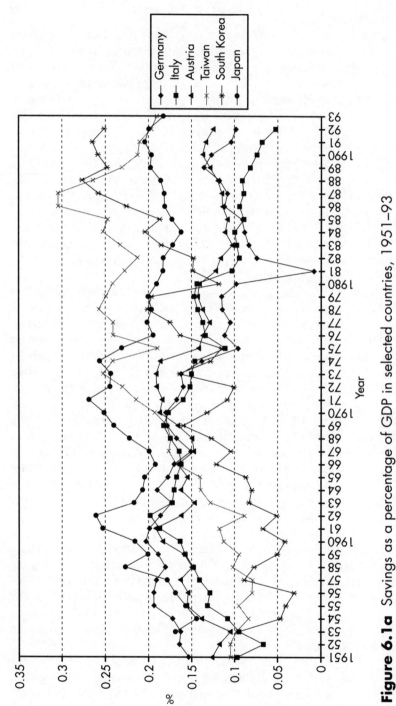

Figure 6.1a Savings as a percentage of GDP in selected countries, 1951–93

Sources: OECD (various years b); Bank of Korea (various years); Executive Yuan (various years).

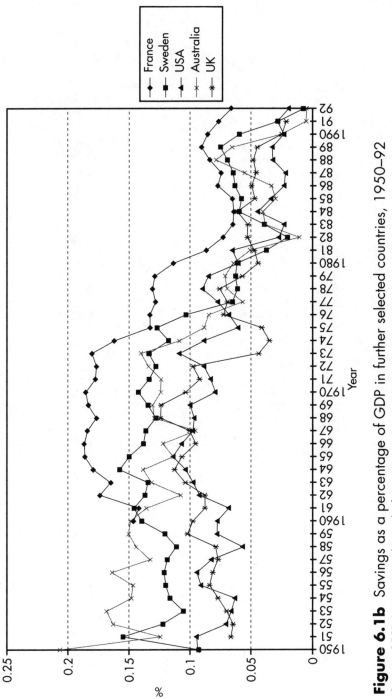

Figure 6.1b Savings as a percentage of GDP in further selected countries, 1950–92

Sources: OECD (various years b); Bank of Korea (various years); Executive Yuan (various years).

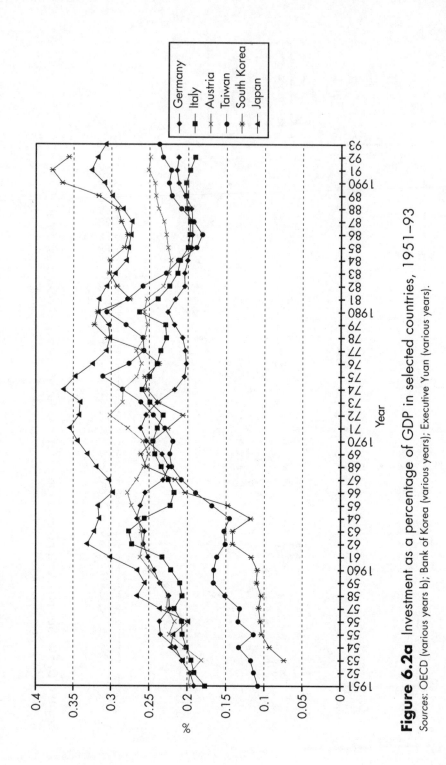

Figure 6.2a Investment as a percentage of GDP in selected countries, 1951–93

Sources: OECD (various years b); Bank of Korea (various years); Executive Yuan (various years).

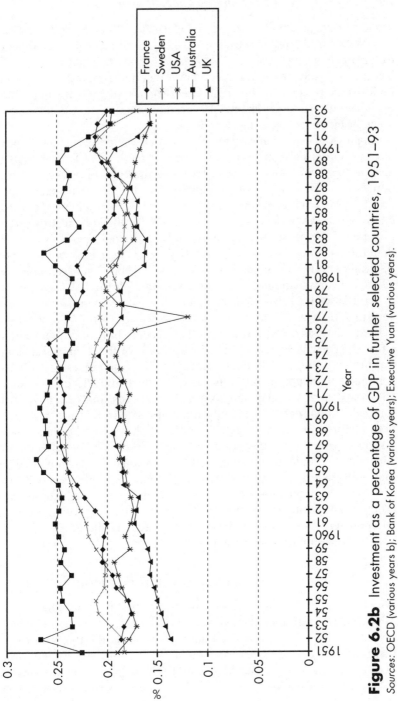

Figure 6.2b Investment as a percentage of GDP in further selected countries, 1951–93

Sources: OECD (various years b); Bank of Korea (various years); Executive Yuan (various years).

economy of production, to deploy Fingleton's (1995: 155) useful distinction. With the exception of exchange rates, the financial market appears to have become increasingly disconnected from the product market.[10] Yet it is precisely on the product market that domestic institutions continue to exert considerable influence. All this suggests an important qualification to 'global' finance. Domestic institutions continue to exert a significant impact on domestic outcomes.

Finally, it is worth pausing to reiterate that while the current volume of cross-border flows appears novel, neither the level of financial openness nor the vulnerability of states to the vicissitudes of market integration is new. Historical evidence dating from at least the eighteenth century reveals a high degree of international capital mobility. This produced virtually 'perfect' financial markets throughout north-western Europe, in the sense of price uniformity. Financial openness appears therefore to have *oscillated* historically, reaching a high point in the classical period of the gold standard, up until 1914. From then until the 1970s, the combination of depression and war, followed by strong political consensus for Keynesianism, helped to weaken financial integration and strengthen policy autonomy (Zevin 1992).

From an historical perspective, there seems little inevitable about either the current degree of financial openness or the level of state control in the future. As the final chapter of this book argues, states have continued to adapt in different ways to fluctuating levels of policy autonomy, and one may suppose, *pace* globalists, that the history of state adaptation has not suddenly come to a standstill in the late twentieth century. While financial liberalization has unleashed extremely disruptive forces upon the world economy, pre-existing patterns do not allow one to predict that financial integration will continue unabated, or that uniformly passive or undifferentiated national responses will prevail. While re-regulation may not be given serious consideration by a group of nation-states like the G7, the possibility of imposing a tax on all short-term international financial transactions should not be discounted as an option open to states in the future (Epstein: 1995).

How 'transnational' are multinationals?

We come, finally, to the second aspect of capital mobility, that of the MNC. These are frequently assumed to have the same footloose quality as global finance. And it is this quality – above all the threat of exit – that is seen to pose the greatest threat to territorially constituted forms of governance. As Held and McGrew (1993: 268) note, the 'disjuncture between the formal authority of the state and the spatial reach of contemporary systems of production, distribution and exchange' is incontestable. For many, this disjuncture translates into zero-sum power, whereby the power of multinationals and other market actors has ostensibly grown at the expense of the power of national authorities to govern the economy. Are we witnessing a final uncaging of economy and society as large corporations take advantage of the economic environment beyond their national domain of origin? Have multinationals genuinely become footloose, operating without regard to a home base? For the current orthodoxy there is little doubt about the answers to such questions.

Globalists assume that the world economy is now so integrated that the constraints of location and of institutional frameworks are increasingly irrelevant; that corporations (whether satisfied or disgruntled with a particular national environment) can simply take a 'random walk' in the world market, escaping the confines of any one nation-state.

In such a world, dominated by the truly global firm, the state's economic powers would indeed appear slight. The reality, however, is somewhat at odds with this vision. On a limited number of criteria, it is true that many MNCs do exhibit some 'transnational' features (e.g. in their pattern of sales, investment flows and production). But by concentrating on such features one can easily paint a false picture. For on virtually all the important criteria, such as share of assets, ownership, management, employment, and R&D held at home or abroad, the importance of a home base remains inescapable (Wade 1996a; Tyson 1991; Kapstein 1991; Hu 1992; Hirst and Thompson 1996). Especially important is the finding that most firms still concentrate their most important value-adding activities at home, thus ensuring a strong contribution to the nation's standard of living. According to existing estimates, the extent of value-added being produced at home is in the range of 70–75 per cent (Wade 1996a; Hirst and Thompson 1996: 96). Overall, these studies conclude that most 'MNCs' are 'national' firms which operate internationally while retaining a home base.

While laying claim to being 'global' is seen as a mark of respectability for the modern company, the number of genuinely transnational companies is rather small. Moreover, where genuine cosmopolitanism exists, this appears to be itself a 'nationally' determined trait.[11] In a confirmation of this finding, Ruigrok and van Tulder's (1995: 168–9) careful assessment of the world's 100 largest core companies concludes that

> not one of these can be dubbed truly 'global', 'footloose' or 'borderless'. . . .
> Thus far, no core firm has managed to overcome its dependence on its home
> base. Globalisation remains a myth – but one which performs a function.

Piven (1995: 111) comes to a similar conclusion with regard to the United States, where huge domestic changes have occurred in the past two decades. While such changes – including trade union decline, rightward shifts in policies and rollbacks in welfare programmes – are 'often read as symptoms of globalization', her data show that America's productive capital 'has in fact remained within national borders'.

Conventional wisdom nevertheless tells us that cost reduction is the driving force that compels MNCs towards a footloose career, and that new transport and information technology liberates and encourages MNCs to exploit low-cost production sites, resulting in a globalization of production. Yet, if cost reduction were the major push factor behind the mobile MNC, we would expect to find most, or at least a very sizeable chunk of, FDI going to the developing (cheap-labour) countries. As we have seen, however, the evidence provides little support for that expectation. As of 1991, a good 81 per cent of world stock of FDI was located in the high-wage (and relatively high-tax) countries: principally the USA, followed by the UK, Germany and Canada. Moreover, this figure represents an *increase* of 12 points since 1967. Indeed, the stock of FDI in the UK and the USA exceeds the stock in Asia and the entire South.

Such figures underline the point that MNCs do not by and large invest where wages and taxes are lowest. Why not? Three considerations seem relevant. In combination, they suggest that the advantages of maintaining a strong 'home' or regional base may be stronger than ever, perhaps for most companies outweighing those to be gained from 'going global'.

Advantages of a national or regional base

These advantages are as follows:

1 New technologies place a premium on fixed costs (i.e. equipment, machinery, etc.) while reducing the importance of variable costs (wages, raw materials). Indeed certain types of labour (especially knowledge-intensive labour) tend to be treated increasingly as a fixed cost. The general effect of this transformation, most notably in the highly developed countries, is to reduce the cost savings to be gained by moving to low-income sites. Notwithstanding post-Plaza Japanese penetration of the Asian region, this tendency is to some degree reflected in the general slowdown of offshore production in cheaper sites by developed countries (Oman 1994).

2 Many new production methods emphasize the growing importance of physical proximity between producers and suppliers (especially in

non-assembly operations). Such methods tend to privilege local supplier networks, thus providing a counter-trend towards the constitution of regional rather than global sourcing networks.

3 Domestic linkages – national institutional frameworks – enmesh business in support relationships with trade associations, training and financial institutions, and national and local governments, as discussed in chapters 3 and 5.[12] In sustaining high-wage economies, one of the most important of these support systems is the government–business relationship. Being generally exclusive rather than open to all, support relationships of this kind constitute a competitive advantage.

It would seem therefore that the advantages of mobility as well as its incidence have been overstated. The embeddedness of companies in national institutions, and especially the quality of those institutions, appear to remain critical components of an effective response to the new competition. The case of Singapore, a city-state founded on MNC investment, can perhaps serve to underline the general point: literally hundreds of MNCs have set up operations on the island over the past three decades. Most have stayed in spite of rising labour costs, which have put Singapore's per capita income ahead of Britain's. Indeed, along with Hong Kong and Japan, Singapore is now one of the most expensive locations in the region. By contrast, in Britain, for example (and one could add Australia), the threat of multinational withdrawal or failure to renew investment has been an oft-repeated story. No doubt there remains much research to be done on locational differences in MNC behaviour; but one suspects that these crude differences in levels of MNC stability have more to do with the degree of corporate embeddedness in institutional frameworks than with more transient differences in cost structures or short-term incentive packages.

Conclusion

The conclusion must be, first, that national economies are in some ways highly integrated with one another. However, with the partial exception of money markets, the result is not so much a globalized world (where national differences virtually disappear) as a more internationalized one, where national and regional interaction networks remain vibrant and continue to highlight the importance of institutions and place. What does such an internationalized world imply for the power of governments to govern? It is to this question that we turn in the final chapter.

7

THE MYTH OF THE POWERLESS STATE

Introduction

Whereas the previous chapter evaluated the extent of globalization as an economic phenomenon, this chapter focuses on its alleged political effects. In particular, I shall assess the veracity of the claim that transnational capital is displacing national political and economic power networks. Many changes have taken place inside nation-states in recent times. On the social front, there has been a general slide towards more fiscally conservative policies, both on the left and on the right, with reforms to taxation systems and the trimming of social programmes. On the economic front, governments have moved towards greater openness in trade and investment policies. These changes are often represented as evidence of the emergence of a new global 'logic of capitalism'. According to this logic, states are now virtually powerless to make real policy choices; transnational markets have so narrowly constrained policy options that more and more states are being forced to adopt similar fiscal, economic and social policy regimes. Globalism therefore predicts convergence on neoliberalism as more and more states adopt the low-taxing, market-based ideals of the American model. As if bolstering this widespread conviction, the Western press continues to offer confident reports about Japan's fading industrial vitality and the death of the Japanese model, on the one hand, and the resurgence of the American economy on the other. More careful (and less polemical) reports, however, suggest that these judgements are superficial.[1]

This chapter seeks to show why the modern notion of the powerless state, with its accompanying reports about the decline of the welfare state and the death of industrial policy, is fundamentally misleading. This is not merely for *empirical* reasons: i.e. because a strong globalization tendency is far from obvious (as argued in chapter 6). One can also argue on *theoretical* grounds that even if economic integration were far more advanced than at present, the predicted emasculation of state powers would not necessarily come about. This is for two related reasons. First, the effects of integration on governing capacities would not be uniform. As earlier chapters have indicated, this is partly because nation-states themselves exhibit considerable adaptability and variety – both in their responses to change and in their capacity to mediate and manage international and domestic linkages, including in particular the government–business relationship. Second, continued divergence can be expected also because, as the present chapter will seek to show, in some key instances globalization is being advanced through the nation-state, and hence depends on the latter for its meaning and existence.

The Extent of Government Powerlessness

If, as shown in chapter 6, trade, production and investment are not subject to a strong globalization tendency whereby an open world market displaces institutional and locational constraints, the same cannot be said of finance. Whichever way we look, it is hard to escape the reality of global money markets where enormous sums are traded daily. This is the 'casino' face of capitalism, unleashed by national governments which now appear powerless to contain its destabilizing effects.

For many commentators, the power of the bond market to undermine the monetary and fiscal policies of governments is taken for granted. It is also viewed as the key constraining feature of a globalized economy, forcing all governments to adopt similar neoliberal (deflationary, fiscally conservative) policies. From this perspective, two conclusions follow. First, global money markets are all-powerful, forcing fiscal conservatism (read 'powerlessness') on governments. Second, it matters not whether a state is weak or strong; all national governments are impotent in the face of global finance. This section and the following will examine each of these claims in turn.

The problem with the 'powerlessness' argument is not that it is wrong about the new constraints on government capacity to make and implement policy. Rather, the problem is the tendency to see such constraints as absolute rather than relative, and as representing 'the end of state history' rather than an evolving history of state adaptation to both external and internal challenges. Three weaknesses in particular deserve highlighting.

Overstating earlier state powers

First, globalists tend to exaggerate state powers in the past in order to claim feebleness in the present. While it is widely believed that financial globalization has made macro-economic policy (of the Keynesian refla-tionary variety) more difficult for governments, there is some dispute about how effective Keynesian demand management ever was.[2] While the Bretton Woods system, by fixing exchange rates, in theory provided a more stable policy-making environment, there is little compelling evi-dence that the state once had the sorts of power that it is now deemed to have surrendered.

What can be said is that expansionary macro-economic policies by postwar governments certainly seemed to produce results while rapid growth provided the fiscal surpluses to spend. But more than two decades of troubled growth, recession and falling real income in the OECD have removed the fiscal surpluses. One consequence of eco-nomic stagnation is that governments need to raise more taxes to pay for more jobless and for more of their citizens retiring from productive work. And these pressures on the public purse are occurring at a time of stagnant living standards. In such a context, and in the absence of national emergency or external threat, electorates are therefore increas-ingly reluctant to sustain tax and spending increases (Mann 1996).

The contextual point about national emergency is an important one. From a wholly contemporary vantage point, it has appeared to many that the pressures on governments generally to reduce the tax burden and restructure the tax system are a result of globalization tendencies: viz. ultra-mobile capitalists who can shop around the globe for the best tax environment. But from a much longer historical perspective, such pressures are the norm. As Michael Mann (1996: 10) argues on the basis of earlier work

> at least since the 13th century, citizens have only consistently agreed to pay a higher proportion of their incomes in taxes during wartime. Their reluc-tance to stump up during the peaceful 1970s and later, in a period of reces-sion (when their real incomes were stagnant or falling), is hardly surprising. It is the historical norm, not the unique product of 'postmodernity' or 'globalism'.[3]

But prolonged peace provides only one contextual variable for the new conservative agenda. Of equal importance in explaining apparent policy convergence, at least after 1973, are the common effects of the oil shocks and the inflation they accelerated. Zevin's (1992: 73) authoritative analysis concludes that whatever policy convergence has occurred can best be explained as the result not of a sudden strengthening of international interdependence, but of 'common responses to the inflation and perceived policy errors of the 1970s'.

Thus, many of the difficulties national policy-makers have experienced with macro-economic management (e.g. balancing budgets, mobilizing sufficient revenue to fund programmes and so on) would seem to have more to do with *internal* fiscal difficulties caused by the recession than with 'globalization'. This is not to deny that some forms of global finance can play havoc with government policy. The important point is that such 'havoc' might prove relatively innocuous in the context of renewed and sustained growth. In so far as sustained growth fails to resume, however, the difficulties for governments will remain and this will continue to nourish the idea of an all-powerful global finance.

Overstating uniformity of state response

At the same time, we do not find all governments following fiscally restrictive measures. At least two nation-states, Germany and Japan, cast doubt on the powerless hypothesis. Germany (i.e. formerly West Germany), where Keynesianism was not well entrenched in the postwar period, has recently sustained a massive tax levy, the so-called solidarity tax, to help finance unification.[4] Also, as the German banks pursue increasingly conservative investment strategies, the German federal government has stepped into the breach, acting as primary source and coordinator of industrial investment in the east (see chapter 5). In Japan, where the importance of various government programmes to protect employment has been evident at least since the two oil shocks, the unpopular consumption tax was also increased sharply in April 1997, ostensibly to help fund further such programmes in this phase of adjustment.

While such examples suggest that 'strong' states like Germany and Japan adapt to their external environment, finding new ways of pursuing their programmes, so too do weaker states.[5] Thus despite the pervasive rhetoric of 'economic rationalism' in Australian policy in recent years, the Labor government pursued an expansionary policy, using deficit spending to fund welfare, labour-market and industrial policies. It was not the power of money markets that undermined these particular policies, but an electoral shift from Labour to the long-excluded conservative coalition pursuing a neoliberal agenda.

A similar pattern of diversity in state response has emerged from the so-called deregulation movements of the 1980s and 1990s in the advanced industrial countries. Steven Vogel's (1996) comparative study of regulatory reforms in Britain and Japan makes the compelling case that governments have responded to similar market pressures in remarkably different ways, reorganizing rather than abandoning control of private-sector behaviour. He finds that 'In most cases of "deregulation", governments have combined liberalization [the introduction of more competition into markets] with reregulation, the reformulation of old rules and the creation of new ones' (1996: 3).

Indeed, the very extent of the domestic changes invoked by proponents of globalization is the subject of serious contention. The topic of welfare state decline is a case in point. Herman Schwartz's useful study (1994) of changes in public service provision in four small states, Australia, Denmark, New Zealand and Sweden, is seen by some to offer support for a logic of globalization. However, Schwartz's study documents changes to the internal organization of public service provision, not to the level of services provided. There is, for instance, no discussion of transfer payments, which constitute the bulk of welfare-state expenditure. In sharp contrast with the argument of Schwartz, Pierson's study of four cases, Britain, Germany, the United States and Sweden, which does focus on social programmes, finds little evidence of radical change. In spite of the harsher economic climate and the pressures on governments for fiscal restraint, it is the 'relative stability' of the welfare state, not radical change, that leaps to the eye:

> What is striking is how hard it is to find radical changes in advanced welfare states. Retrenchment has been pursued cautiously: whenever possible, governments have sought all-party consensus for significant reforms and have chosen to trim existing structures rather than experiment with new programs or pursue privatization. (1996: 174)

If there is a new logic of global capitalism forcing convergence of national policy models, Pierson does not find evidence of fundamental overhaul. Popular support for the welfare state endures, he suggests, in spite of scholarly speculation, and this makes retrenchment electorally difficult. Of course this does not mean that the welfare state will survive in its present form. But the pressures for change may have more to do with life-cycle changes (as discussed in chapter 5) that have occurred since the original regime was conceived half a century ago.[6]

These observations suggest that global finance has not exerted the uniformly debilitating effects on public policy so often claimed for it. Why then, we may ask, has the idea of the powerless state seemed so persuasive to so many?

The political construction of helplessness

Perhaps more than anything, it was the rise of monetarist policies in the 1980s, the emergence of fiscal retrenchment in bulwarks of social democracy like Sweden, and the various speculative attacks on national currencies that have contributed most to the current conviction that – while governments may reign – the global economy rules.

It must be said, however, that political leaders – especially in the English-speaking world dominated by neoliberal economic philosophy – have themselves played a large part in contributing to this view of government helplessness in the face of global trends. In canvassing support for policies lacking popular appeal, many OECD governments have sought to 'sell' their policies of retrenchment to the electorate as being somehow 'forced' on them by 'global economic trends' over which they have no control, a point with which even the free market's champion, *The Economist* ([1995] 7 October), concurs.

While governments are no doubt responding to similar pressures in the world economy (such as the long slump in world-wide demand, and stagnant or falling living standards), one cannot conclude that these pressures derive solely or largely from 'globalization' tendencies, or that the latter produce a uniformity of response. One reason for expressing scepticism about this causal logic has simply to do with the recent history of policy diffusion. As one study has nicely illustrated, economic policy is very often influenced by 'the mood of the time'. For example, as Graham (1990: 3) summarizes the main findings,

> the UK's interest in planning in the 1960s was a conscious aping of the planning in France a few years earlier and similar moves were occurring at the same time in Italy and even, on some readings, in West Germany. Similarly, in the late 1960s and early 1970s many countries experimented with prices and incomes policies of one sort or another and then in the 1980s we observe de-regulation and a renewed emphasis on markets (at least in domestic markets ... [and] at the international level the 1980s is notable for the renewed use of protectionist policies). This last swing in policy occurs on both sides of the Atlantic, both sides of the English Channel, and even both sides of the Iron Curtain.

While allowing for the possibility that all such shifts in policy were carefully considered responses to shared external pressures, it is also hard to avoid the alternative conclusion that 'there is an element of fashion to economic policy' (ibid.).

Convergence *Versus* Varieties of State Capacity

Globalists have not only overstated the degree of state powerlessness. They have also *overgeneralized* it. This is the final weakness in the globalist argument that we now turn to examine.

Varieties of 'national capitalism' (Continental European, East Asian and Anglo-American) find a parallel in the diversity of 'state capacity' for domestic adjustment strategies. At issue here is the variety as opposed to the convergence of state capabilities. Contrary to globalist predictions, I propose that national differences are likely to become more rather than less pronounced in a highly internationalized environment, thus exacerbating rather than diminishing current differences between strong and weak states.

It is worth noting that even those who agree that 'globalization' has been highly exaggerated nevertheless part company when considering the effects of economic internationalization on state capacity. While some accounts conclude that the nation-state persists as an important locus of accumulation, and that national (and international) actors and institutions continue to structure economic space (e.g. Wade 1996a; Mann 1996), others see state powers much more circumscribed through the shedding and shifting of traditional responsibilities. Thus in their recent study, Hirst and Thompson propose that certain traditional powers are declining: 'The power of nation states as administrative and policy-making agencies has declined' while the state's role as an economic manager is 'lessening'. In this respect they appear to overlap with the globalists. Taking a more nuanced approach, however, they insist on the enduring importance of the nation-state – not in traditional terms as sovereign power or as economic manager, but as key source of legitimacy and delegator of authority to powers above and below the national level. Its territorial centrality and constitutional legitimacy assure the nation-state of a distinctive and continuing role in an internationalized world economy, even as conventional sovereignty and economic capacities lessen. 'Nation-states should be seen no longer as "governing" powers ... Nation-states are now simply one class of powers and political agencies in a complex system of power from world to local levels' (Hirst and Thompson 1996: 190).

According to this interpretation of current tendencies, state power is being reduced and redefined on a broad scale, stripped to the basics, becoming even a shell of its former self: still the supreme source of legitimacy and delegator of authority, but exercising no real capacity over its economic domain. The question is whether one can identify unambiguously clear cases which might fit this conception, and whether, having identified them, they represent not simply a group of tradition-ally 'weak' states, but a group where real power shifts are in train.

It seems that the 'basic state' hypothesis is inspired largely by the EU experience, which has been highly influential in informing this kind of reasoning. But the fit is far from clear even here. It would be too easy to conclude from the mere existence of the EU that differences in state–economy relations and policy regimes have been ironed out with increasing rounds of integration. We have seen that the German approach to industry, analysed at length in chapter 5, differs in interest-ing ways from the Japanese. Nevertheless, it has strikingly little in com-mon with that of neoliberal Britain. Moreover, while old-style subsidy packages may no longer be permissible in the leading EU states, the German case shows that there is more than one way to skin the prover-bial cat of industrial policy. Comparative studies of particular industry sectors also show for Germany and France that neither sub-national nor supra-national agencies have supplanted the national state's coordinat-ing capacities in the crucial area of foreign investment (cf. Jenkins 1991).

Although Hirst and Thompson do insist on the state's continuing importance as source of legitimacy and rule of law, and would therefore probably reject the 'weak state' characterization of their position, it is hard to see what kinds of substantive power the state will retain if it is no longer where the action is. If the state is becoming more and more simply the place from which law is promulgated, authority delegated and powers devolved, then is that not simply a form of power shrinkage by stealth (somewhat akin to the centrifugal tendencies of feudalism)? After all, their image of the evolving role of the state (as *rechtsstaat*) has much in common with the role envisaged by eighteenth-century liber-als: hence, the result is not an eclipse of state power as globalists are led to claim, but certainly a very narrowly defined power.

This view of the way state power is evolving seems to me mistaken, for it is blind to state variety and to adaptation. I too would emphasize change, but change is hardly novel to the state: it is the very essence of the modern state, by virtue of the fact that it is embedded in a dynamic economic and inter-state system (even the evolving forms of warfare must be seen in that context).

Thus in what follows I propose that nation-states will matter more rather than less and, by implication, that this will advance rather than retard development of the world economy. The argument is in three parts, emphasizing: (1) state adaptation rather than decline of functions;

(2) strong states as 'midwives' not victims of internationalization; and (3) the emergence of 'catalytic' states consolidating national and regional networks of trade and investment.

Adaptivity of the State

The whole issue of state capacity for economic adjustment has most often been cast as a choice between Keynesian and neoliberal policies. Since they are both macro-economic in focus, they offer to say the least a choice between highly restricted alternatives. Yet, as the East Asian experience has shown, there is much more to governing the economy than macro-economic policy. Industrial policy, as argued in chapter 3 and in more detail below, continues to play a large role in the Asian region. Even in the EU, where one would most expect to find uniformity, industrial policy is far from dead. It has simply changed its character. In Germany, as chapter 5 showed, the state still has a major impact on corporate strategies in particular industries through policies shaping strategic partnerships and innovation strategies. More generally, the federal government provides financial and infrastructural support for 'steady-state' industries through the self-governing national system of innovation. But it takes an active role where a steady state no longer applies: at points of crisis management relating to issues of industry decline, or industry creation (as in the east), or competitive pressures for new technology (e.g. in response to the Japanese challenge).

Vogel demonstrates powerfully this notion of state *adaptivity* of policy instruments in the way MITI and MOF turned liberalization to their own ends. By being able 'to determine the timing and conditions of new market entry', the Japanese ministries generated 'a powerful new source of leverage over industry' (Vogel 1996: 257). More generally, Vogel argues that regulatory reform has been shaped fundamentally by pre-existing institutions, and thus reinforced rather than flattened national differences. In market-led settings 'deregulation' has become an 'exercise in disengagement'; but in countries with close government-industry ties, the reform process has been structured 'to maintain critical government capacities and protect valued institutional arrangements' (1996: 269).

Used to treating states as 'prisoners of a fixed genetic code', to use Ikenberry's phrase (1995: 125), many commentators have also readily chorused the 'death of industrial policy' in Japan. Japan's industrial bureaucrats in the MITI have understandably played a key role in cultivating this myth, largely to assuage American complaints about 'unfairness' in trade disputes. Thus in recent years, the foreign visitor to MITI in Kasumigaseki in downtown Tokyo could expect to be greeted with the solemn statement that MITI's main function in these times is to promote imports. If this were true, one would have to wonder why MITI's renowned prowess in promoting exports has not translated as well to imports.

Of course MITI no longer needs to promote exports, or preside over industry creation. It may have 'lost' many of its former policy instruments (e.g. capital, foreign exchange and licensing controls), as all the standard accounts repeatedly tell us, but this is by no means the end of the story. For MITI continues to create new tools, ones more suited to the new environment and to the new tasks that this engenders: promoting (and diffusing) technological innovation through cooperative arrangements (Fransman 1990; Anchordoguy 1988), as well as facilitating the internationalization of corporate activity through the use of Official Development Assistance (ODA) and other instruments (see below). Indeed 'industrial policy' may have become more important (and indeed more complicated) than in the 1980s when the yen's value was lower. A high yen makes it more urgent for companies to adjust quickly: not only by relocating labour-intensive parts of production to cheaper-cost sites, but also by competing on innovation, especially in the higher-value-added areas of production. So industry continues to profit from the guidance and coordination that MITI can provide in the way of institutional support for research and for offshore investment strategies.

The tendency to expect institutional convergence and the failure to recognize state variety are two sides of the same coin. Both are based on a 'policy instrument' theory of state capacity in which the relevant instruments are somehow predetermined and fixed in character. Any diminution in the importance of a particular policy tool is taken as evidence of a loss of state power.

But it is important to distinguish between state capacity for adjustment strategy and the tools or instruments of policy. Economic integration does not so much enfeeble *the state* as weaken the efficacy of specific *policy instruments*. In particular, financial liberalization destabilizes macro-economic adjustment strategies which focus almost exclusively on fiscal and monetary policies. Both Keynesian and neoliberal policies are similar in this one major regard. Both imply a focus on short-term macro-economic objectives. In both cases the instruments of intervention are predetermined; there is little room for creative adjustment. This may of course account for the greater appeal of macro-economic policy in settings lacking strong state traditions.

But the very opposite is the case with *industrial policy*. In so far as industry itself is constantly changing, 'industrial policy' must of necessity be creative. Hence it cannot be defined once and for all in static, 'snapshot' terms. Thus many commentators have looked for 1960s-style Japanese industrial policy in the 1990s and unsurprisingly concluded that it does not exist. It must be stressed, however, that *the very capacity for industrial policy is one that requires the state constantly to adapt its tools and tasks*.

It would of course be foolish to claim that financial liberalization destabilizes only macro-economic policy. As the case of France has shown, it also weakens those approaches to industrial policy that rely predominantly on state leadership through the targeting of credit to particular sectors or firms. Thus, as William Coleman has argued, when France began to liberalize its financial and banking markets in 1979 and throughout the 1980s, it gradually undermined its own capacity to engage in this kind of strong state leadership in industrial policy.[7] What this suggests is not that states are incapable of engaging in industrial policy. Rather it says that one particular approach to industry policy – state leadership through controlling access to credit – has been severely undermined in settings which have experienced financial liberalization. Accordingly, states will have to use other instruments to pursue industry policy. This is the thrust of the argument that follows.

Has the bell tolled for industrial policy? Japan in comparative perspective

Let us examine one position which has become increasingly influential in studies of the Japanese political economy.[8] According to this view, Japan's industrial policy and MITI's capacity to coordinate change are of relevance only to an earlier era. The Japanese system of industrial policy may have worked well in the phase of catch-up with the West when Japan had clear models to follow, but it has become obsolete now that the technological frontier has been reached. Bureaucrats and public agencies can therefore no longer offer guidance or provide useful coordination. Callon's (1995) study of high-tech offers the most recent statement of this position and can be taken as typical.

Like others who chorus the demise of the Japanese model, Callon contends that MITI's industrial policy regime has broken down.[9] This contention rests on three claims: (1) that Japan's high-tech consortia (e.g. for the Supercomputer and Fifth Generation computer) are riven by conflict and competition, rather than driven by cooperation; (2) that the 1980s consortia did not reach the high level of effectiveness demonstrated by the very large-scale integration (VLSI) consortium in the 1970s; and (3) that Japan's emergence as a leading high-tech economy in the 1980s has undermined the conditions for an effective industrial policy.

The first point is by no means novel or, let it be said, particularly well formulated. By emphasizing the prevalence of conflict over cooperation, the author is claiming that Japan's national system of innovation has changed and ceases to offer any distinctive advantages that might come from inter-firm collaboration. These include the willingness of firms to engage in more ambitious technology strategies that the pooling of resources and sharing of risks can promote, as well as the rapid diffusion of technologies and the advantages of scale economies that collaborative research permits (cf. Levy and Samuels 1991: 143). But the presence of conflict by no means vitiates the reality or benefits of cooperation. It is already well understood in the literature that both conflict and competition abound in Japanese research consortia. In their richly nuanced study of the role of research collaboration in Japan's technology strategy, Levy and Samuels (1991: 129) report that 'Japanese firms, ever distrustful of their competitors, have by no means cast away all their fears and embraced full-scale cooperation. Rather, they have developed a set of practices which allow them to pool resources while keeping their partners at arm's length.' This is what the Japanese call 'distributed cooperation', whereby participant firms take responsibility for a specific task which is then researched independently in the firm's own laboratory, with the technological results exchanged through shared patents. By focusing only on the conflict, studies like that of Callon misunderstand the significance of this pervasive practice.

Levy and Samuels find that in a variety of forms, inter-firm collaboration has become 'ubiquitous' since the end of war. Moreover, while about four-fifths of all inter-firm research collaboration occurs vertically, 'involving firms at different phases of production' (e.g. steel firms and vehicle manufacturers), the number of 'horizontal' alliances (between competitors) has increased and 'their forms have diversified'. In fact, in the 1980s, all legislation governing high-technology initiatives sought to encourage this horizontal form of inter-firm collaboration. More than ever before it seems that Japanese firms are now participating in several dozen such consortia, seconding researchers as well as giving direct financial support. Levy and Samuels's conclusion that 'collaboration has transformed the landscape of Japanese technology' (1991: 326) thus seems much at odds with the obsolescence thesis advanced by Callon.

One final point worth emphasizing in this context is that in absolute amounts, MITI is directly funding and coordinating more cooperative R&D than ever. While this may seem counter-intuitive in view of the increased wealth of Japanese corporations, it is precisely the transition from technological follower to a leadership position – where the technology payoffs are less certain – that redefines a pivotal role for a public agency like MITI.[10]

The second claim is true but inconclusive. *Relative* to the extraordinary success of the VLSI consortium, the more recent ventures seem much less fruitful, especially if measured in terms of market or product success, the only criteria Callon considers (1995: 212). But while rapid, profitable payoffs have been elusive, technical breakthroughs have nevertheless been achieved (Hane 1992). The question of course is what if anything can be concluded from striking successes in the 1970s followed by some not so striking successes in the 1980s? The obsolescence thesis concludes that Japan is exhibiting the classical 'frontier' symptoms. Projects which do not lead to commercial success are construed as evidence that once at the technological frontier, industrial strategy is no longer feasible for a given country. Like a suit of clothes one has outgrown, it must therefore be discarded.

One might set against this contemporary American evaluation of Japan's relative failures a more long-term view of the R&D enterprise. For as the head of one of Taiwan's government-funded research laboratories at ITRI put it lucidly in a recent interview, 'R&D is about taking large risks; failure is therefore an indispensable part of the R&D process. *If there are only success stories, one is probably not doing very good R&D*' (emphasis added).[11]

This leads to the final proposition of the obsolescence argument. It resonates strongly within the neoliberal community, reiterating a deeply held faith in the power of free markets to maximize national prosperity. This is the oft-repeated notion that advanced economies have neither need, nor instruments, nor support for an industrial strategy. Consequently, Japan, as a member of the group of technologically advanced countries, can no longer hope to conduct or benefit from a national technology policy.

The first part of this claim is hard to fault: undoubtedly the task of economic management is made easier when there are models to follow. But the conclusion is unsubstantiated. If the logic of keeping up or staying ahead could be simply narrowed down to the quest for 'breakthrough' technologies, then industrial strategy would indeed become more difficult and uncertain. Clearly, however, technology policy, as the centrepiece of modern industrial strategy, covers a range of measures and programmes – not just the unpredictable 'break-through' innovations. This basic truth is sometimes lost sight of. It therefore deserves a great deal more emphasis than it has received to date.

In principle, one can identify in the advanced countries at least five major areas where coordination of industrial change remains important and continues to operate to the advantage of industry.[12] These are:

1 tracking areas with *new product and technological potential*, for example, MITI's leading role in promoting robotics in the 1980s;
2 promoting *new infant industries* (so-called high-tech industries of the future), specifically biotechnology, micro-electronics and new materials (Goto and Irie 1990). In August of 1996, for instance, MITI announced its plan to expand support for growth industries radically from 250 million yen to 4.25 billion for financial year (FY) 1997;[13]
3 maintaining a continuous long-term programme of investment for *mature industries*, whether through new purchases or upgrading of existing plant and equipment, as in the case of Japan's machine tool industry (cf. Sarathy 1989: 148);
4 regaining critical ground lost to competitors in *strategic industries*, for example, the US Defense Department's successful sponsorship of Sematech, the public–private consortium for restoring semiconductor capacity lost to Japan (cf. Grindley et al. 1994);
5 assisting an orderly retreat for *industries in decline* – whether due to falling demand or to the loss of competitive advantage – so-called 'industrial adjustment' policy. In Japan, 'structural adjustment policy' is aimed at shifting resources (both capital and labour) from such sectors to others, and at assisting firms to diversify into new related fields or into other promising areas.[14]

It is of course the rising and declining industries, not those in their prime, that are the principal subject of industrial policies. It should also be understood that in an advanced country like Japan, 'technological autonomy' – as distinct from what is normally understood as 'economic development' – is the central objective of such a regime (Samuels 1994).[15]

More generally, it must be emphasized that this list is merely indicative of the range of transformative tasks that states can, in principle, undertake in the advanced industrial economies. It makes no presumptions about the actual willingness or capacity of states in general to undertake those tasks. The whole thrust of the argument in earlier chapters has been that willingness and capacity, which tend to go hand in hand, are not widely institutionalized outside East Asia in contemporary capitalism, and are more and more *ideologically* constrained in the European setting.

The contrast with the Japanese perspective (and perhaps within the East Asian region in general) could not be more striking. Reflecting on the future of Japan's industrial policy in the new international environment, MITI's own research institute has produced a theoretical treatise. *Strategic industrial policy*, according to the MITI authors, is not only possible for countries like Japan which have 'no more countries to imitate for further development'; *it is essential as a means of avoiding protectionism*:

> As long as the establishment of industries incurs set-up costs, policy intervention will be essential, and laissez-faire policies would constrain the expansion of the frontiers of industry, and would become an obstacle to the development of the world economy. If the frontiers of industry are not extended, advanced nations will be unable to smoothly transfer the industries in which they have a comparative disadvantage to developing countries seeking to catch up, and will tend to resort to import restrictions and other protectionist measures. This may mean that instead of developing, the world economy will contract. (Goto and Irie 1990: 58)

With the claim that national strategy is vital for an expanding world economy, Japan therefore seeks to justify its industrial-technological policy in terms of a win–win logic.

If these observations offer us any guidance at all, they would seem to say: do not be led by the 'end of industrial policy' school. The Japanese are certainly doing things differently today from say twenty or thirty years ago. But one should not make the mistake of assuming that the baby has been thrown out with the bath water. The bath water has been changed. However, the baby remains firmly in the tub and is as healthy as ever; it is simply being washed afresh in new ways.

Institutional arrangements, domestic linkages and state capacity

My argument to this point implies that the capacity for domestic adjustment strategy does not stand or fall with macro-economic capacity, whether of the reflationary or deflationary variety. It rests, perhaps more than ever, on industrial strategy: the ability of policy-making authorities to mobilize savings and investment and to promote their deployment for the generation of higher-value-added activities.

This capacity for a strategic response to economic change depends, in turn, not so much on a fixed set of policy 'instruments' or level of 'integration into the world economy'. As argued in earlier chapters, primarily it rests on core orientations and institutional arrangements which make key decision-makers in the economic bureaucracies at once 'autonomous' and in some important respects 'accountable'. The character of 'autonomy' applies in so far as decision-making is largely (though never perfectly) insulated from clientelistic political pressures, and from the plurality of special interests that in most liberal democracies tend to privilege the politics of distribution over the politics of growth. This is not to suggest that growth and equity (or indeed welfare) are incompatible – quite the contrary, as shown in chapter 5. Rather, the issue is one of national priorities. No less contentious in discussions of East Asian bureaucracy, 'accountability' nevertheless can be said to apply in so far as the effectiveness of industry policies depends on domestic linkages: notably, institutionalized structures for the exchange of information and for the participation of the business groups whose involvement is central to successful implementation.[16] In the East Asian Three (Japan, Korea and Taiwan) the institutional arrangements in question concern the core economic bureaucracies as well as the financial sector, together with a host of agencies for technology development and diffusion, and the acquisition and exchange of industrial information (Johnson 1984a; Wade 1990a; Evans 1995; Weiss and Hobson 1995). These arrangements, which pull together state and industry in close (albeit not tension-free) cooperation, have underpinned rapid structural change and technological learning in the region (Mathews 1997a).

Economic integration and state capacity

Differences in state adaptivity are not readily explained in terms of whether states are weakly or strongly integrated into the world economy. Consider, for example, the contrasting cases of Singapore and Britain. Highly integrated Singapore (whose per capita GDP now exceeds that of Britain) maintains strong control over its savings and investment rates, thus engineering upward mobility in the international system. By contrast, highly integrated Britain, with little capacity for industrial adjustment, has failed to arrest its downward slide in the international order (Britain's traditional strength in promoting its financial sector being part of that drama).[17]

Such comparisons can be expanded. What they suggest is that one cannot read off from the level of integration the level of state strength. High integration does not necessarily mean the displacement of 'national' economies as the locus of accumulation, or the weakening of national economic management.

Globalization has been widely conceived as inimical to state capacity.

The Singaporean case, to be discussed further, suggests a different interpretation. As we shall see, it provides support for the notion that 'globalization' (*qua* 'internationalization') and state strength may be mutually reinforcing rather than antagonistic. The core issue would therefore appear to be the character of state capacity, not the level of 'integration' *per se*.

Rather than attributing the current proclivities for macro-economic adjustment to 'globalization', one should look in the first instance domestically, to a country's governing institutions, and thus to differences in national orientations and capabilities. This leads to the second strand of my argument as to why the state's importance is, in principle if not always in practice, increasing rather than diminishing in ensuring more equitable participation in the world economy.

The State as Victim or Midwife of 'Globalization'?

Failure to differentiate state capacities has blinded global enthusiasts to an important possibility: that states may at times be facilitators (even perhaps perpetrators) rather than mere victims of so-called 'globalization'. Although this possibility has not yet been canvassed by those researching in the field, there is sufficient evidence to indicate this would offer a promising line of enquiry. Such evidence as exists for Japan, Singapore, Korea and Taiwan indicates that these states are acting increasingly as catalysts for the 'internationalization' strategies of corporate actors. As 'catalytic' states (to be discussed later) Japan and the NICs are in many ways taking the bull by the horns, offering a panoply of incentives to finance overseas investment, to promote technology alliances between national and foreign firms, and to encourage regional relocation of production networks.

Institutionally strong states like Japan and Singapore have for many years been promoting the offshore relocation of certain parts of the production process, providing corporate actors with similar developmental infrastructure, inducements and government–business relations abroad to those they offer at home. In certain industries, such as microelectronics, MITI has for some years sought to manage trade imbalances with the United States by assisting companies to localize production offshore. 'Internationalization' is thus a key strategy of the Japanese bureaucracy, implemented through agencies such as MITI.

While many governments represent their firms abroad, the Japanese government has taken this process some steps further, to the point where it has become meaningful to speak of the internationalization of

Japan's industrial policy. A host of government agencies – from MITI and the Economic Planning Agency to JETRO and the Export–Import Bank – now ensure that firms are assisted in choosing appropriate foreign investment locations and in establishing their operations abroad. Such involvement has generally assumed a low profile in the advanced economies. In the emerging market economies of Vietnam, Cambodia and Laos, however, MITI has been centrally involved in the selection and planning of model cities as free-trade zones which will serve as incubators for the transition to a market economy.

ODA is another tool which the Japanese state has used creatively, in part as a means of externalizing its domestic alliances. Throughout the Asian region (and beyond to Eastern Europe), bureaucrats from the MOF and other agencies have been teaching Japanese-style economics to governments responsive to advice. ODA has thus become an instrument not only for extending the Japanese market, but also for externalizing Japan's model of governed market coordination.[18] As a condition of ODA disbursement, Japan has not simply stipulated the import of Japanese goods. It has also involved the placement of Japanese bureaucrats in government offices abroad, ostensibly to proselytize and ensure a more receptive environment for its own model of economic management.[19]

While institutional differences may thwart Japan-style developmentalism in South East Asia (most notably in the Philippines, Malaysia and Indonesia), it would seem at least that through Japan's influence, many nations in the region are bound to absorb some of the lessons of Japanese industrial policy and its institutions. Thus, writes *Business Week* (April 1994), by early next century, this sort of 'missionary work' could exert 'a profound effect on world capitalism'. As a result, regionalism in this part of the world will look quite different from neoclassical American-style capitalism.

More robust capacity still underlies MITI's encouragement of corporate relocation to the Asian countries, a coordinated move beginning in the 1980s. This sought not only to offset high production costs due to an appreciating yen, but also to reduce Japan's trade surplus with the United States. MITI's role in fostering and supporting the relocation of Japanese production to other parts of the region should not be underplayed. Evidence for the micro-electronics sector shows that MITI has for some time been prodding Japanese companies into action by requiring them to submit plans detailing how they intend to reduce their trade surplus over a five-year period, and providing assistance in relocation (SIA 1992: 244–5). Initially, compared with the post-Plaza period, however, Japanese companies remained relatively slow to take up MITI's inducements and set up operations throughout the region. Yet once the

Plaza Accord was in place and the value of the yen soared, business response to the relocation project was dramatic.

The point is not that MITI alone achieved this outcome, or that business was pushed by the state to relocate, or even that relocation was simply a response to the intensification of American pressure over trade imbalances. The important point is that relocation to the region was much more a publicly coordinated effort than an ad hoc response by individual firms acting alone. It therefore provides a useful example of *how a government itself may be part of the 'globalization' process.* While the latter is so often invoked as the enemy of state power, here we see state capacity as a condition of successful internationalization.

There is a larger point that the use of such measures illustrates. This is that domestically strong states may be able to adapt, and to assist firms to adjust, more effectively to the external environment by 'internationalizing' state capabilities. As already noted, for example, Japan has externalized aspects of its model of government–business relations beyond the home territory as part of the integration process. In the Asian region at least, this conclusion casts a rather new light on the old truism that bureaucrats, unlike large multinationals, are territorially bound in their operations.

The case of Singapore adds to this point. For here we see a new phase in the state's 'internationalization' strategy, from an emphasis on attracting foreign companies to Singapore to encouraging locally based companies to expand overseas (cf. Ramesh 1995). As a consequence of growing affluence and diminishing space, the Singaporean government has for several years been prodding its local companies and MNCs to move offshore to Singaporean-created industrial parks throughout the region (chiefly to China, Malaysia, Hong Kong, Indonesia, and more recently Thailand and Vietnam). When some years ago Dr Goh Keng-Swee, then Minister for Economics, announced the project to shift more business operations offshore, few Singaporean firms were willing to take the plunge. In Goh's words, firms have to be 'pushed'.[20] More recently, the former prime minister Lee Kuan Yew has argued that

> The task of Singapore was to achieve regionalization during the 1990s. If our economy is to maintain an optimal growth rate, Singapore's corporations must go beyond their home borders ... In order to more actively advance into foreign countries, they are now seeking to form partnerships with Korea. (*Korean Business Review* 1995, October: 9)

As Goh's statement and the measures that lie behind it indicate, the 'regionalization' of the Singaporean economy has been much more a directly top-down affair, with the government driving the process through the creation of the Singapore Technologies Industrial Corporation (STIC). The city-state not only initiated government–business visits

to the region to explore investment opportunities; it also set up govern-
ment-to-government bodies (like the China–Singapore Joint Steering
Council) to facilitate relocation of Singaporean companies, and
financed and administered the industrial parks and infrastructural projects abroad. At home the government provides potential offshore
investors with economic data, incentives, capital infusions, investment
guarantees and training programmes. Thus, led by the STIC, a great
string of industrial parks is now under construction, stretching from
Indonesia to China and Vietnam, some of them already linked to the
island's service industries. The China–Singapore Suzhou Industrial Park
is described as 'an extraordinary experiment [which] ... essentially
amounts to operating an entire Chinese township using Singapore
expertise' (*Far Eastern Economic Review* [1996], 25 April: 25). If successful, these ventures are most likely to advance regional integration
not at the expense of state power, but by its internationalization via
reproduction *in extenso* of the Singaporean model.

Similar moves appear to be under way in Japan, where MITI is
preparing to select candidates for 'model cities' in Cambodia, Laos and
Vietnam which will provide free-trade zones and lead the transition to a
market economy. Parallel stories can be told for Korea and Taiwan,
where the state has not only abolished many of the restrictions on outbound capital flows, but also moved directly to promote the globalization strategies of national firms. At least three strategies can be
distinguished.[21] First, the state has encouraged local firms to finance
their investment projects through the overseas issue of corporate bills
and convertible bonds. Government approval, however, is still required,
and monetary ceilings apply. More than 100 Korean firms were thus
permitted to raise money in foreign capital markets by 1991.

Second, state agencies supplement private overseas investment with
ODA to assist business expansion in developing countries. In this respect,
the management of ODA tends to follow Japanese practice, being tightly
linked to trade and investment and focused on infrastructure projects of
significance to the investment activities of national firms.

Third, local firms receive strong financial support to enter joint ventures or technology partnerships with MNCs in strategic sectors (e.g.
aerospace, semiconductors, telecommunications and biotechnology). In
Taiwan, for example, the state's financial support, according to Chu (Y.
Chu 1995: 222), 'was behind every major merger and takeover plan of
Taiwanese firms in the US high-tech industries'; while in Korea, similar
concerns are reflected in the dramatic policy reorientation of the
Export–Import Bank, which has been authorized to shift from export
financing to the support of overseas investment.

Finally, one can add a fourth category of state-facilitated internation-alization. This involves direct on-the-ground assistance for firms to relo-cate operations overseas, as in the case not only of Singapore, but of the Taiwanese government establishing a quasi offshore version of its Hsinchu Science Park at Subic Bay in the Philippines.

This sort of evidence is hard to square with the favoured image of states as passive victims of powerful 'transnational' forces. There is no attempt to suggest that all states are thus engaged in facilitating corpor-ate internationalization. The point is that some are – amongst them the more industrially vibrant and highly coordinated market economies – and that this attests to state *adaptiveness* and to the *increasing* rather than diminishing salience of state capacity.

From such evidence it would appear that with some caveats for Korea (chapter 3), core capacities are alive and well in East Asia. Behind the 1997 turmoil of currency fluctuations, banking failures and, in the case of Korea, bankruptcies of overextended *chaebol*, the fundamentals of these coordinated economies remain strong – especially compared with the uncoordinated market economies of Anglo-America. State capacity remains high in the crucial areas of mobilizing savings and investment required to sustain growth and continue the process of industrial upgrad-ing into higher value-added activities. Thus, paradoxically, the financial turmoil of 1997 should serve to re-emphasize the advantages of co-ordinated market economies and the dangers of 'undisciplined support' (see chapter 3) being brought to bear on the business sector. To this extent, potential adaptors of the coordinated model, at least in the Asian region, are more likely to emerge than faithful followers of the neoliberal model of capitalism. One might attempt a similar argument for the EU in the light of the German state's considerable, if somewhat more muted, transformative capacity, as argued at length in chapter 5.

More generally, so-called 'globalization' needs to be viewed as a politically rather than technologically induced phenomenon. It is politi-cal, first, in the general sense that the opening up of capital markets has occurred as a direct result of governments, either willingly or unwill-ingly, ceding to pressure from financial interests, seeking to prevent international crises, and eschewing implementation of effective controls (cf. Banuri and Schor 1992; E. Helleiner 1995). But it is political also in the more specific sense discussed here: that a number of states are seek-ing directly to promote and encourage rather than constrain the inter-nationalization of corporate activity in trade, investment and production. From this perspective, the internationalization of capital may not merely restrict policy choices, but expand them as well.[22]

The Emergence of 'Catalytic' States

The final strand in my argument is that we are witnessing changes in state power; but these changes have to do not with diminution but with reconstitution of power around the consolidation of domestic and international linkages. As macro-economic tools appear to lose their efficacy, as external pressures for homogenization of trade regimes increase, and as cross-border flows of people and finance threaten the domestic base, a growing number of states are seeking to increase their control over the external environment. State responses to these pressures have not been uniform. They have varied according to politico-institutional differences. But in general one of two strategies has prevailed. Both involve building or strengthening power alliances: 'upwards' via inter-state coalitions at the regional and international level, and/or 'downwards' via state–business alliances in the domestic market.

To the extent that states are seeking to adapt and reconstitute themselves in these ways, they can perhaps best be seen as 'catalytic', to apply a term coined by Michael Lind (1992). Catalytic states seek to achieve their goals less by relying on their own resources than by assuming a dominant role in coalitions of states, transnational institutions and private-sector groups.

> As a catalyst, this kind of state is one that seeks to be *indispensable* to the success or direction of particular strategic coalitions while remaining substantially *independent* from the other elements of the coalition, whether they are other governments, firms, or even foreign and domestic populations. (Lind 1992: 3)

Far from relinquishing their distinctive goals and identity, states are increasingly using collaborative power arrangements to create more real control over their economies (and indeed over security). As such, these new coalitions should be seen as gambits for augmenting rather than shedding state capacity.

There are many who would support the claim that we are witnessing the end of an era marked by the 'integral state', with assured territorial control over the means of legitimacy, security and production. But at a time when serious analysis of 'state power' or the 'state's role' has become academically unfashionable, there will undoubtedly be less support for Lind's assertion that in place of the integral state we are now witnessing the rise of the catalytic state.

To what extent can the catalytic state be generalized? The first point to make is that 'catalytic' is being contrasted with 'integral'. It is a way of highlighting the tendency of states to seek adaptation to new challenges (e.g. internationalization) by forging or strengthening partnerships with other (state *and* non-state) power actors, rather than going it alone. Consolidation of such alliances is taking place primarily at regional and international level, between states, though also domestically, between states and corporate actors. The proliferation of regional agreements between nation-states (including *inter alia* the EU, APEC [Asia–Pacific Economic Cooperation] and NAFTA [North American Free Trade Agreement]) can be seen as one manifestation of this tendency. The evolving character of close domestic government–business cooperation, most notably in the cases examined in this book – Japan, the NICs and Germany – is another. Between these formations, there are others evolving in unexpected ways in response to the regulatory gaps created by financial liberalization. Thus, new forms of interstate collaboration are emerging as specialized national agencies become enmeshed in regulating cross-border financial transactions. As Lutz (1996: 33) notes, observing the newly acquired powers of the federal state in this arena, 'Even securities markets, seen as the most fluid and mobile segments of financial capital, have to be organized.'

The second point, however, is that even catalytic states have differential capabilities: some, like Japan and Germany, have both domestic and international clout, and hence are able to use their domestic leverage to position themselves advantageously, for example, in regional coalitions. Others, like the United States, exploit strong international leverage but at the expense of domestic adjustment capacity. Still others, like Russia, are so lacking in domestic capability that they are not even serious candidates for the kinds of regional coalition they might aspire to lead or join.[23]

Recent examples of states using international agreements as a means of pursuing domestic economic goals include such initiatives as NAFTA and APEC. While both weak and strong states enter into such alliances, it is often the domestically weaker states which take the lead in seeking out this external path, aspiring to constrain others to adopt their own more hands-off approach to trade and industry. Australia's enthusiastic efforts in seeking to establish APEC, and the United States' leadership of NAFTA, can each be interpreted in this light. But these states, with their traditional arm's-length approach to the corporate sector, lack the more strategic capacities of their East Asian counterparts. In the absence of a normative and institutional base for strengthening developmental capabilities at home, both countries have sought instead to level the playing field outside their domain. To this extent, one might agree with the conclusion that, unlike the case with the EU, such moves are driven not by a supra-national vision but by 'insecure governments' seeking 'new tools to stimulate growth, employment, and a stable regional policy community' (Ikenberry 1995: 124). To make the point in slightly different language, to pursue regionalism (inter-state coalitions) without domestic capacity (public–private coalitions) is only half the story, akin to a war of movement without having established a war of position.[24]

What this analysis suggests is that the most important power actors in these new inter-state coalitions will not necessarily be those initiating them (e.g. the USA and Australia), but those who participate in them on the basis of a position of domestic strength. For the major solidity of Japan and even of Germany as catalytic states in international coalitions is that they have developed robust capability at home via domestic (government–business) linkages. By contrast, the major weakness of the United States may well be the under-development of such linkages, reinforced by the over-development of external strength. This statement may of course seem counter-intuitive to some, especially in view of the apparent 'reversal of fortune' experienced by Japan and the US in the 1990s. But as the evidence presented in chapter 5 suggested, it is well to be sceptical of such appearances.

If this reasoning is accepted, then we must enter a caveat to the notion of the rise of the catalytic state. Domestically strong states will be more likely to act in concert with others, while domestically weak states (especially larger ones like the United States) will not completely lose their 'integral' character. In such cases, rather than a concentration on power sharing we can expect to find *oscillation*, as weak states shift between acting alone (e.g. defensive protectionism or bilateralism) and with others.

In this new era therefore the most successful states will be those which can augment their conventional power resources with collaborative power: engaging others (whether states, corporations or business associations) to form cooperative agreements and 'consortia' for action on this or that issue. But by far the most important of these coalitions will be partnerships of government and business, for as this book has argued this goes to the very heart of state capacity.

This contrasts with Hirst and Thompson's (1996) conception, discussed earlier. The proliferation of domestic and international (regional) coalitions implies that the state is not so much 'devolving' power – in a negative-sum manner – to other power actors from whom it then maintains a passive distance. Rather, contemporary states are constantly seeking power-sharing arrangements which will give them scope for remaining an *active centre*, hence 'catalytic' states.

Conclusion

'Globalization' is a big idea resting on slim foundations. Its main basis would seem to be the financial deregulation of the post-Bretton Woods era. But big ideas excite. This may partly explain why enthusiasm has transcended the evidence.

There are now sufficient grounds to suggest that globalization tendencies have been exaggerated, and that we need to employ the language of internationalization to understand better the changes taking place in the world economy. In this kind of economy, the nation-state retains its importance as a political and economic actor. So rather than a uniformity of national responses producing convergence on a single neoliberal model, we can expect to find a firming up of the different varieties of capitalism with their correspondingly varied state capacities for domestic adjustment.

My analysis has suggested that globalization arguments, with their image of a borderless world economy, have obfuscated some of the more fundamental processes whereby 'strong' states themselves have altered the rules of the game. Thus the European integration process is to a significant degree being driven by and in the image of Europe's strongest state, Germany. In parallel manner, Japan has been leading the regional integration of production in Asia. While the corporation continues to be seen as the main motor of economic integration, the German and Japanese cases suggest that not all capital is equal, that there is, in short, a 'hierarchy' to the integration process. As the argument of this book implies, the hierarchical aspect of integration is one which has a basis in strong transformative capability, and hence is supported by robust domestic linkages between government and industry.

Not only the rise of East Asia and the responses to that challenge from countries like Germany, but also the spread of regional agreements, suggest that we can expect to see more and more of a different kind of state taking shape in the world arena, one that is reconstituting its power at the centre of alliances formed either within or outside the nation-state. For these states, building or augmenting state capacity rather than discarding it would seem to be the lesson of dynamic integration. It seems likely that as we move into the twenty-first century, the ability of nation-states to adapt to internationalization (so-called 'globalization') will continue to heighten rather than diminish national differences in state capacity and the associatiated advantages of national economic coordination.

NOTES

Chapter 1 The state is dead: long live the state

1 This tendency has been attributed in part to the pervasive influence of functionalist and utilitarian approaches, especially evident in American political science and economics (March and Olsen 1989; Skocpol 1985: 4). While an alternative to the reductionism of liberal pluralism and Marxism emerged in the period prior to World War II, this literature on the state tended to be written by Germans and was therefore largely ignored because of its associations with authoritarianism.

2 Most notable in this early batch of historical comparative studies are the works of P. Anderson (1974), C. Tilly (1975), Mann (1977/1988), Poggi (1978), Skocpol (1979) and, later, Giddens (1985). Equally important, though more for refocusing attention on the state's contribution to economic performance, were the studies of neocorporatism: in particular, Crouch (1979, 1985), Schmitter and Lehmbruch (1979) and Goldthorpe (1984). Among the earlier attempts to explain why advanced industrial states responded so differently to common economic problems, see especially Zysman (1977), Katzenstein (1978a), and Krasner (1978a).

3 Thus, what I refer to below as the tradition of 'state denial' suddenly found itself in the rearguard. As one prominent political scientist put it, '[t]he state, a concept that many of us thought had been polished off a quarter of a century ago, has now risen from the grave to haunt us once again' (Easton 1981: 303).

4 See the collection by Evans et al. (1985). As the chapters in that text make clear, 'bringing the state back in' (BSBI) was aimed at reductionist social science: the tendency to explain the policies, interests and activities of the state solely in terms of 'society-centred' or non-state variables. At the time of its publication, the thrust of the critical response was that the claim to novelty was overplayed, and that BSBI merely harked back to an earlier literature in which states and thus institutions were held to be consequential. More recent criticisms, however, take a different tack, rejecting the BSBI school for its apparent state-centrism. The claim here is that there has been a preoccupation with state structure to the neglect of state–society relations (cf. Migdal 1996). For an interesting survey which finds that the so-called 'state-centric' literature 'has always recognized that state–society relations are critical to understanding state action', see Barkey and Parikh (1991: 523).

5 Economic globalization is of course not the only tendency that is claimed to threaten the nation-state. Michael Mann's (1996) discussion of four globalization tendencies casts some fresh light on a debate that threatens to become overly technical and repetitious.

6 This paradoxically reverses the earlier emphasis of eighteenth-century theorists of economic and political liberalism, for whom the exercise of state power was something to be carefully delimited and constrained.

7 Many excellent studies have argued along similar lines, maintaining that industrial policy is a vital component of national competitiveness in an interdependent world economy. See in particular Johnson (1984b), Scott (1985, 1992), Thurow (1985), Zysman (1983), Freeman (1987), Kentworthy (1990), and further references in Kentworthy. For an economist's view that government relations with business can be an important competitive advantage, see Porter (1986: 53).

8 See the productive collection by Hollingsworth et al. (1994), which discusses different coordination systems at work in different sectors and countries.

9 For a remarkable illustration of the problems of bounded rationality and short-time horizons assisting in the demise of an industry, see Magaziner and Patinkin's discussion of the US steel industry (1990: 5–6). For a more comprehensive justification of state coordination, see the World Bank (1993a: 90–100).

10 World Bank (1993a: 90–2).

11 For a discussion of the 'new institutionalist theory of state intervention', emphasizing the role of state coordination in reducing transaction costs, see Chang (1994: ch. 2). The business and organizational argument is lucidly outlined in Lazonick (1991).

12 For a comparative analysis of extractive capacity, see Kugler and Domke (1986).

13 The distinction between infrastructural and despotic powers was first theorized by Mann (1984/1988) as a means of differentiating the power of modern and pre-industrial states. For a development of the concept of infrastructural power in contemporary settings, see Weiss and Hobson (1995: esp. chs 1, 6, 7).

14 Mann (1993a: 796) has theorized this lack of coherence through the notion of diverse 'political crystallizations'. See also chapter 2.

15 Andrew Gamble has rightly insisted that in differentiating models of capitalism, it is not national culture but 'particular institutional complexes' that are the key factors to consider (1995: 527). In this book, the defining institutional complex is 'state capacity' and the particular set of state–society relationships that informs and underpins it.

Chapter 2 The sources of state capacity

1 The literature on corporatism is vast. Among the outstanding studies of comparative performance, which focus on institutional arrangements and domestic policy, see Schott (1984), Goldthorpe (1984), Katzenstein (1984, 1985) and Crouch (1993a).

2 Soskice (1990) draws the distinction between cost-driven and innovation-led competition very effectively. For a ground-breaking argument along these lines, see Abernathy et al. (1981).

3 The 'developmental state' literature on East Asia is extensive. In addition to the path-breaking 'classics' by Johnson (1982), Amsden (1989), Y. Woo (1991) and Wade (1990a), worthy collections include Deyo (1987), White (1988), Appelbaum and Henderson (1992) and, most recently, the important volume edited by Woo-Cumings (forthcoming).

4 For a recent attempt to conceptualize the state's political capacity, see Jackman (1993). His conclusion that powerful states rely on legitimacy (cooperation) rather than force is a useful antidote to the conventional wisdom. It runs parallel in certain important respects with my own argument about economic capacity. More theoretically productive is Hobson (1997).

5 For a useful discussion along these lines, applied to the South Korean case, see Haggard and Moon (1990).

6 Buchanan (cited in Chang 1994: 27) defines rent as 'that part of the payment to an owner of resources over and above that which those resources could command in any alternative use'.

7 On pre-industrial states as 'revenue-maximizers' see Levi (1981); on third world states see Evans (1989).

8 For a discussion of institutionalization in terms of depth and breadth, see Krasner (1989: 84).

9 See Peter Evans's major study (1995) for an elaboration and application of these concepts to late industrializing countries.

10 For a skilful exposition and critique of the so-called government-failure literature, see Chang (1994: ch. 1).

11 To talk of states as 'liberal' or otherwise implies that basic orientations are non-partisan, and thus relatively stable whether governments are conservative or social democratic.

12 See Ian Verrender 1996: *Rip-off Yarns, Sydney Morning Herald* (28 December): 7.

13 On the role of the Pentagon in the development of high-tech industry in the US, see the informative study by Markusen and Yudken (1992: ch. 3).

14 The question of origins no doubt merits a study of its own. None the less, thanks to ground-breaking work on late industrialization in Europe, Meiji Japan and South Korea since World War II (Gerschenkron 1962; Samuels 1994; Y. Woo 1991), one can readily grasp the general importance for the formation of state orientations of a country's developmental timing, location, and point of entry into the international system, as well as geopolitical factors more generally. On the transformation of regime goals as a result of military weakness, see Kuisel's (1981) study of France.

15 Atkinson and Coleman (1989: 58) have argued that the label 'corporatism' should be reserved for tripartite networks and distinguished from 'concertation' networks of government and business in which the role of labour is marginal. The assumption here is that the action of state agencies is much more circumscribed in corporatist networks, and rather more autonomous in concertation networks.

16 Among the more influential and sophisticated statements of the strong-state thesis see Katzenstein (1976) and Krasner (1978a).

17 For a critique of the strong–weak formulation from a 'coalitional' perspective, see Gourevitch (1978: 900–7).

18 Both Ikenberry (1986) and Katzenstein (1976, 1978a) tend to see policy instruments as relatively fixed in so far as they are said to be shaped by the

larger structures of state and society. As Katzenstein (1976: 5) puts it: 'The number and range of policy instruments emerge from the differentiation of state and society and the centralization of each.'

19 On Taiwan, see Wade (1990a). On how Japan used its tax system creatively to assist developing industries, see Johnson (1982: 233–6). Johnson cites a Japanese director of the National Tax Agency and vice-minister of finance who insists that from the point of view of implementation, taxes are better than subsidies, 'because a tax advantage is valuable only after an enterprise has done what the government wants it to do, whereas a subsidy is paid prior to performance and sometimes does not produce any improvement in performance' (1982: 233).

20 For a comprehensive recent study analysing the makings and evolution of the Japanese civil service, see the collection edited by H.-K. Kim et al.

21 Focusing on state structure (or state autonomy) in itself is insufficient for explaining state capacity. Historically, the most autonomous states had little capacity to transform 'their' societies because there was almost no connection with (i.e. embeddedness in) their surrounding social structure. See chapter 3 in Mann 1988.

22 Though it is probably not in keeping with the spirit of Evans's larger objectives, one is none the less reminded here of the functionalist component in certain versions of Marxism whereby the state is inconceivable as a power means in its own right; where it exists only to serve capital; and where once capital is up and running, the state is no longer needed and eventually retires into the background.

23 For a more detailed discussion and development of Mann's notion of infrastructural power, see Weiss and Hobson (1995).

Chapter 3 Transformative capacity in evolution: East Asian developmental states

1 On the concept of a 'producer economics', as compared with 'consumer economics', see Lester Thurow (1992), who applies these respectively to Japan and the United States.

2 Friedrich List, a German scholar and civil servant who lived much of his life in exile, wrote this in 1842, in his best-known book, *The National System of Political Economy* (1966), a treatise on economic nationalism. For a recent analysis by a political scientist, see Levi-Faur (1997).

3 This is perhaps most explicit for Japan. On List's influence on Japanese policy-makers, see Samuels (1994). In discussions, Robert Wade has remarked that List's books are readily available in campus bookshops in Seoul.

4 See references in n. 6; for a full list see Weiss (1995), which represents an earlier and shorter version of the present chapter.

5 This is evident in recent reports issued by the World Bank; e.g. *The East Asian Miracle: Economic Growth and Public Policy* (1993a), especially ch. 4 on the institutional bases of growth; and *Government, Policy and Productivity Growth: Is East Asia an Exception?* (1993b). For a short but cogent critique of the 1993 'Miracle' report, see Lall (1993).

6 Exemplary texts include Wade (1990a), Amsden (1989), Y. Woo (1991),

Johnson (1982, 1984a) and Evans (1989, 1995).

7 As David Soskice has done for certain economies of Continental Europe, though for somewhat different reasons (1990).

8 Useful descriptions of the coordinated and highly selective interventions of Japan and the NICs can be found in Lall (1993) and Chang (1994). Selective interventions in East Asia include targeting sectors, products and technologies to deepen industrial capabilities; intervening in 'factor markets' to create specialized education and technology institutes; and screening foreign investment and foreign technology for local impact. Coordinated intervention is an integral feature of East Asian industrial policy, yet neoclassical economists have been unable to evaluate its contribution because of their focus on particular interventions, analysed separately. As Lall (1993: 17) explains, 'Credit market interventions, for instance, could not have worked if they had not been integrated with protection, technological promotion, selective skill creation, and so on.'

9 In spite of some striking misreadings of his 'developmental state' concept, Chalmers Johnson was in fact among the first to highlight the cooperative and consultative basis of Japanese industrial policy, especially with regard to its strengths (1982: e.g. 70, 113–15, 195–7, 239–40, 256, 310–12, 318; 1984a: 9–10). For Johnson, *'The fundamentional political problem of the state-guided high-growth system is that of the relationship between the state bureaucracy and privately owned businesses. If this relationship is overbalanced in favor of one side or the other, it will result in either the loss of the benefits of competition or the dilution of the state's priorities'* (1982: 196). In this light, recent studies highlighting the importance of government–business cooperation in Japan (e.g. Okimoto 1989; Samuels 1987), while providing richer accounts of that relationship, nevertheless appear to be extending, not overturning, the thrust of Johnson's argument.

10 In private discussion, Wade has indicated a preference for the notion of 'guidance' or 'leadership', rather than coordination, because the latter suggests the lack of a focal point for action. I do not wish to exclude guidance from the state's role as coordinator; on the contrary, it seems to me that the task of coordinating actors, actions, resources, policy measures and so on would not be possible without some sense of the goals to be accomplished (i.e. a focal point). Thus, when I use the term 'coordination' I also intend 'guidance through coordination'.

11 This conception is indebted to the work of Michael Mann (1984/1988). For a more extended discussion with comparative and historical applications, see Weiss and Hobson (1995).

12 For an argument that meritocratic criteria of recruitment do not always outweigh political considerations in fostering homogeneity and cohesion among the state elite, see Barnett (1992). On Israel, Barnett notes that conversion to more professional appointments actually weakened elite cohesion, 'for these new appointments were not concerned with the state's adherence to socialist–Zionist norms' (1992: 178).

13 For an important collection which examines the makings of Japan's famed civil service, see H.-K. Kim et al. (1995).

14 Steel is a much-studied early example of MITI's strengths in technology analysis (Lynn 1985). Recent examples include biotechnology and new materials. For a study of Japanese biotechnology see Fransman and Tanaka (1990).

15 KOTRA was modelled after the Japanese External Trade Organization (JETRO), the MITI-created organization for export promotion which was set up in the 1950s as an international intelligence service to provide, *inter alia*, the detailed market information that companies needed in order to address the problem of trading blindly.

16 Based on interviews conducted in Taiwan in September 1994 with the Industry Development Bureau, ERSO within ITRI, and the Taiwan Electrical Appliance Manufacturers' Association (TEAMA).

17 On the organization and development of the Korean bureaucracy, see Woo-Cumings (1995).

18 In Korea, inter-ministerial conflicts have increased as ministries have jockeyed for policy leadership. Jurisdictional conflicts between the EPB and individual ministries have also mounted in recent years in conjunction with the EPB's efforts to quicken liberalization in the financial sector and in imports.

19 This is not to deny that industrial bureaus are vital to industrial policy. As Johnson puts it, 'without them a ministry would not be close enough to industry to exercise real guidance or control and could achieve no more than general economic policy' (1982: 126).

20 For a persuasive argument along these lines, see Samuels's (1994) accomplished analysis of the development of 'technonationalism' in Japan. National systems of production and innovation, he argues, 'are more than aggregate expressions of domestic institutions and sectoral networks. They comprise shared values and beliefs that are confirmed and reconfirmed by the intimacy of shared national experience' (1994: 330).

21 For an informative discussion of the role of deliberative or consultative councils in general (*shingikai*), see F. Schwartz (1993). The role of deliberative councils is controversial. In the sphere of industry, it is often believed that council meetings merely authorize the draft guidelines presented by bureaucrats, while the real process of consultation, negotiation and decision-making takes place informally and bilaterally between ministry officials and the corporate actors concerned (e.g. Argarwala 1983: 22). On the other hand, however important the process of prior informal consultation, there seems little doubt that the most important economic councils, such as MITI's Industrial Structure Council, do make an important contribution to the policy-making process. But rather than handing down authoritative decisions, the significance of such councils appears to be that of encouraging 'expression and reconciliation of public and private interests' (F. Schwartz 1993: 241).

22 This and the following paragraph are based on Kuo (1995: 95–111, 169–91).

23 Initiated by the Ministry of Commerce and Industry, the meetings included business representatives (mainly trade associations and the conglomerates), along with labour leaders, economic ministry officials, legislators and ruling party representatives.

24 This and the following paragraph are based on Kuo (1995: 102ff).

25 On Japan's vigorous pursuit of technological autonomy, diffusion and nurturance as a way of achieving national security, see Samuels (1994). On the NICs' distinctive efforts as latecomers to create advantage in high-tech, see Mathews (1997a) and Mathews and Cho (forthcoming).

26 For an argument critical of the 'end of Japanese industrial policy' thesis, see chapter 7.

27 For fuller discussion of this concept, see chapter 7.
28 In the most recent obituary on the Japanese model, the *Wall Street Journal* proclaims (not for the first time) 'the fall of Japan as an economic role model', adding that this has 'the clarifying effect of showing who was right and wrong, and who we should heed in the future'. Having proclaimed the failure of socialism, the 'European welfare state' and 'Asian mercantilism', the article continues: 'All that's left now is American-style capitalism, more or less' (P.A. Gigot [1997] 'The Great Japan Debate is Over. Guess Who Won?', reprinted in *Asian Wall Street Journal*, 3 February). For a more sober view of the Japanese model's continuing viability, see the analysis of Sakakibara, writing as director-general of the Ministry of Finance's International Finance Bureau (1997: 79).
29 Moreover, there is some doubt as to how far one can generalize from the Japanese energy industry, given its quite special status (cf. Wade 1990a: 326–7).
30 Calder's (1993) business-led account of Japan's success has this quality. Callon's (1995) is the most recent study in this vein (see below).
31 However, Wade adds further categories of leadership and followership with the qualifiers 'big' and 'small'. 'Big followership' is when government helps firms to do more than they would have done anyway. However, as his definition suggests, it would seem that only 'big leadership' counts: i.e. 'government initiatives on a large enough scale to make a real difference in investment and production patterns in an industry' (1990b: 28).
32 On the importance of disciplined support in Korean development, see Amsden (1989) and Y. Woo (1991: 165); on Taiwan, see Y. Chu (1995: 790–1) and Wade (1993: 434).
33 If firms are eligible for a given form of assistance, they become beneficiaries of state support regardless of whether they achieve the outcomes for which the measure was intended. For this reason, what passes for industrial policy in Anglo-American settings is often described as 'hand-outs'. The World Bank (1993b: 167) makes a similar point in contrasting the policies of East Asia with the 'pork-barrel subsidies' of less successful industrializing countries.
34 Based on interviews with the TTF, Taipei, September 1994.
35 For this argument, see Tilton (1996), McKean (1993), Johnson (1982) and Okimoto (1989).
36 For a more detailed description of these alliances, see Mathews (1997b).
37 For a powerful portrayal 'from below' of the desperate conditions of the Brazilian poor, see Hecht (1994). On the topic of East Asian 'growth with equity', see Campos and Root (1996: esp. ch. 6).
38 This is an adaptation of Michael Mann's historical categories to more contemporary concerns; see chapter 1, n. 13. John Hall's (1985) historical and comparative analysis provides an early creative application of these concepts.
39 The relevant measures include inducements and disincentives to encourage the *chaebol* to divest themselves of certain subsidiaries and to concentrate on core activities; the promotion of small industry; and an emphasis on industry representation in policy deliberation councils. Interview with the secretary to the president for trade, industry, energy and communications affairs, Seoul, September 1994.

Chapter 4 Limits of the distributive state: Swedish model or global economy?

1 This distinction between goals and outcomes is neatly made by Bruce Scott (1985) in an illuminating discussion of the relationship between national strategies and economic performance.

2 For a comparison of national strategies which employs this concept, see Scott (1985: 106).

3 Sweden spends between 1.5 and 3 per cent of GDP annually on labour-market programmes, including public relief work, training, youth and disability programmes.

4 Whether or not one regards the pre-1990s Swedish system as 'corporatist' – to indicate negotiated wage setting between industry and labour on one hand, and negotiated policy-making between government, industry and labour on the other – it is clear that its functioning rested on the presence of highly centralized, encompassing organizations. Colin Crouch and others point out that neocorporatism goes well beyond Keynesianism. It is not just about demand management (or centralized wage setting). It is also a model of 'improving the quality of the labour force' and of providing other infrastructural public goods (Crouch 1993a: 345).

5 'Prominent examples', writes Pierson, 'include expansion of waiting days for unemployment and sickness benefits, a lowering of replacement rates of unemployment benefits (from 90 percent to 80 percent), a freeze on adjustments in child allowances, and a raise in the retirement age, from sixty-five to sixty-six' (1996: 172).

6 As a result of recent tax reforms, the revenue structure has shifted towards a more conservative system that taxes consumption. Whereas in 1989/90, income tax accounted for 27 per cent, social insurance 14 per cent and consumption taxes 42 per cent of public revenue, in 1991/92, the shares were 11 per cent, 18 per cent and 50 per cent, respectively (Auer and Riegler 1994: 23, n. 5).

7 In this period, Sweden recorded sharp declines in economic growth and industrial production, a more rapid rise in wage costs and domestic inflation than that experienced internationally, falling levels of savings and investment, and soaring budget and current account deficits financed by foreign borrowing (Henrekson et al. 1993: 21).

8 By comparison, over the next decade, foreign employment jumped 11 points to 37 per cent of the corporate total in 1987 (Pontusson 1992a: 322).

9 For data and further references, see Henrekson et al. (1993: 45 *passim*).

10 On problems with the functioning of the Swedish model, see Glyn (1995: 17–18).

11 For an argument which stresses the lessening of competitive pressure, rather than the intensification of international pressures, as the source of Sweden's economic weakness, see Henrekson et al. (1993).

12 This section is based on Colin Crouch (1993a: 224ff).

13 Andrew Glyn suggests this fact has received insufficient emphasis. He notes that because of falling productivity, 'consumption out of the average worker's earnings fell by nearly 2% per year', or 20 per cent all told for the 1973–85 period. While consumption grew with the credit boom and rising transfers in the latter part of the 1980s, this occurred in the context of falling

productivity growth, so that 'by 1990 consumption out of the average pay-packet was still 17% less than in 1973' (Glyn 1995: 17).

14 From the 1970s up to 1982, 'Hourly earnings rose at roughly the same rate in Sweden as in other OECD countries, or slightly less ... but between 1982 and 1986 were rising 2.5 per cent faster' (Crouch 1993a: 225). In the 1980s Swedish wage costs rose more rapidly than those of its main competitors – e.g. from 1982 to 1989, they rose by 76.5 per cent, compared with 64.9 per cent in Britain and 36.6 per cent in West Germany (Fulcher 1994: 205).

15 A large share of the pension funds initially went to endangered firms for bail-out operations and to Sweden's traditional paper and pulp industry. Thus the terms 'reactive', 'incoherent', 'bailout' and 'preservation of exist-ing structure' are those one most readily finds in the literature on Swedish 'industrial policy' (cf. Katzenstein 1985: 66, 67). See also Carlsson (1983: 3, 10) for a discussion of the industrial subsidy programme, which averaged $US2.4 billion per year throughout the 1970s, roughly 50 per cent more than the cost of labour-market measures.

16 More generally, for a detailed study which finds no clear evidence that high welfare state spending is related to competitive decline, see Pfaller et al. (1991).

17 The state's dependence on individual firms for industry intelligence has often had negative consequences, as in the case of shipbuilding, where mas-sive resources were channelled to firms with few prospects of recovery.

18 For an interesting contrasting argument, which suggests the adequacy of active labour-market policy in the Swedish case as a partial reason for its abstention from capital formation, see Pontusson (1991: 177).

19 Protection could be eschewed because Taiwan's own domestic market was not at the time significant for semiconductors. Electronics producers were dependent on foreign markets for advanced semiconductors while Taiwan was gearing up for simpler devices. See Mathews and Cho (forthcoming).

20 For a thoughtful exposition of this argument, see Kentworthy (1990), who in the end takes the view that while corporatist arrangements 'are not well suited for implementing industrial policies', selective intervention 'is neither logically nor institutionally precluded' (1990: 258). See also Pontusson's conclusion to his larger study (1992b: 236).

21 It contrasts directly with the Japanese approach, which has been to subsi-dize and upgrade smaller, 'inefficient' firms in particular sectors, in order to maintain earnings and employment (whether waged or self-employed) in the private sector rather than expanding public employment (see chapter 5).

22 Between 1976 and 1980 shipbuilding and steel companies received some $US7 billion in loan guarantees, many of which were subsequently national-ized; another $US4 billion was allocated in direct grants and equity infu-sions 'to support bankrupt companies'. Such massive expenditures 'in a government budget already in serious deficit made support programs for growing industries and for R&D and training hard to fund adequately' (Magaziner and Patinkin 1990: 352).

23 Winton Higgins (1996: 7) maintains that the original Rehn–Meidner model contained an industry policy component but that this was quickly sup-pressed and remained so for three related reasons: strong and sustained resistance from private industry; the experience of full employment since World War II, which removed one important justification for such intervention;

and the growing influence of economic liberalism within the political elite, including the SDP.

Chapter 5 Dualistic states: Germany in the Japanese mirror

1 On increasing inequality in Korea, see various chapters in Borregos et al. (1996). On income distribution in the region, see Campos and Root (1996).
2 In spite of well-known similarities in German and Japanese development patterns, there is surprisingly little literature that directly compares these, past or present. For suggestive material, see Johnson (1995: 54–5) and Wever and Allen (1993: 190).
3 On the critical role of the state in fostering the development of long-term credit, see R. Tilly (1989), Vitols (1995) and Deeg (1997).
4 This section is based on Allen (1989).
5 While 'this stress on capital goods and exports left many workers without access to consumer goods', healthy growth rates of 8 to 9 per cent annually paved the way for higher wages, while the system of social welfare 'provided tangible benefits for the working class' (Allen 1989: 287). For further discussion of postwar German economic policy and its odd relationship to Keynesianism, see Matzner and Streeck (1991).
6 Further suggestive evidence of a 'producer economics' in Germany (as contrasted with consumer-oriented Britain and America) can be found in King and Fullerton's (1984) comparative study of how governments take different approaches to the taxation of income from capital, creating powerful incentives either to reinvest or to consume or export profits.
7 On government targeting of sectors and technologies in the postwar period, see Katzenstein (1985: 68–92).
8 Reich argues that the BFM, whose leading officials were Christian Democratic Union (CDU) members, housed the strongest opponents of Erhard's neoliberal policies. They stressed a strategic approach to industrial development based on collaboration with organized labour and business (1990: 187).
9 Germany's report to the OECD in 1975, concerning the aims and instruments of its industrial policy, states that there is no concept of an 'independent industrial policy' in that country (cited in Abromeit 1990: 61). In addition to Abromeit, see also Streeck (1989) for an account which argues along similar lines.
10 See Coleman (1990: 244–5) for an analysis of the role of Germany's comprehensive business associations.
11 On technology policy see Ziegler (1995: 362), discussed in more detail below.
12 On the state's role in the national system of innovation see Ziegler (1995), Keck (1993), Burton and Hansen (1993) and Collis (1988). On the concept of a national innovation system, see Nelson (1993).
13 The three agencies involved are the Ministries for Education and Science (BMBW), Defence (BMVg) and Economics (BMWI), which together commanded 37 per cent of the budget in 1989.
14 Engineers are certainly a major component of the state-sponsored innovation conducted by the FI, which also house a 'mission-oriented' capacity,

but because the FI must be partly self-funding through industry contracts, there has until recently been little industry support for the riskier, long-term kinds of research whose commercial payoffs are uncertain. This too suggests that the distribution of expertise is not a rigid determinant, but that the state can and does make a difference.

15 For a contrasting account of the bank's role which updates this understanding, see Deeg (1994, 1997).

16 The lack of venture capital for new start-ups is often cited as a cause of technology conservatism in Germany, but the same could be said of Japan, where the outcomes are quite different. Hence a different explanation is required.

17 At the same time of course Japan has expanded dramatically into high-tech markets. World high-tech trade expanded ninefold between 1975 and 1986. During this period, Japan doubled its share of high-tech exports, displacing the USA as the leading nation (Ruigrok and van Tulder 1995: 143).

18 Pre-unification Germany always had a massive trade surplus, amounting to 64 billion ECU in 1989, and an estimated 47 billion in 1995.

19 Germany's costs are about 15 per cent above the EU average; EU costs are 9 per cent above US costs, and 20 per cent higher than in Japan (Aiginger 1995).

20 This section is based on Richard Deeg (1997: 53–74).

21 To the extent that German banks still play an important role in industrial finance compared to other countries, Deeg (1997) argues that this is because they are a crucial source of capital for the *Mittelstand*.

22 As supplier to the large metal-working industry, this sector's health is vital to that of manufacturing as a whole. Ziegler (1994) notes how the ministry brought the different actors together, publicized the problem to be tackled, and devised the necessary instruments and programmes for the task at hand.

23 Simon Reich (1990: 319) provides an illuminating account of the saga of preserving Daimler-Benz from foreign acquisition.

24 Ziegler (1995) argues that the precedent for this approach was the SDP programme for micro-electronics instituted in 1979; the Christian Democrats simply extended it to other technologies. Since the early 1980s, the government has targeted four priority technologies – biotechnology, production engineering, information technology/microsystems and materials research – via such measures as encouragement of inter-firm collaboration on science and technology, a greater public role in technology transfer, and promotion of small and medium-sized industry (Burton and Hansen 1993: 46).

25 On policy-making as a 'negotiated model of adjustment' which gives the state considerable capacity for coordinating change, see Wever and Allen (1993: 185, 186, 197, 198) and Huelshoff (1992: 11, 12) on adjustment in steel. On 'institutionalized access' which allows industry associations close involvement in the formulation and administration of relevant public programmes, see Burton and Hansen (1993: 44) and Abromeit (1990: 63). On the 'extensive communication between policy experts and technical experts' in the framing of technology programmes, see Ziegler (1995).

26 Under the new technology drive from the centre, it seems that key federal agencies have maintained considerable coordinating capacity. The Ministry of Education and Technology has broken with the practice of distributing

federal grants in turns rather than on merit. Instead, states now have to compete for grants (*The Economist* [1995], 28 October).

27 Allen comments on the disciplinary nature of the Federal Republic of Germany's (FRG) tax policies used to stimulate investment-led growth, as compared with the lax approach towards tax cuts under the Reagan administration (1989: 286), where no performance outcomes of any kind were stipulated. Similarly, Huelshoff (1992: 11–13) observes how the FRG government was more effective than its European Community (EC) neighbours in restructuring the steel industry, minimizing subsidization while tying this to capacity reductions. By contrast, in France, Italy and Belgium, firms drew huge state subsidies while failing to meet capacity cuts.

28 Pierson (1996: 166). Pierson argues that Germany's welfare state, in contrast to Sweden's, is based not on maximizing employment but on subsidizing 'the "outsiders" who are encouraged to leave the labor market to those who are highly productive. ... by far the largest and most expensive group of outsiders consisting of former insiders: pensioners and early retirees' (p. 167).

29 For an overly pessimistic account, see Crouch and Streeck (1997); for a rejoinder, see Dore (1997).

30 Reported in the *International Herald Tribune* (1997: [24 May]). Compare also the important public statement of MOF official, Eisuke Sakakibara, otherwise known as 'Mr Yen', writing recently as director general of the International Finance Bureau in *The Economist* (1997: [February]).

31 In a moment of pessimism Crouch and Streeck (1997) have tended to interpret Germany's rising unemployment and Japan's long recession as evidence that alternative models to neoliberal capitalism are no longer sustainable. Much of their argument assumes competition between high-cost Germany with Western Europe and the 'cheap-labour' economies of East Asia (from which they exclude the high-wage economy of Japan). However, this loses sight of the fact that for Germany, the most serious competition has come not from low-cost East Asia in general, but from Japan in particular. This makes Crouch and Streeck's argument and conclusions somewhat problematic and their pessimism misplaced.

32 In this respect, and unlike the Scandinavian idea of universal rights to a 'citizen's wage', Japan's public programmes are more similar to those of the United States (cf. S. Anderson 1993: 153).

33 These programmes provided subsidies to both large and small employers to retain their employees (with somewhat larger subsidies to smaller firms).

34 Reported in the *Washington Post* (1997), 5 May.

35 According to Pempel and Muramatsu (1995: 36), Japan's ruling conservatives have sought precisely this outcome. For a comparison of social policies in Japan and Germany which uses the concept of 'welfare society', see Leibfried (1994).

36 Some analysts suggest that the IT boom is too contained to generate multiplier effects in the form of an economy-wide upgrading of skills, wages and standards of living. Indeed, the absence of any evidence of productivity growth suggests that the current boom is based on a greater number of people working, longer working hours, falling wages, and a lower dollar (cf. Economic Policy Institute 1996).

37 Though there is surely no reason why institutional learning and adaptation

should be all one way. After all, the Japanese have been past masters at borrowing, and above all at *adapting* and *learning* from the developmental practices of their Western competitors.

Chapter 6 The limits of globalization

1 For an influential argument along these lines emphasizing the social and political consequences of state decline, see Vivien Schmidt (1995).
2 For a fresh perspective on globalization more generally, see Michael Mann (1996).
3 Orthodox globalists include Ohmae (1990), R. Reich (1992) and Horsman and Marshall (1994). For a more complex version, which suggests a hierarchy rather than convergence of national power relative to MNCs, see Perraton et al. (1997).
4 This position is best expressed by *The Economist* (e.g. [1995], 7 October), which holds that the state never had the (macro-economic planning) powers it is said to have lost, and that those powers it continues to have are still (regrettably) significant.
5 This position is exemplified by Hirst and Thompson's study (1996).
6 For studies supporting such a conclusion, see the excellent volume edited by Banuri and Schor (1992). Further references can be found in Hirst and Thompson (1996: 28).
7 This and the following paragraph are based on Griffith-Jones and Stallings (1995).
8 See, for example, papers by Lynne Guyton and Anuwar Ali in Borregos et al. (1996).
9 The following two paragraphs are based on Wade's account.
10 According to the Federal Reserve Board of New York, some $US650 billion each day is transacted in foreign exchange dealings in London, Tokyo and New York. Of these transactions, Howard Wachtel writes that 'only about 18 percent support either international trade or investment – the ostensible reasons for foreign-exchange markets. The other 82 percent is speculation' (1995: 36).
11 In their concluding chapter, Hollingsworth et al. (1994: 295) point out that the only example of an MNC in their entire set of studies 'that seems to be abandoning its home base' is Britain's chemical company ICI, as it moves more activities to the United States. 'But this apparent cosmopolitanism may itself be a national trait, given the historical footlooseness of British capital and the notorious inhospitability of the British institutional environment to manufacturing industry.' Nor does movement from one Anglo-Saxon setting to another appear to warrant the 'cosmopolitan' label.
12 For a useful collection which shows how European multinational firms are embedded in national contexts, see Whitley and Kristensen (1996); also Sally (1994). The importance of national institutions for firm advantage is also highlighted by Hirst and Thompson (1996) and Porter (1986).

Chapter 7 The myth of the powerless state

1 Compare, for example, recent accounts of the 'end of the Japanese model'

in the *Wall Street Journal* (November 1996) with the more sober outlook of MOF chief Eisuke Sakakibara (1997), the so-called 'Mr Yen', in *The Economist*. While Japan has clearly been going through an adjustment crisis in recent years, seeking to temper productivism with a greater emphasis on a consumption-based developmental pattern, one cannot readily deduce from this that fundamental changes to its model of economic management are afoot. For an analysis critical of what it sees as 'current distortions', see Itoh (1994).

2 See for example, *The Economist* ([1995], 7 October: 15). For an argument that demand management policies worked most effectively at the level of investor expectations rather than through 'mechanistic plugging in of a certain quantity of expenditure', see Graham (1990: 4).

3 The contrasting 'globalist' argument can be found in Sven Steinmo (1994).

4 On 'The Underdevelopment of Keynesianism in the Federal Republic of Germany', see Allen (1989).

5 It should be clear from preceding chapters that by a 'strong' state I mean not a coercive state but one with the organizational capacity for governing industrial transformation. For a larger comparative and historical discussion of strong and weak states, see Weiss and Hobson (1995) and Hobson (1997).

6 Gøsta Esping-Andersen and his international colleagues are currently working on a large project relevant to this issue, documenting the life-cycle changes that have occurred as a result of labour-market developments.

7 I am indebted to William Coleman for this observation, which was made in a personal communication. As he shows in his studies of banking policy in France (1996), the French state's ability to pursue a credit-led industrial strategy relied not simply on micro-economic tools, but on a particular approach to monetary policy in combination with a highly segmented, regulated banking sector, and hence on a mix of macro- and micro-policy instruments.

8 The reference in this section's heading is to the title of Sanjaya Lall's critique of the World Bank (1993a) *East Asian Miracle* study (Lall 1993).

9 For an earlier version of this theme stressing the 'end of industrial policy', see Saxonhouse (1983) and Yamamura (1986).

10 For a more detailed argument along these lines, focusing on Japan's industrial policy in the 1990s, see OTA (1991).

11 Interviews conducted in Taipei, March–April 1997.

12 For a succinct account of the continuing advantages of an industrial policy, see Kentworthy (1990). A lucid statement of the transformative role that states can play beyond that of protection for infant industry is provided by David Levi-Faur (1997), on the basis of an analysis of Friedrich List's political economy.

13 Under MITI's guidance companies can request up to two-thirds of the cost of commercializing technology developed by universities and government research institutes; similar measures apply to small firms for technology development (JPRI 1996: 2).

14 In the 1980s, Japan's industrial adjustment policy was primarily concerned with industries where Japan had lost comparative advantage. Typical forms of support included low-interest loans, special tax measures, and promotion of cartels to help small firms to innovate, upgrade and find new markets

(typically in textiles), to assist large firms to diversify via development of new high-tech materials (as in the steel industry), and to facilitate the smooth transfer of resources from endangered sectors (mining, aluminium smelting, shipbuilding and so forth) to other industries. Under the 1983 Temporary Measures Law for the Structural Adjustment of Specific Industries, the government designated twenty-six industries, where 'structural improvement' policies were implemented. The success of these measures is indicated to some degree by the fact that 'Actual scrapped capacity amounted to an average of 98.4% of the initial targets in 26 sectors, before the law was abolished in 1988.' In tandem with these measures, government funded between a quarter and two-thirds of the costs related to the retraining and transfer of workers to other jobs (Goto and Irie 1990).

15 For an overview of MITI's industrial strategies in the 1980s and 1990s, focusing on areas of technology development, see Komiya and Yokobori (1991). As part of its 'technology development policy', in 1988 MITI allocated almost 70 billion yen, dedicated to projects in four major areas: on 'Basic Technologies for Future Industries' (superconductivity, new materials, biotechnology and future electron devices), on the 'National Research and Development Program (Large-Scale Project)', on alternative energy sources (the so-called 'Sunshine Project') and on energy-saving technology (the 'Moonlight Project'). Of these, the last two consumed more than half the budget (35.4 billion). The grand total of almost 70 billion yen can be compared with the government's share of 29 billion for the famous 1970s VLSI project, spent over four years.

16 For an account of the East Asian developmental experience which emphasizes this feature of accountability in decision-making, see Root (1996).

17 The literature on this topic is vast. For an important synthesis see Michael Mann's chapter on 'The Decline of Great Britain' (in Mann 1988); also Weiss and Hobson (1995: ch. 7); and Hobson (1997).

18 For an intriguing account of the contests between Japanese and World Bank officials, representing opposing models of capitalism, in the making of the controversial World Bank *East Asia Miracle Report*, see Wade (1996b).

19 On MITI's influence on foreign aid as an export tool, see Orr (1990).

20 As cited in the *Far Eastern Economic Review* collection (1991: 116–17).

21 The three strategies are described in Y. Chu (1995: 221).

22 For a suggestive analysis of Singaporean economic and social policy choices along these lines, see Ramesh (1995).

23 I am grateful to Victor Sumsky for the observation about Russia.

24 See Jenkins (1991) for a productive application of these concepts to an analysis of the role of states in determining comparative advantage in telecommunications.

BIBLIOGRAPHY

Abelshauser, Werner 1983: *Wirtschaftsgeschichte der Bundesrepublik Deutschland (1945–1980)*. Frankfurt: Suhrkamp.

Abernathy, William J., Clark, Kim B. and Kantrow, Alan M. 1981: The New Industrial Competition. *Harvard Business Review* (Sept.–Oct.), 68–81.

Abromeit, Heidrun 1990: Government–Industry Relations in West Germany. In Chick (1990).

Aiginger, Karl 1995: A Framework for Evaluation: The Dynamic Competitiveness of Countries, *Working Paper No. 3*. Birmingham: Research Centre for Industrial Strategy.

Allen, Christopher 1989: The Underdevelopment of Keynesianism in the Federal Republic of Germany. In Peter Hall (ed.) *The Political Power of Economic Ideas: Keynesianism across Nations*, Princeton NJ: Princeton University Press.

Amsden, Alice H. 1988: Private Enterprise: The Issue of Business–Government Control. *Columbia Journal of World Business* (Spring), 37–42.

Amsden, Alice H. 1989: *Asia's Next Giant*. New York: Oxford University Press.

Amsden, Alice H. 1992: A Theory of Government in Late Industrialization. In L. Patterman and D. Reuschemeyer (eds) *State and Market in Development: Synergy or Rivalry?*, Boulder CO: Lynne Rienner.

Amsden, Alice H. 1993: Asia's Industrial Revolution. *Dissent* (Summer), 40, 324–32.

Amsden, Alice H. 1994: The Specter of Anglo-Saxonization is Haunting South Korea. In Cho and Kim (1994).

Anchordoguy, Marie 1988: Mastering the Market: Japanese Government Targeting of the Computer Industry. *International Organization*, 42 (3), 509–43.

Anderson, Perry 1974: *Lineages of the Absolutist State*. London: Verso.

Anderson, Stephen 1993: *Welfare Policy and Politics in Japan: Beyond the Developmental State*. New York: Paragon House.

Appelbaum, R. and Henderson, J. (eds) 1992: *States and Development in the Asian Pacific Rim*. London: Sage.

Argarwala, R. (ed.), 1983: *The Japanese and Korean Experiences in Managing Development*. Washington DC: World Bank.

Atkinson, Michael M. and Coleman, William D. 1989: Strong States and Weak States: Sectoral Policy Networks in Advanced Capitalist Economies. *British Journal of Political Science*, 19, 47–67.

Audretsch, David B. 1993: Industrial Policy and International Competitiveness. In P. Nicolaides (ed.) *Industrial Policy in the European Community: A Necessary Response to Economic Integration?*. The Hague: European Institute of Public Administration.

Audretsch, David B. 1995: The Innovation, Unemployment and Competitiveness Challenge in Germany. *Discussion Paper*. Berlin: WZB.

Auer, Peter and Riegler, Claudius H. 1994: Sweden: The End of Full Employment. *InforMISEP* (European Commission) (Summer), 46, 16–23.

Bank of Korea, various years: *Economics Statistics Yearbook*. Seoul: Bank of Korea.

Banuri, Tariq and Schor, Juliet B. (eds) 1992: *Financial Openness and National Autonomy*. Oxford: Clarendon Press.

Barkey, Karen and Parikh, Sunita 1991: Comparative Perspectives on the State. *Annual Review of Sociology*, 17, 523–49.

Barnett, Michael 1992: *Confronting the Costs of War: Military Power, State and Society*. Princeton NJ: Princeton University Press.

Berger, Suzanne and Dore, Ronald (eds) 1996: *National Diversity and Global Capitalism*. Ithaca NY: Cornell University Press.

Bergsten, C. Fred and Noland, Marcus (eds) 1993: *Pacific Dynamism and the International Economic System*. Washington DC: Institute for International Economics.

Bernard, Mitchell and Ravenhill, John 1995: Beyond Product Cycles and Flying Geese: Regionalization, Hierarchy, and the Industrialization of East Asia. *World Politics*, 47 (2), 171–210.

Best, Michael 1990: *The New Competition*. Cambridge MA: Harvard University Press.

Blank, Stephen 1978: Britain: The Politics of Foreign Economic Policy, the Domestic Economy, and the Problem of Pluralistic Stagnation. In Katzenstein (1978b).

Borregos, J., Bejar, A.A. and Jomo, K.S. (eds) 1996: *Capital, the State and Late Industrialization*. Boulder CO: Westview Press.

Braunthal, G. 1963: *The Federation of German Industry in Politics*. Ithaca NY: Cornell University Press.

Burton, Daniel F. and Hansen, Kathleen M. 1993: German Technology Policy: Incentive for Industrial Innovation. *Challenge!* (Jan.–Feb.), 37–47.

Calder, Kent 1988: *Crisis and Compensation: Public Policy and Political Stability*. Princeton NJ: Princeton University Press.

Calder, Kent E. 1993: *Strategic Capitalism*. Princeton NJ: Princeton University Press.

Callon, Scott 1995: *Divided Sun: MITI and the Breakdown of Japanese High-Tech Industrial Policy, 1975–1993*. Stanford CA: Stanford University Press.

Campos, J. and Root, H. 1996: *The Key to the Asian Miracle*. Washington DC: Brookings Institution.

Carlin, Wendy and Soskice, David 1997: Shocks to the System: The German Political Economy Under Stress. *National Institute Economic Review* (January), 159, 57–76.

Carlsson, Bo 1983: Industrial Subsidies in Sweden: Macro Economic Effects and an International Comparison. *Journal of Industrial Economics*, 32 (1), 1–23.

Casper, Steven and Vitols, Sigurt 1997: The German Model in the 1990s: Problems and Prospects. *Industry and Innovation*, 4 (1), 1–14.

Chan, S. 1993: *East Asian Dynamism*. Boulder CO: Westview Press.

Chang, Ha-Joon 1994: *The Political Economy of Industrial Policy*. London: Macmillan.

Cho, Lee-Jay and Kim, Yoon Hyung (eds) 1994: *Korea's Political Economy: An Institutional Perspective*. Boulder CO: Westview Press.

Choi, Byung-Sun 1987: The Structure of Economic Policy-making Institutions in Korea and the Strategic Role of the Economic Planning Board. *Korean Journal of Policy Studies*, 2 (1), 1–28.

Choi, Byung-Sun 1991: The Politics of Financial Control and Reform in Korea. *Korean Journal of Policy Studies*, 6 (1), 41–73.

Chu, Wan-Wen 1994: Import Substitution and Export-led Growth: A Study of Taiwan's Petrochemical Industry. *World Development*, 22 (5), 790–1.

Chu, Yun-han 1989: State Structure and Economic Adjustment of the East Asian Newly Industrializing Countries. *International Organization*, 43 (4), 647–72.

Chu, Yun-han 1995: The East Asian NICs: A State-led Path to the Developed World. In Stallings (1995).

Colander, D. (ed.) 1984: *Neoclassical Political Economy*. Cambridge MA: Ballinger.

Coleman, William D. 1990: State Traditions and Comprehensive Business Associations: A Comparative Structural Analysis. *Political Studies*, 38, 231–52.

Coleman, William D. 1996: *Financial Services, Globalization, and Domestic Policy Change: A Comparison of North America and the European Union*. Basingstoke: Macmillan.

Collis, David 1988: The Machine Tool Industry and Industrial Policy, 1955–82. In A. Spence and H. Hazard (eds) *International Competitiveness*, Cambridge MA: Harper and Row.

Crouch, Colin (ed.) 1979: *State and Economy in Contemporary Capitalism*. London: Croom Helm.

Crouch, Colin 1985: Conditions for Trade Union Wage Restraint. In L. Lindberg and C. Maier (eds) *The Politics of Inflation and Economic Stagnation*. Washington DC: Brookings Institution.

Crouch, Colin 1993a: *Industrial Relations and European State Traditions*. Oxford: Clarendon Press.

Crouch, Colin 1993b: Co-operation and Competition in an Institutionalised Economy: The Case of Germany. In Colin Crouch and David Marquand (eds) *Ethics and Markets: Co-operation and Competition within Capitalist Economies*, Oxford: Blackwell.

Crouch, Colin forthcoming: The Terms of the Neo-liberal Consensus. *Political Quarterly*, special post-election issue.

Crouch, Colin and Streeck, Wolfgang (eds) 1996: *Modern Capitalism or Modern Capitalisms?*. London: Francis Pinter.

Crouch, Colin and Streeck, Wolfgang 1997: Il futuro della diversità dei capitalismi. *Stato e Mercato* (Apr.), 49, 3–30.

Dankbaar, B. 1994: Sectoral Governance in the Automobile Industries of Germany, Great Britain, and France. In Hollingsworth et al. (1994).

Deeg, Richard 1994: Banking on the East: The Political Economy of Investment

Finance in Eastern Germany. *Discussion Papers FS 194–303*, Berlin: Wissenschaftszentrum Berlin fur Sozialforschung (WZB).

Deeg, Richard 1997: Banks and Industrial Finance in the 1990s. *Industry and Innovation*, 4 (1), 53–74.

Deyo, F. (ed.) 1987: *The Political Economy of the New Asian Industrialism.* Ithaca NY: Cornell University Press.

Doner, Richard F. 1992: Limits of State Strength: Toward an Institutionalist View of Economic Development. *World Politics*, 44 (3), 398–431.

Dore, Ronald 1987: *Taking Japan Seriously*. Stanford CA: Stanford University Press.

Dore, Ronald 1996: La globalizzazione dei mercati e la diversità dei capitalismi. *Il Mulino* (Nov.–Dec), 368, 1017–26.

Dore, Ronald 1997: Un commento. *State e Mercato* (Apr.), 49, 31–8.

Dyson, Kenneth 1980: *The State Tradition in Western Europe: A Study of an Idea and Institution*. Oxford: Martin Robertson.

Easton, D. 1981: The Political System Besieged by the State. *Political Theory* (Aug.), 9, 303–25.

Economic Policy Institute 1996: *The State of Working America 1996–97*. Washington DC: Economic Policy Institute.

Edquist, Charles and Lundvall, Bengt-Ake 1993: Comparing the Danish and Swedish Systems of Innovation. In R. Nelson (ed.) *National Innovation Systems*, New York: Oxford University Press.

Epstein, G. 1995: International Financial Integration and Full Employment Monetary Policy. *Review of Political Economy*, 7 (2), 164–85.

Esping-Andersen, Gøsta 1990: *Three Worlds of Welfare Capitalism*. Cambridge: Polity Press.

Esping-Andersen, Gøsta 1996: Positive-Sum Solutions in a World of Trade-Offs? In G. Esping-Andersen (ed.) *Welfare State in Transition: National Adaptations in Global Economies*. London: Sage.

Esser, Josef and Fach, Wolfgang 1989: Crisis Management 'Made in Germany': The Steel Industry. In Katzenstein (1989).

Esser, Josef and Fach, Wolfgang with Dyson, Kenneth 1987: 'Social Market' and Modernization Policy: West Germany. In Kenneth Dyson and Stephen Wilks (eds) *Industrial Crisis: A Comparative Study of the State and Industry*. New York: St Martin's Press.

Evans, Peter 1989: Predatory, Developmental and Other Apparatuses: A Comparative Political Economy Perspective on the Third World State. *Sociological Forum*, 4, 233–46.

Evans, Peter B. 1992: The State as Problem and Solution: Predation, Embedded Autonomy, and Structural Change. In S. Haggard and R.R. Kaufman (eds) *The Politics of Economic Adjustment*, Princeton NJ: Princeton University Press.

Evans, Peter B. 1995: *Embedded Autonomy: States and Industrial Transformation*. Princeton NJ: Princeton University Press.

Evans, Peter B., Reuschemeyer, Dieter, and Skocpol, Theda 1985: *Bringing the State Back In*. New York: Cambridge University Press.

Executive Yuan, various years: *Statistical Yearbook of the Republic of China*. Taipei: Directorate-General of Budget, Accounting and Statistics, Executive Yuan.

Fallows, James 1994: *Looking at the Sun*. New York: Pantheon.

232   *Bibliography*

Far Eastern Economic Review 1991: *Japan in Asia.* Hong Kong: FEER.
Ferguson, Charles and Morris, Charles 1995: *Computer Wars: The Fall of IBM and the Future of Global Technology.* Harmondsworth: Penguin.
Fingleton, Eamonn 1995: *Blindside.* New York: Simon and Schuster.
Fishlow, Albert 1990: The Latin American State. *Journal of Economic Perspectives,* 4 (3), 61–74.
Fong, Glenn R. 1990: State Strength, Industry Structure, and Industrial Policy: American and Japanese Experiences in Microelectronics. *Comparative Politics* (Apr.), 22, 273–99.
Fransman, Martin 1990: *The Market and Beyond: Information Technology in Japan.* Cambridge and New York: Cambridge University Press.
Freeman, Christopher (ed.) 1987: *Technology Policy and Economic Performance: Lessons from Japan.* London: Pinter.
Friedman, D. 1988: *The Misunderstood Miracle.* Cambridge MA: MIT Press.
Fulcher, James 1991: *Labour Movements, Employers and the State: Conflict and Co-operation in Britain and Sweden.* Oxford: Clarendon Press.
Fulcher, James 1994: The Social Democratic Model: Termination or Restoration? *Political Quarterly,* 65 (2), 203–15.
Gamble, Andrew 1981: *Britain in Decline.* London: Macmillan.
Gamble, Andrew 1995: The New Political Economy. *Political Studies,* XLIII, 516–30.
Garon, Sheldon and Mochizuki, Mike 1993: Negotiating Social Contracts. In A. Gordon (ed.) *Postwar Japan as History,* Berkeley: University of California Press.
Garrett, Geoffrey and Lange, Peter 1991: Political Responses to Interdependence: What's Left for the Left? *International Organization,* 45 (4), 539–64.
Garrett, Geoffrey and Lange, Peter 1986: Performance in a Hostile World: Economic Growth in Capitalist Democracies, 1974–1982. *World Politics* (July), 38, 517–45.
Gerschenkron, Alexander 1962: *Economic Backwardness in Historical Perspective.* Cambridge MA: Harvard University Press.
Giddens, Anthony 1985: *The Nation State and Violence.* Cambridge: Polity Press.
Giersch, H., Paque, K., and Schmieding, H. 1992: *The Fading Miracle: Four Decades of Market Economy in Germany.* New York: Cambridge University Press.
Glyn, Andrew 1995: Social Democracy and Full Employment. *Discussion Paper No. FS 195–302.* Berlin: WZB.
Godet, Michel 1989: West Germany: A Paradoxical Power. *Futures* (Aug.), 344–60.
Gold, Thomas B. 1986: *State and Society in the Taiwan Miracle.* New York: M.E. Sharpe.
Goldthorpe, John H. (ed.) 1984: *Order and Conflict in Contemporary Capitalism.* Oxford: Clarendon Press.
Goto, Fumihiro and Irie, Kazutomo 1990: *The Theoretical Basis of Industrial Policy: Toward a New Horizon in the 1990s.* Tokyo: MITI Research Institute.
Gourevitch, Peter 1978: The Second Image Reversed: The International Sources of Domestic Politics. *International Organization,* 32 (4), 881–911.
Graham, Andrew 1990: Introduction. In A. Graham and A. Seldon (eds) *Government and Economies in the Postwar World.* London, New York: Routledge.

Grant, Wyn, Paterson, William and Whitson, Colin 1988: *Government and the Chemical Industry: A Comparative Study of Britain and West Germany.* Oxford: Clarendon Press.

Griffith-Jones, Stephany and Stallings, Barbara 1995: New Global Financial Trends: Implications for Development. In Stallings (1995).

Grindley, P., Mowery, D. and Silverman, B. 1994: Sematech and Collaborative Research: Lessons in the Design of High Tech Consortia. *Journal of Policy Analysis and Management,* 13 (4), 723–58.

Haggard, S. and Kaufman, Robert. 1989: The Politics of Stabilization and Structural Adjustment. In Jeffrey Sachs (ed.), *Developing Country Debt and Economic Performance I: The International Financial System,* Chicago: University of Chicago Press.

Haggard, Stephan and Moon, Chung-In 1990: Institutions and Economic Policy: Theory and a Korean Case Study. *World Politics,* 42 (2), 210–37.

Hall, John A. 1985: *Powers and Liberties.* Oxford: Blackwell.

Hall, John A. (ed.) 1986: *States in History.* Oxford: Blackwell.

Hall, Peter A. 1986: *Governing the Economy: The Politics of State Intervention in Britain and France.* New York: Oxford University Press.

Hall, Peter 1995: The Political Economies of Europe in an Era of Interdependence. Paper presented to a Roundtable of the International Political Science Association, Kyoto, Japan, 12 March 1994.

Hane, G.J. 1992: Research and Development Consortia in Innovation in Japan: Case Studies in Superconductivity and Engineering Ceramics. PhD thesis, Harvard University.

Hart, Jeffrey A. 1986: West German Industrial Policy. In C.E. Barfield and W.W. Schambra (eds) *The Politics of Industry Policy,* Washington, DC: American Enterprise Institute for Public Policy Research.

Hart, Jeffrey A. and Tyson, Lara 1989: Responding to the Challenge of HDTV. *California Management Review,* 31 (4), 132–45.

Hecht, Susanna B. 1994: Love and Death in Brazil. *New Left Review* (Mar./Apr.), 204, 129–37.

Held, David 1991: Democracy, the Nation-state and the Global System. *Economy and Society,* 20 (2), 138–72.

Held, David 1995: *Democracy and the Global Order: From the Modern State to Cosmopolitan Governance.* Cambridge: Polity Press.

Held, David and McGrew, Anthony 1993: Globalization and the Liberal Democratic State. *Government and Opposition,* 28, 261–85.

Helleiner, Eric 1995: Explaining the Globalization of Financial Markets: Bringing States Back In. *Review of International Political Economy,* 2 (2), 315–41.

Helleiner, G.K. (ed.) 1994: *Trade Policy and Industrialization in Turbulent Times.* London: Routledge.

Henrekson, Magnus, Jonung, Lars and Stymne, Joakim 1993: Economic Growth and the Swedish Model. *Working Paper No. 118.* Stockholm: Trade Union Institute for Economic Research (FIEF).

Herrigel, Gary B. 1989: Industrial Order and the Politics of Industrial Change: Mechanical Engineering. In Katzenstein (1989).

Herrigel, Gary B. 1994: Industry as a Form of Order: A Comparison of the Historical Development of the Machine Tool Industries in the United States and Germany. In Hollingsworth et al. (1994).

Higgins, Winton 1996: Which Swedish Model? Unpublished manuscript, Macquarie University, Sydney.
Hirono, Ryokichi 1988: Model for East Asian Industrialisation? In H. Hughes (ed.) *Achieving Industrialisation in East Asia*, New York: Cambridge University Press.
Hirst, Paul and Thompson, Grahame 1995: Globalization and the Future of the Nation State. *Economy and Society*, 24 (3), 408–42.
Hirst, Paul and Thompson, Grahame 1996: *Globalization in Question*. Cambridge: Polity Press.
Hobson, John M. 1997: *The Wealth of States: A Comparative Study of International Economic and Political Change*. New York: Cambridge University Press.
Hollingsworth, J. Rogers, Schmitter, Philippe C., and Streeck, Wolfgang 1994: *Governing Capitalist Economies*. New York: Oxford University Press.
Horn, Ernst-Jurgen 1987: Germany: A Market-led Process. In F. Duchene and G. Shepherd (eds) *Managing Change in Western Europe*, New York: Pinter.
Horsman, M. and Marshall, A. 1994: *After the Nation State*. London: HarperCollins.
Hu, Yao-Su 1992: Global or Stateless Corporations are National Firms with International Operations. *California Management Review* (Winter), 107–26.
Huelshoff, Michael G. 1992: Corporatist Bargaining and International Politics: Regimes, Multinational Corporations, and Adjustment Policy in the Federal Republic of Germany. *Comparative Political Studies*, 25 (1), 3–25.
Ikenberry, G. John 1986: The Irony of State Strength: Comparative Responses to the Oil Shocks in the 1970s. *International Organization*, 40 (1), 105–37.
Ikenberry, G. John 1988: *Reasons of State: Oil Politics and the Capacities of American Government*. Ithaca NY: Cornell University Press.
Ikenberry, G. John 1995: Funk de Siècle: Impasses of Western Industrial Society at Century's End. *Millenium*, 24 (1), 113–26.
IMF 1995a: *Government Finance Statistics Yearbook*. Washington DC: IMF.
IMF 1995b: *Government Finance Statistics Yearbook*. Washington DC: IMF.
Itoh, Makoto 1994: Is the Japanese Economy in Crisis? *Review of International Political Economy*, 1 (1), 29–51.
Iversen, Torben 1996: Power, Flexibility, and the Breakdown of Centralized Wage Bargaining: Denmark and Sweden in Comparative Perspective. *Comparative Politics*, 28 (4), 399–436.
Jackman, R. 1993: *Power without Force*. Ann Arbor: University of Michigan.
Jenkins, Barbara 1991: Strategic Partnerships in Telecommunications: The Role of States in Determining Comparative Advantage. In Mytelka (1991).
JETRO (Japan External Trade Organization) 1993: *Industrial Policy in East Asia*. Tokyo: Japan External Trade Organization.
Johnson, Chalmers 1982: *MITI and the Japanese Miracle*. CA: Stanford: Stanford University Press.
Johnson, Chalmers 1984a: The Institutional Foundations of Japanese Industrial Policy. *California Management Review*, 27 (1), 59–69.
Johnson, Chalmers 1984b: The Industrial Policy Debate Re-examined. *California Management Review*, 27 (1), 71–90.
Johnson, Chalmers 1994: What Is the Best System of National Economic Management for Korea? In Cho and Kim (1994).

Johnson, Chalmers 1995: *Japan: Who Governs?: The Rise of the Developmental State in East Asia*. New York: Norton.

Johnson, Chalmers (forthcoming): The Developmental State: Odyssey of a Concept. In Meredith Woo-Cumings (ed.) *The Developmental State in Historical Perspective*, Ithaca NY: Cornell University Press.

Jones, L.P. and Sakong, Il 1980: *Government, Business, and Entrepreneurship in Economic Development: The Korean Case*. Cambridge MA: Harvard University Press.

JPRI (Japan Policy Research Institute) 1996: Government Investment in Commercial Technology. *JPRI Critique*, 3 (8), 1–2.

Junne, Gerd 1989: Competitiveness and the Impact of Change: Applications of 'High Technologies'. In Katzenstein (1989).

Kapstein, Ethan B. 1991: We are Us. *National Interest* (Winter), 55–63.

Katzenstein, Peter J. 1976: International Relations and Domestic Structures: Foreign Economic Policies of Advanced Industrial States. *International Organization* (Winter), 30, 1–45.

Katzenstein, Peter J. 1978a: Conclusion: Domestic Structures and Strategies of Foreign Economic Policy. In Katzenstein (1978b).

Katzenstein, Peter J. (ed.) 1978b: *Between Power and Plenty*. Madison WI: University of Wisconsin Press.

Katzenstein, Peter J. 1984: *Corporatism and Change*. Ithaca NY: Cornell University Press.

Katzenstein, Peter J. 1985: *Small States in World Markets*. Ithaca NY: Cornell University Press.

Katzenstein, Peter J. (ed.) 1989: *Industry and Politics in West Germany*. Ithaca NY: Cornell University Press.

Keck, Otto 1993: The National System for Technical Innovation in Germany. In Nelson (1990).

Keips (Korea Electronics Industry Promotion Society) 1967: *The Implementation Plan*. Seoul: KEIPS.

Kentworthy, Lane 1990: Are Industrial Policy and Corporatism Compatible? *Journal of Public Policy*, 10 (3), 233–65.

Kim, Eun Mee 1987: From Dominance to Symbiosis: State and Chaebol in Korea. *Pacific Focus*, 3, 105–21.

Kim, Hyung-Ki, Muramatsu, Michio, Pempel, T.J. and Yamamura, Kozo (eds) 1995: *The Japanese Civil Service and Economic Development*. Oxford: Clarendon Press.

Kim, Ji-Hong 1991: Korea: Market Adjustment in Declining Industries, Government Assistance in Troubled Industries. In H. Patrick and L. Meissner (eds) *Pacific Basin Industries in Distress*, New York: Columbia University Press.

Kim, Kihwan and Leipziger, Danny M. 1993: Korea: A Case of Government-led Development. 'The Lessons of East Asia' series. Washington DC: World Bank.

King, M. and Fullerton, D. 1984: *The Taxation of Income from Capital: A Comparative Study of the US, UK, Sweden and West Germany*. Chicago: University of Chicago Press.

Koechlin, Thomas 1995: The Globalization of Investment. *Contemporary Economic Policy*, 13 (1), 92–100.

Komiya, R. and Yokobori, K. 1991: *Japan's Industrial Policies in the 1980s*. Tokyo: MITI Research Institute.

Krasner, Stephen D. 1978a: United States Commercial and Monetary Policy: Unravelling the Paradox of External Strength and Internal Weakness. In Katzenstein (1978b).

Krasner, Stephen D. 1978b: *Defending the National Interest: Raw Materials Investment and US Foreign Policy.* Princeton NJ: Princeton University Press.

Krasner, Stephen D. 1989: Sovereignty: An Institutional Perspective. In James A. Caporaso (ed.) *The Elusive State.* New York: Sage.

Kreile, Michael 1978: West Germany: The Dynamics of Expansion. In Katzenstein (1978b).

Kugler, Jack and Domke, William 1986: Comparing the Strength of Nations. *Comparative Political Studies,* 19 (1), 39–69.

Kuisel, R. 1981: *Capitalism and the State in Modern France.* Cambridge: Cambridge University Press.

Kuo, Cheng-Tian 1995: *Global Competitiveness and Industrial Growth in Taiwan and the Philippines.* Pittsburgh: University of Pittsburgh Press.

Kurzer, Paulette 1993: *Business and Banking: Political Change and Economic Integration in Western Europe.* Ithaca NY: Cornell University Press.

Kwan, C.H. 1994: *Economic Interdependence in the Asia-Pacific Region.* London, New York: Routledge.

Lall, Sanjaya 1993: 'The East Asian Miracle' Study: Does the Bell Toll for Industrial Strategy? *Development Studies Working Papers, No. 67.* Oxford: International Development Centre.

Lee, C.H. and Yamazawa, I. (eds) 1990: *The Economic Development of Japan and Korea.* New York: Praeger.

Leibfried, Stephan 1994: 'Sozialstaat' oder 'Wohlfahrtsgesellschaft'? Thesen zu einem japanisch–deutschen Sozialpolitikvergleich. ['Welfare State' or 'Welfare Society'? Theses on Japanese–German Social Policy Similarities.] *Soziale Welt-Zeitschrift fuer Sozialwissenschaftliche Forschung undo Praxis,* 45 (4), 389–410.

Levi, Margaret 1981: The Predatory Theory of Rule. *Politics and Society,* 10, 431–65.

Levi-Faur, David 1997: Friedrich List and the Political Economy of the Nation-state. *Review of International Political Economy,* 4 (1), 154–78.

Levy, Jonah D. and Samuels, Richard J. 1991: Institutions and Innovation: Research and Collaboration as Technical Strategy in Japan. In Mytelka (1991).

Lim, L.Y.C. 1983: Singapore's Success: The Myth of the Free Market Economy. *Asian Survey,* 23 (6), 752–64.

Lind, Michael 1992: The Catalytic State. *National Interest* (Spring), 27, 3–12.

List, Friedrich 1966: *The National System of Political Economy.* Trans. S. Lloyd. New York: Augustus Kelley.

Lodge, George and Walton, Richard 1989: The American Corporation and its New Relationships. *California Management Review,* 31 (3), 9–24.

Lundberg, E. 1985: The Rise and Fall of the Swedish Model. *Journal of Economic Literature* (Mar.), 12, 1–36.

Lütz, Suzanne 1996: The Revival of the Nation-State? Stock Exchange Regulation in an Era of Internationalized Financial Markets. *MPIFG Discussion Paper,* 96/9. Koln: Max Planck Institute for the Study of Societies.

Lynn, Leonard H. 1985: Technology Transfer to Japan: What We Know, What We Need to Know, and What We Know That May Not Be So. In N. Rosenberg and C. Frischtak (eds) *International Technology Transfer: Concepts, Measures, and Comparisons*, New York: Praeger.

Mabuchi, Masaru 1995: Financing Japanese Industry. In H.-K. Kim et al. (1995).

Magaziner, Ira and Patinkin, Mark 1990: *The Silent War: Inside the Global Business Battles Shaping America's Future*. New York: Vintage Books.

Mann, Michael 1977/1988: States, Ancient and Modern. In Mann (1988).

Mann, Michael 1983/1988: State and Society, 1130–1815: An Analysis of English State Finances. In Mann (1988).

Mann, Michael 1984/1988: The Autonomous Power of the State: Its Origins, Mechanism, and Results. In Mann (1988).

Mann, Michael 1988: *States, War and History*. Oxford: Blackwell.

Mann, Michael 1993a: *The Sources of Social Power. Vol. 2*. Cambridge and New York: Cambridge University Press.

Mann, Michael 1993b: Reconstructing Nations and States. *Daedalus*, 122 (3), 115–40.

Mann, Michael 1995: As the Twentieth Century Ages. *New Left Review* (Nov./Dec.), 214, 104–25.

Mann, Michael 1996: The Global Future of the Nation State. Revised version of a paper for the 'Direction of Contemporary Capitalism' Conference, University of Sussex, 26–9 April 1996.

March, James G. and Olsen, Johan P. 1989: *Rediscovering Institutions: The Organizational Basis of Politics*. New York: Free Press.

Markusen, Ann and Yudken, Joel 1992: *Dismantling the Cold War Economy*. New York: Basic Books.

Maschke, Erich 1969: Outline of the History of German Cartels from 1873 to 1914. In F. Crouzet, W.H. Chaloner and W.M. Stern (eds) *Essays in European Economic History 1789–1914*, London: Edward Arnold.

Mathews, John A. 1997a: An Emerging Silicon Valley of the East: How Taiwan Created a Semiconductor Industry. *California Management Review*, 39 (4), 26–54.

Mathews, John A. 1997b: Technological Upgrading through Organizational Collaboration: The Case of Taiwan's R&D Alliances. Unpublished manuscript, University of New South Wales.

Mathews, John A. and Cho, Dong-Sung (forthcoming): *Tiger Chips: High Technology Industrialization in East Asia: The Case of the Semiconductor Industry, 1975–1995*. Cambridge: Cambridge University Press.

Matzner, E. and Streeck, W. (eds) 1991: *Beyond Keynesianism*. Aldershot: Edward Elgar.

McFaul, Michael 1995: State Power, Institutional Change, and the Politics of Privatization in Russia. *World Politics*, 47: 210–43.

McKean, Margaret 1993: State Strength and the Public Interest. In G. Allinson and Y. Sone (eds) *Political Dynamics in Contemporary Japan*, Ithaca, NY: Cornell University Press.

McLennan, Gregor 1989: *Marxism, Pluralism and Beyond: Classic Debates and New Departures*. Cambridge: Polity Press.

Meidner, R. 1993: Why Did the Swedish Model Fail? *Socialist Register 1993*, 211–28.

Migdal, Joel S. 1987: Strong States, Weak States: Power and Accommodation. In M. Weiner and S.P. Huntington (eds) *Understanding Political Development*, Boston: Little, Brown.

Migdal, Joel S. 1996: Studying the State. Paper presented at the annual meeting of the American Political Science Association, San Francisco, 29 August.

Migdal, Joel S., Kohli, Atul and Shue, Vivienne (eds) 1994: *State Power and Social Forces: Domination and Transformation in the Third World*. Cambridge and New York: Cambridge University Press.

Mitchell, Deborah 1990: Comparing Income Transfer Systems: Is Australia the Poor Relation? *Discussion Paper No. 18*. September, ANU Graduate Program in Public Policy.

Mjoset, Lars 1987: Nordic Economic Policies. *International Organization*, 41 (3), 403–56.

Moon, Chung-in 1988: The Demise of a Developmentalist State? The Politics of Stabilization and Structural Adjustment. *Journal of Developing Societies*, 4, 67–84.

Moon, Chung-in 1994: Changing Patterns of Business–Government Relations in South Korea. In A. MacIntyre (ed.) *Business and Government in Industrializing Asia*, Sydney: Allen and Unwin.

Moore, Barrington 1977: *The Social Origins of Dictatorship and Democracy*. Harmondsworth: Penguin.

Moses, Jonathan W. 1994: Abdication from National Policy Autonomy. What's Left to Leave? *Politics and Society* (June), 22, 125–48.

Mowery, David C. and Rosenberg, Nathan 1989: New Developments in U.S. Technology Policy: Implications for Competitiveness and International Trade Policy. *California Management Review*, 32 (1), 107–24.

Mytelka, Lynn Krieger (ed.) 1991: *Strategic Partnerships: States, Firms and International Competition*. London: Pinter.

Nagatani, Keizo 1992: Japanese Economics: The Theory and Practice of Investment Coordination. In J.A. Roumasset and S. Barr (eds) *The Economics of Cooperation*, Boulder CO: Westview Press.

Nelson, Richard R. 1991: Diffusion of Development: Post-World War II Convergence Among Advanced Industrial Nations. *American Economic Review*, 81 (2), 271–75.

Nelson, R. (ed.) 1993: *National Innovation Systems: A Comparative Analysis*. Oxford: Oxford University Press.

Noble, Gregory W. 1989: The Japanese Industrial Policy Debate. In Stephan Haggard and Chung-in Moon (eds) *Pacific Dynamics: The International Politics of Industrial Change*, Boulder CO: Westview Press.

Nordlinger, Eric A. 1987: Taking the State Seriously. In M. Weiner and S.P. Huntington (eds) *Understanding Political Development*, Boston, Toronto: Little, Brown.

O'Brien, Patricia 1994: Governance Systems in Steel: The American and Japanese Experiences. In Hollingsworth et al. (1994).

OECD various years a: *Historical Statistics*. Paris: OECD.

OECD various years b: *National Accounts*. Paris: OECD.

Ohmae, Kenichi 1990: *The Borderless World*. New York: Collins.

Ohmae, Kenichi 1995: Putting Global Logic First. *Harvard Business Review*, 73 (1), 119–25.

Okimoto, Daniel I. 1989: *Between MITI and the Market: Japanese Industrial Policy for High Technology*. Stanford CA: Stanford University Press.

Oman, C. 1994: *Globalisation and Regionalisation: The Challenge for Developing Countries*. Paris: OECD.

Orr, Robert M., Jr 1990: *The Emergence of Japan's Foreign Aid Power*. New York: Columbia University Press.

OTA (Office of Technology Assessment) 1991: *Competing Economies: America, Europe and the Pacific Rim*. Report OTA-ITE-498. Washington DC: Office of Technology Assessment, Congress of the United States.

Pempel, T.J. and Muramatsu, Michio 1995: The Japanese Bureaucracy and Economic Development: Structuring a Proactive Civil Service. In H.-K. Kim et al. (1995).

Perraton, Jonathan, Goldblatt, David, Held, David and McGrew, Anthony 1997: The Globalisation of Economic Activity. *New Political Economy*, 2 (2), 257–77.

Pfaller, A., Gough, I. and Therborn, G. 1991: *Can the Welfare State Compete? A Comparative Study of Five Advanced Capitalist Countries*. London: Macmillan.

Pierson, Paul 1996: The New Politics of the Welfare State. *World Politics*, 48 (2), 143–80.

Piven, Frances Fox 1995: Is it Global Economics or Neo-Laissez-faire? *New Left Review*, 213, 107–14.

Poggi, Gianfranco 1978: *The Development of the Modern State*. Stanford CA: Stanford University Press.

Poggi, Gianfranco 1990: *The State: Its Nature, Development and Prospects*. Stanford CA: Stanford University Press.

Pontusson, Jonas 1991: Labor, Corporatism and Industrial Policy: The Swedish Case in Comparative Perspective. *Comparative Politics*, 23 (2), 163–79.

Pontusson, Jonas 1992a: At the End of the Third Road: Swedish Social Democracy in Crisis. *Politics and Society*, 20 (3), 305–32.

Pontusson, Jonas 1992b: *The Limits of Social Democracy*. Ithaca NY: Cornell University Press.

Porter, Michael 1986: Competition in Global Industries: A Conceptual Framework. In M. Porter (ed.) *Competition in Global Industries*, Boston: Harvard Business School Press.

Pringle, Robert 1992: Financial Markets versus Governments. In Banuri and Schor (1992).

Ramesh, M. 1995: Economic Globalization and Policy Choices: Singapore. *Governance*, 8 (2), 243–60.

Reich, Robert B. 1988: Bailout: A Comparative Study in Law and Industrial Structure. In A. Spence and H. Hazard (eds) *International Competitiveness*. Cambridge MA: Ballinger.

Reich, Robert B. 1991: Who Do We Think They Are? *American Prospect* (Winter), 4, 49–53.

Reich, Robert B. 1992: *The Work of Nations*. New York: Vintage.

Reich, Simon 1990: *The Fruits of Fascism: Post War Prosperity in Historical Perspective*. Ithaca NY: Cornell University Press.

Rhodes, Martin 1996: Globalization and West European Welfare States: A Critical Review of Recent Debates. *Journal of European Social Policy*, 6 (4), 305–27.

Root, Hilton 1996: *Small Countries, Big Lessons: Governance and the Rise of East Asia*. New York: Oxford University Press.

Rosovsky, Henry 1961: *Capital Formation in Japan, 1868–1940*. Glencoe IL: Free Press.

Ruigrok, Winfried and van Tulder, Rob 1995: *The Logic of International Restructuring*. London, New York: Routledge.

Sakakibara, Eisuke 1997: Reforming Japan: The Once and Future Boom. *The Economist* (22 March), 79–80.

Sako, Mari 1994: Neither Markets nor Hierarchies: A Comparative Study of the Printed Circuit Board Industry in Britain and Japan. In Hollingsworth et al. (1994).

Sally, Razeen 1994: Multinational Enterprises, Political Economy and Institutional Theory: Domestic Embeddedness in the Context of Internationalization. *Review of International Political Economy*, 1 (1), 161–92.

Sally, R. 1995: The Economics and Politics of the German Miracle. *Government and Opposition*, 30 (4), 541–54.

Samuels, Richard J. 1987: *The Business of the Japanese State: Energy Markets in Comparative and Historical Perspective*. Ithaca NY: Cornell University Press.

Samuels, Richard J. 1994: *Rich Nation, Strong Army: National Security and the Technological Transformation of Japan*. Ithaca NY: Cornell University Press.

San, Gee 1995: An Overview of Policy Priorities for Industrial Development in Taiwan. *Journal of Industry Studies*, 2 (1), 27–56.

Sarathy, Ravi 1989: The Interplay of Industrial Policy and International Strategy: Japan's Machine Tool Industry. *California Management Review* (Spring), 132–60.

Sato, Hiroki 1997: Still Going? Continuity and Change in Japan's Long-Term Employment System. *Social Science Japan* (August), 10, 16–18.

Saxonhouse, Gary R. 1983: What Is All This About 'Industrial Targeting' in Japan? *World Economy*, 6, 253–73.

Schmidt, Vivien A. 1995: The New World Order, Incorporated: The Rise of Business and the Decline of the Nation-state. *Daedalus*, 124 (2), 75–106.

Schmitter, Philippe and Lehmbruch, Gerhard (eds) 1979: *Trends towards Corporatist Intermediation*. London: Sage.

Schott, Kerry 1984: *Policy, Power and Order: The Persistence of Economic Problems in Capitalist States*. New Haven CT: Yale University Press.

Schwartz, Frank 1993: Of Fairy Cloaks and Familiar Talks: the Politics of Consultation. In G.D. Allinson and Y. Sone (eds) *Political Dynamics in Contemporary Japan*, Ithaca NY: Cornell University Press.

Schwartz, Herman 1994: Small States in Big Trouble: State Reorganization in Australia, Denmark, New Zealand, and Sweden in the 1980s. *World Politics*, 46 (4), 527–55.

Scott, Bruce R. 1985: National Strategies: Key to International Competition. In Bruce Scott and George Lodge (eds) *US Competitiveness in the World Economy*, Boston: Harvard Business School Press.

Scott, Bruce R. 1992: Economic Strategy and Economic Performance. *Harvard Business School Note N9-792-086*.

Shaw, Martin 1997: The State of Globalization: towards a theory of state transformation. *Review of International Political Economy*, 4 (3), 497–513.

SIA (Semiconductor Industry Association) 1992: *Creating Advantage: Semiconductors and Government Industrial Policy in the 1990s*. Washington DC: SIA.

Skocpol, Theda 1979: *States and Social Revolutions*. Cambridge: Cambridge University Press.

Skocpol, Theda 1985: Bringing the State Back In: Strategies of Analysis In Current Research. In Evans et al. (1985).

Sone, Yasunori 1993: Structuring Political Bargains: Government, *Gyokai* and Markets. In G.D. Allinson and Y. Sone (eds) *Political Dynamics in Contemporary Japan*. Ithaca: Cornell University Press.

Soskice, David 1990: Reinterpreting Corporatism and Explaining Unemployment: Co-ordinated and Non-co-ordinated Market Economies. In Renato Brunetta and Carlo Dell'Aringa (eds) *Labour Relations and Economic Performance*, London: Macmillan.

Stallings, Barbara (ed.) 1995: *Global Change, Regional Response: The New International Context of Development*. New York: Cambridge University Press.

Stallings, Barbara and Streeck, Wolfgang 1995: Capitalisms in Conflict? The United States, Europe, and Japan in the Post-Cold War World. In Stallings (1995).

Steinmo, Sven 1994: The End of Redistribution? International Pressures and Domestic Tax Policy Choices. *Challenge!*, 37 (6), 9–17.

Streeck, Wolfgang 1983: Between Pluralism and Corporatism: German Business Associations and the State. *Journal of Public Policy*, 3 (3), 265–83.

Streeck, Wolfgang 1989: Successful Adjustment to Turbulent Markets: The Automobile Industry. In Katzenstein (1989).

Streeck, Wolfgang and Schmitter, Philippe C. 1985: *Private Interest Governance: Beyond Market and State*. Beverley Hills: Sage.

Therborn, Goran 1987: Does Corporatism Really Matter? *Journal of Public Policy*, 7 (3), 259–84.

Thompson, Grahame 1992: Economic Autonomy and the Advanced Industrial State. In A. McGrew, P. Lewis et al., *Global Politics: Globalization and the Nation State*, Cambridge: Polity Press.

Thurow, Lester 1985: The Case for Industrial Policies in America. In T. Shishido and R. Sato (eds) *Industrial Policy and Technological Change*, London: Croom Helm.

Thurow, Lester 1992: *Head to Head*. Sydney: Allen and Unwin.

Tillotson, Amanda R. 1989: Open States and Open Economies: Denmark's Contribution to a Statist Theory of Development. *Comparative Politics*, 21 (3), 339–54.

Tilly, Charles 1975: *The Formation of National States in Western Europe*. Princeton NJ: Princeton University Press.

Tilly, Richard 1989: German Industrialization and Gerschenkronian Backwardness. *Rivista di Storia Economica* (June), 6, 139–64.

Tilton, Mark 1996: *Restrained Trade: Cartels in Japan's Basic Material Industries*. Ithaca NY: Cornell University Press.

Tonelson, Alan 1994: Beating Back Predatory Trade. *Foreign Affairs*, 73 (4), 123–35.

Trimberger, Ellen 1978: *Revolution from Above: Military Bureaucrats and Development in Japan, Turkey, Egypt and Peru*. New Brunswick NJ: Transaction Books.

Tyson, Laura D'Andrea 1991: They are Not Us: Why American Ownership still Matters. *American Prospect* (Winter), 4, 37–53.

UNCTAD (United Nations Conference on Trade and Development) 1994: *World Investment Report*. New York.

Vitols, Sigurt, 1995: The German Industrial Strategy. Paper prepared for the Workshop on Innovation and Industrial Strategy in Germany and the New Europe. Wissenschaftszentrum. Berlin, September.

Vitols, Sigurt 1997: German Industrial Policy: An Overview. *Industry and Innovation*, 4 (1), 15–36.

Vogel, Steven K. 1996: *Freer Markets, More Rules: Regulatory Reform in Advanced Industrial Countries*. Ithaca NY: Cornell University Press.

Wachtel, Howard M. 1995: Taming Global Money. *Challenge!*, 38 (1), 36–40.

Wade, Robert 1990a: *Governing the Market*. Princeton NJ: Princeton University Press.

Wade, Robert 1990b: Industrial Policy in East Asia: Does it Lead or follow the Market? In G. Gereffi and D.L. Wyman (eds) *Manufacturing Miracles*, Princeton NJ: Princeton University Press.

Wade, Robert 1993: The Visible Hand: The State and East Asia's Economic Growth. *Current History*, 92 (578), 431–40.

Wade, Robert 1996a: Globalization and its Limits: Reports of the Death of the National Economy are Greatly Exaggerated. In Suzanne Berger and Ronald Dore (eds) *National Diversity and Global Capitalism*, Ithaca NY: Cornell University Press.

Wade, Robert 1996b: Japan, the World Bank, and the Art of Paradigm Maintenance: The East Asian Miracle in Political Perspective. *New Left Review* (May/June), 217, 3–36.

Weiss, Linda 1988: *Creating Capitalism*. Oxford: Blackwell.

Weiss, Linda 1993: War, the State, and the Origins of the Japanese Employment System. *Politics and Society*, 21 (3), 325–54.

Weiss, Linda 1995: Governed Interdependence: Rethinking the Government–Business Relationship in East Asia. *Pacific Review*, 8 (4), 589–616.

Weiss, Linda and Hobson, John M. 1995: *States and Economic Development*. Cambridge: Polity Press.

Wever, Kirsten S. and Allen, Christopher S. 1993: The Financial System and Corporate Governance in Germany: Institutions and the Diffusion of Innovations. *Journal of Public Policy*, 13 (2), 183–202.

Whang, In-Joung 1971: Leadership and Organizational Development in the Economic Ministries of Korea. *Asian Survey*, 11 (10), 992–1004.

White, Gordon (ed.) 1988: *Developmental States in East Asia*. London: Macmillan.

Whitley, Richard and Kristensen, Peer Hull 1996: *The Changing European Firm*. London, New York: Routledge.

Wilks, Stephen and Wright, Maurice 1987: *Comparative Government–Industry Relations: Western Europe, the United States and Japan*. Oxford: Clarendon Press.

Williams, David 1994: *Japan: Beyond the End of History*. London, New York: Routledge.

Woo, Wing Tye 1990: The Art of Economic Development: Markets, Politics, and Externalities. *International Organization*, 44 (3), 403–29.

Woo, Yung-en (Woo-Cumings, Meredith) 1991: *Race to the Swift*. New York: Columbia University Press.

Woo-Cumings, Meredith 1995: The Korean Developmental State. In H.-K. Kim et al. (1995).

Woo-Cumings, Meredith (forthcoming): *The Developmental State in Historical Perspective*. Ithaca NY: Cornell University Press.

World Bank 1991: *World Development Report 1991*. New York: Oxford University Press.

World Bank 1993a: *The East Asian Miracle: Economic Growth and Public Policy*. New York: Oxford University Press (for the World Bank).

World Bank 1993b: *Government, Policy and Productivity Growth: Is East Asia an Exception?*. 'The Lessons of East Asia' series. Washington DC: World Bank.

World Bank 1995: *World Development Report 1995*. Washington DC: World Bank.

World Bank 1997: *World Development Report 1997*. Washington DC: World Bank.

Yamamura, K. 1986: Caveat Emptor: The Industrial Policy of Japan. In P. Krugman (ed.) *Strategic Trade and the New International Economics*. Cambridge MA: MIT Press.

Yin, K.Y. 1954: The development of the textile industry in Taiwan. *Industry of Free China*, 1 (1), 1–6.

Yoon, Jeong-Ro 1989: The State and Private Capital in Korea: The Political Economy of the Semiconductor Industry, 1965–1987. PhD thesis, Harvard University.

Zevin, Robert 1992: Are World Financial Markets More Open? If So, Why and with What Effects? In Banuri and Schor (1992).

Ziegler, J. Nicholas 1994: Technology Policy and Social Partnership in Unified Germany. Revised version of a paper prepared for workshop on Political Economy of the New Germany, Ithaca NY, 14–15 October.

Ziegler, J. Nicholas 1995: Institutions, Elites, and Technological Change in France and Germany. *World Politics*, 47 (3), 341–72.

Zysman, John 1977: *Political Strategies for Industrial Order: State, Market, and Industry in France*. Berkeley CA: University of California Press.

Zysman, John 1978: The French State in the International Economy. In Katzenstein (1978b).

Zysman, John 1983: *Governments, Markets and Growth: Financial Systems and the Politics of Industrial Change*. Ithaca NY: Cornell University Press.

INDEX

Page references in bold type (e.g. **158–9**) refer to the major discussion of a topic.

Theoretical and general discussions of a topic are indexed under the topic (e.g. industrial policy); applications to a particular state are indexed under the name of the state (e.g. Germany: industrial policy).

248   *Index*

   state compared, 83–6, 104, 114–15,
   117, 220; *see also* dual capabilities
domestic linkages, 33, 35, 55–9, 210;
   see also government–industry
   relations
Dore, Ronald, 56, 59, 76, 224
dual capabilities (developmental and
   distributive): Germany and Japan
   as dualistic states, 4, 12, **116–66**,
   222–5; national prosperity, **150–7**;
   power, **153–7**; *see also* growth with
   equity
Dyson, Kenneth, 126

East Asian developmental states:
   bureaucratic structures, 35–6, 44,
   46, 48, **49–54**, 55–9, 65, 81, 203;
   business organization, **59–64**, 72,
   76–7, 133; cartels, 72, 76; catalytic
   states, 46, 204, 210–11; cooperative
   arrangements, 43–5, 49, 55–65,
   60–1, 74–5, 203–4, 207–8;
   coordination systems, 42–5, 47–8,
   49–54, 55, 110, 143, 217;
   corporatism, 48, 103; delegation of
   authority, 40, 72, 76–7; disciplined
   support, 43–4, 71, **73–5**, 78–9, 137,
   219; distributive state capacity,
   54–5, 86, 117; economic
   performance, **46–9**; embedded
   autonomy, 34–5, 37–8, 49, 55, 63–5,
   69; finance, 47, 74, 203–4, 207;
   foreign direct investment, 175, 204,
   207–8, 217; German competition
   and comparisons, 137–9, 142–3,
   148, 163, 166; globalization, 43,
   174–5, 177, 179–80, 182, 204,
   207–8; governed interdependence,
   37–8, 43–6, 48–9, 55–65, **69–80**,
   81–2, 137, 148; government–
   industry linkages, 33, 41, 43, 45–52,
   55–9, 65, 69–70, 81, 116, 203, 210;
   growth with equity, 5, 80, 116–17,
   153, 219; high technology, 46, 71,
   78, 120, 207–8, 218; income
   distribution, 83–4, 154, 222;
   industrial policy, **41–9**, 55, 69, 148,
   153, 203, 208, 210, 219;
   industrial–technological

   transformation, **49–64**;
   industrialization, 23, 66, 215, 218;
   information-gathering, **50–2**, 54–5,
   203; infrastructural power, 38, 72,
   81; innovation, 33, 42–3, 47–8,
   50–2, 137; institutions, 42–5, **46–94**,
   201, 203; intervention, 41–4, 69, 79,
   217; national capitalism, 194;
   policy instruments, 33, 61, 74,
   197–8; politics, 50, **54–5**, 117;
   predictions of demise, 37, **64–5**,
   117; private-sector governance,
   76–8, 131–3; R&D, 33, 47; risk-
   sharing, 48, 71, **75**, 116, 137; social
   solidarity, 54–5, 112, 117; state
   adaptivity, 48, 196, 201–3; state
   effectiveness, 42–3, 46, 48–9, 64;
   state power, 45, **80–2**; state
   structure, 49–50, 54; 'strong state'
   thesis, 44–8, 64; structural
   transformation, 47, 66, 76, 203;
   studies of, 215; technology policy,
   203; trade policy, 42, 47, 76, 79, 83;
   transformative capacity
   ('developmentalism'), 12–13, 15,
   37, 40, **43–6**, **64–71**, 83, 110, 117,
   119–20, 124, 166, 201, 203, 212,
   218; *see also* Japan, Korea, Taiwan
East Asian model, 49, 116–17
Eastern Europe, 126, 145, 205
Easton, D., 213
economic bureaucracy *see*
   accountability of
economic ideology: East Asia, 54–5;
   Europe, 201; Germany, 16, 129,
   163, 166, 222, 226; *see also*
   liberalism
economic integration: financial
   markets, **178–84**; state capacity, 5,
   7–8, 12, 167–8, 170, 175, 177–8,
   189, 195, 197, 202, **203–4**
economic nationalism: List, Friedrich,
   216
economic openness *see* 'open'
   economy
economic rationalism (Australia), 191
economic transformation: types of
   state power and, 65, **66–8**
The Economist, 149, 154, 168, 193,
   224–6